The Nature of Race

D0874862

The Nature of Race

HOW SCIENTISTS THINK
AND TEACH ABOUT HUMAN
DIFFERENCE

ANN MORNING

UNIVERSITY OF CALIFORNIA PRESS
Berkeley   Los Angeles   London

University of California Press, one of the most distinguished
university presses in the United States, enriches lives around the world
by advancing scholarship in the humanities, social sciences, and
natural sciences. Its activities are supported by the UC Press Foundation and by philanthropic contributions from individuals and
institutions. For more information, visit www.ucpress.edu.

University of California Press
Berkeley and Los Angeles, California

University of California Press, Ltd.
London, England

© 2011 by The Regents of the University of California

Library of Congress Cataloging-in-Publication Data

Morning, Ann Juanita, 1968–
    The nature of race : how scientists think and teach about human
difference / Ann Morning.
        p.   cm.
    Includes bibliographical references and index.
    ISBN 978-0-520-27030-5 (cloth : alk. paper)
    ISBN 978-0-520-27031-2 (pbk. : alk. paper)
    1. Race.   2. Racism in anthropology.   3. Racism in education.
    4. Racism in textbooks.   I. Title.
    GN269.M675   2011
    305.8—dc22   2011000291

20   19   18   17   16   15   14   13   12   11
10   9   8   7   6   5   4   3   2   1

Contents

Illustrations

FIGURES

Acknowledgments

The people to whom I owe the most for this book are paradoxically those I know the least: the ninety-three individuals I interviewed and quoted extensively in the pages to follow. I probably wouldn't recognize—or be recognized by—any of them on the street now, but their ideas and words have breathed life into mine. I am deeply grateful to these men and women for the time and experiences they shared with me.

Several organizations provided support for this project. I thank the National Science Foundation (and especially John Perhonis) for a Dissertation Improvement Award from the program in Societal Dimensions of Engineering, Science and Technology; the Ford Foundation and National Research Council for Diversity Fellowships at both the doctoral and postdoctoral levels (and Columbia University's Department of Sociology for hosting my postdoctoral year); the Spencer Foundation for a Dissertation Fellowship; and Princeton University's Center for Arts and Cultural Policy Studies as well as its Program (now a Center) in African American Studies for research funding. I am also grateful to my former teachers at the United Nations International School for donating old biology textbooks to my study. Last but not least, I thank the American Sociological Association prize committees that honored me with the ASA Dissertation Award in 2005 and the Section on Racial and Ethnic Minorities' Oliver Cromwell Cox Article Award in 2009.

As a doctoral student at Princeton, I began my exploration of Americans' understandings of race in the most auspicious way possible: with the assistance of a top-notch dissertation committee. The chair, Marta Tienda, combined being a demanding guide with being a tireless supporter. Every time I sit down to write, I benefit from her teaching. Michèle Lamont, now at Harvard, has consistently broadened my intellectual horizons, introducing me to new ideas and people across the globe. Her generous and enthusiastic support for my research is priceless. Last but far from least, Elizabeth M. Armstrong remains an inspiration for me. Not only do I admire her scholarship, but I treasure her professional advice and her friendship. My project benefited as well from the comments of my dissertation readers Paul Starr and especially Robert Wuthnow, who was most encouraging of my efforts. My classmate Marion Carter, my friends Rekha Shukla and Greg Victor, and my cousins Larry and Ingrid Glasco also contributed directly to the dissertation in different ways. Finally, I can't mention Princeton without also expressing my heartfelt thanks to Noreen Goldman and to the wonderful staff at the Office of Population Research.

New York University (NYU) has exposed me to some of the most brilliant scholars in the discipline of sociology, and just as importantly, to a highly supportive intellectual community. I am especially fortunate to work with Troy Duster, who is both a mentor and a role model. He has not only supported my research endeavors and championed my work, but included me in the conversation he keeps going among the foremost experts on the intersection of race and science. This book has also benefited in myriad ways from the assistance of the outstanding staff of NYU's Department of Sociology, and from the knowledge and efficiency of our Sociology librarian Jason Phillips.

I have been fortunate to be able to develop some of the central ideas in *The Nature of Race* by presenting them at a wide range of universities and institutions. Accordingly, I would like to thank my audiences at the annual meetings of the American Sociological Association, the Population Association of America, the Society for the Advancement of Socio-Economics, and the Society for Social Studies of Science; the Russell Sage Foundation; and Columbia University, Drew University, the Massachusetts Institute of Technology, New York University, Northwestern University, Princeton University, Stanford University, the University of Chicago, the University of Minnesota, and Yale University.

Thanks to a Fulbright Scholarship, as well as a Goddard Fellowship from NYU, I had the pleasure of spending the 2008–09 academic year in the Sociology Department at the University of Milan-Bicocca, where I wrote a substantial portion of this book. I am grateful to the colleagues who made such an intellectually engaging experience possible: Guido Martinotti, Giorgio Grossi, Guido Barbujani, Tommaso Vitale, Fabio Quassoli, and especially Marcello Maneri. My Milanese sabbatical gave me the opportunity to reflect on race with academics and students across Europe, and I thank those who shared their thoughts with me in my talks at the University of Milan-Bicocca, the University of Ferrara, the University of Salerno, the Institut d'Etudes Démographiques in Paris, and at special lectures organized by the American Embassy in Rome and by the organizations Felix Meritis and Humanity in Action in Amsterdam.

No one gave more generously than those individuals who read and commented on my work, whether drafts of articles, book chapters, or even the whole manuscript. For such contributions, I am indebted not only to many of the individuals mentioned above, but to Peter Bearman, Melissa Caldwell, Steve Carlton-Ford, Kathleen Gerson, Charles Glock, Ruth Horowitz, Jeff Manza, Molly Martin, Cynthia Miller-Idriss, Susan Moscou, François Nielsen, Daniel Sabbagh, Janelle Scott, Sara Shostak, Mario Small, and Mitchell Stevens.

There are also two special classes of readers to whom I am immensely grateful. First are the participants in a December 2009 manuscript workshop that department chair Jeff Manza organized and funded to provide me with expert and detailed feedback on my manuscript. In attendance were a veritable "dream team" of scholars of racial conceptualization: Lawrence Bobo of Harvard University, Lawrence Hirschfeld of the New

School for Social Research, Pamela Sankar of the University of Pennsylvania, and my NYU colleagues Deirdre Royster and Troy Duster (the workshop chair). I cannot thank them enough for the time they took from their busy schedules to read my work, travel to NYU, and spend the better part of a day discussing it—not to mention following up with written comments and support. This book is much improved for their contribution.

The second group of scholars whose intelligence and insight have benefited this book is my writing circle, which includes Catherine Lee of Rutgers University, Alondra Nelson of Columbia University, and Wendy Roth at the University of British Columbia. We have been discussing each other's work on Skype every month for two years now, even when we were spread out across nine time zones. To a woman, my partners are extraordinarily sharp and articulate scholars whose observations are spot-on, yet they leaven their critiques with empathy, humor, and encouragement.

Working with an editor of the caliber of Naomi Schneider at the University of California Press has been a true pleasure. Not only does she possess patience of biblical proportions, but it is always a delight to sit down with her (something I suspect is not true of all editors). I am also most grateful to assistant editor Kalicia Pivirotto.

Finally, friends and family are an important part of this book's back story. There are the friends who kept asking, "How's the book going?" (Sara Benjamin, Marcia Castro, Jyoti Thottam), the friends who kept saying, "Your book is so interesting, you should be on Oprah!" (Nancy Exumé, Susan John), and the friends who distracted me from writing altogether (Rina Agarwala, Afia Ali). I owe special thanks to Carl Haacke for always being willing to bat around potential book titles (such as *The Nature of Race: Ten Things You Always Wanted to Know but Were Afraid to Ask*).

I have been fortunate to be supported by my family in all kinds of ways. My father, John, the inveterate article-clipper, is my most faithful research assistant; my brother, John, patiently answered all my questions about copyright law; and my mother, Carole, read and commented on drafts of every single chapter in this book. Even my in-laws pitched in; I thank Mario, Rosa, Lucia, and Alberto for all the support and encouragement they have given me, especially on the days when I worried that things would never come together. I am even more indebted to the hardworking women who have helped keep up my home and family; this manuscript would still be an unpublished dissertation were it not for Shermin, Nadya, and Kirene. No one has done more, though, to keep me in pasta than my husband, Andrea. Even better, his intellectual rigor and bilingual eloquence help me work through and refine arguments big and small. And best of all, he has given me the sweetest, sunniest little girls in the world.

This book is dedicated to my daughters Sofia and Gaia, and to their cousins Coleman, Miles, and Anson. I truly wonder what they will make of all this race business one day.

ONE

Introduction

Even before my first child was born, her race—and mine—seemed to matter. Most of the pamphlets my doctor gave me about potential birth defects made reference to groups such as "African Americans" and "Caucasians," or they mentioned "ethnicity." A brochure from a company called Genzyme Genetics, for example, calculated a mother's risk of being a carrier of cystic fibrosis according to whether she was Northern European, Southern European, Ashkenazi Jewish, Hispanic, African American, or Asian American.[1] When I was twelve weeks pregnant, my doctor ordered a blood test that would indicate how likely the baby was to have certain chromosomal disorders such as Down syndrome. Before drawing my blood, a nurse asked me to state my race. Usually I describe myself as African American, but on that day, piqued by curiosity about what race had to do with my unborn child's health, I gave the full version of my ancestry: African, European, American Indian, and Asian. "Oh," the nurse replied as she noted my answer on a form, "So you go in the 'Other' box."

Since her birth, my four-year-old daughter has been racially classified on several occasions. Within twenty-four hours of delivery, Sofia received her first official racial designation: her birth certificate required her mother's and her father's race. Dutifully, I filled in "black," but my Italian-born husband went into a huff, and, muttering that *his* daughter would be "*a*racial," left the item blank. A week or two later, when we took Sofia to a doctor's visit, the hospital admissions clerk insisted that they needed to know her race before she could be seen. For someone who studies race for a living, I was surprisingly unprepared for the question. "Hmmm," I pondered. "Multiracial?" "That's not an option," the clerk told us. "We'll just put 'Race Unknown.'" Since those early days, my daughter's race has even been required on nursery-school applications. It is probably just the beginning of what will be a lifetime of forms, checkboxes, and computer codes that all designate race. In short, a typical American experience.

My own experience offers a sampling of the varied occasions on which Americans are called upon to identify their race. In addition to medical visits, I have had to report my race when submitting school applications, renting an apartment, getting a marriage license, applying for work as a college professor, being fingerprinted for government job clearance, obtaining research funding, and filling out the household census form. Although some of these examples clearly relate to my profession as an academic, several are routine experiences that many if not most Americans share. Categorization by race comes up in our institutional transactions as well as our interpersonal relations.

As common as bureaucratic requests for racial information are, however, they rarely come with any explanation of what race is. In the absence of explicit, straightforward, or accessible definitions of race, individuals are largely left to their own devices to make sense of what they are being asked for. What is it that we think we are revealing about ourselves when we report our race? Are we saying something about our cultural practices, appearance, biological makeup, ancestry, or social class? About our economic status, political leaning, health, or consumer habits? And why do requests for our "ethnicity" so often require that we choose a *racial* label such as "black" or "white"? Sociologists tend to define racial categories as being based on beliefs about physical difference, while ethnicity is thought to involve categories reflecting cultural differences (for example, in language, religious practice, customs, etc.). Yet the term *ethnicity* is frequently treated as a substitute for *race*, and not just in informal conversation.

When I was pregnant, I tried to find out what race meant from a medical perspective: what did it have to do with blood tests or my unborn daughter's health? A couple of the corporate brochures I received explained that the results of my blood tests would be affected by my "weight, ethnic background and age," making my ethnicity seem like a bodily measure akin to how old I was or how heavy. The nurse who drew my blood could not explain how race was relevant to predictions about my baby's health other than to say it somehow affected how my blood work was analyzed. So although I gathered that medical professionals believe race is meaningful for health, it was hard to figure out exactly how or why. What kind of a phenomenon was race that it could be linked to blood, genes, and illness?

SCIENCE, EDUCATION, AND RACIAL CONCEPTUALIZATION

How Americans define what race is—and how science, education, government, and business influence those views—is at the heart of this book. Our understandings of racial difference are undoubtedly shaped by our families, friends, neighbors, and peers. But in a society where racial classification pervades bureaucratic life, our everyday experiences in settings such as schools, companies, state agencies, and medical offices also leave their mark on our notions of race. Being repeatedly asked to report our race conveys the message that it is important—one of the handful of basic facts that people or organizations need to know about us. It also casts race as a permanent and individual characteristic: something that is embedded within us and does not change over time. Finally, the ubiquitous race question presumes a straightforward, self-evident answer: everybody knows his or her race. It does not require any complicated investigation or calculation.

The fundamental objective of this book is to explore how scientists' concepts of race are transmitted to the public through formal education as well as other institutions. The scientific enterprise is central to American thinking about race because its claims are often the bedrock upon which academic, business, and government interpretations of the nature of race purport to rest. The medical tests marketed by companies such as Genzyme Genetics are informed by scientists' research; so are census questionnaires and high-school textbooks. To be sure, the authority of the scientific establishment does not always go uncontested; consider for example the occasional successes of religiously inspired creationism in shaping biology education. Still, in the United States today, science is largely equated with "knowledge of nature," especially as it is acquired through a specialized process (Conner 2005, 2).[2] Indeed, as Yearley (2005, 1) put it, "Science is the exemplar and the measure of knowledge in the contemporary industrialized world." So in our society, the natural and social sciences are ultimately the place where we expect to find answers about what race is.

Despite the special authority that scientists enjoy, their beliefs are by no means independent of the broader society in which they train and practice. If lay people are influenced by what "experts" say about race, the reverse is true too: scientific notions of race are informed by the broader political and social currents of their times. This was the case in the nineteenth century when scientists sought to corroborate popular wisdom concerning the intelligence of whites or the physical frailty of mulattoes, and it still holds true today. This book, then, can be understood as focusing on one section of what is in fact a loop: the flow of scientific thinking to the public, which in turn unquestionably shapes scientists' views in the first place.

As students of "science popularization" know, scientific arguments are not usually conveyed directly to the lay public, but rather are transmitted through intermediate institutions. Organizations that have an obviously communicative function (such as schools, newspaper publishers, or television companies) clearly play a role in the dissemination of scientific thinking to the public, and they receive the lion's share of attention from scholars who study the diffusion of such thinking. Yet other institutions also send messages about the nature of race, either through explicit statements (for example, the Census Bureau providing a working definition of race on its website) or implicitly through their practices, such as using information about a patient's race to help analyze her blood samples. A central premise of this book then is that it is not enough to ponder the role of academic science alone when it comes to studying the impact of scientific expertise on Americans' understandings of human difference; we must also investigate the range of institutional intermediaries—from government agencies to biotech companies—that amplify and interpret scientists' views, putting them into material practice and thus delivering them for public consumption.

Among the institutions that channel scientists' notions of race, formal education provides the focus for this book. Elementary schools, secondary schools, and colleges and universities are in the business of teaching young people about the world, so it is in their classrooms that we might expect to find the most straightforward attempts to explain the concept of race. They are among the organizations most explicitly devoted to disseminating scientists' views to the lay public, and they may well have the greatest impact of any institutions with that mission. Formal schooling is nearly universal in the United States: in 2008, 88 percent of the population aged twenty-five and over had completed high school; only about 1 percent had not finished grade school (National Center for Education Statistics 2009). Moreover, messages delivered through education generally reach their audience at an important stage: in youth, when teaching has the potential to leave profound, lifelong impressions. Finally, the classroom setting, particularly at the college level, actually brings students into direct, face-to-face contact with the scientists whose research forms the core literature that will be disseminated through varied channels. In short, school seems like a natural place to start exploring how contemporary institutions transmit scientists' understandings of race as it enjoys a public reach that is unparalleled in its breadth, depth, and immediacy.

This inquiry about education and the spread of scientific race thinking is organized around three main questions:

1. What concepts of race do scientists hold?
2. What concepts of race do scientists transmit to the public through formal education?
3. How do students (the lay recipients) receive or react to these messages about race?

To answer these questions, I pursued three lines of research. In-depth interviews with over forty professors of anthropology and biology at four universities in the northeastern United States supplied data on how these scientists define race. A sample of over ninety textbooks in the social and biological sciences that were published between 1952 and 2002 illustrated the messages that are broadcast from the ivory tower to the public. Finally, interviews with over fifty undergraduates at the same four campuses where I spoke with professors helped me understand what these young people made of the race-related messages they encountered in the classroom.

LOSS AND REDEMPTION: AMERICAN RACE CONCEPTS AT THE START OF THE TWENTY-FIRST CENTURY

The Nature of Race advances a dual argument: that biological interpretations of race remain powerful in scientific thinking and communications to the public, and that in contrast, the idea that race is socially constructed is not conveyed nearly as widely. Indeed, the message that race is a human invention has been largely "lost in transmission."

These findings will surprise in some quarters. For one thing, they squarely contradict those social scientists who presume that the constructivist perspective on race dominates the academy. When I began my research on scientists' concepts of race, more than one senior scholar was skeptical that I would find any variety to study. "Everyone knows race is a social construct!" was the refrain I got used to hearing.

This book's central argument is at even greater odds with the more widespread belief that the United States has become a "postracial" nation. In the wake of Barack Obama's presidential campaign and election, the claim that "we are now entering a new era in America in which race has substantially lost its special significance" (Pettigrew 2009, 279)—in other words, a postracial era–has gained serious traction. But if race is fading as a dividing line in society, why is it enduring and perhaps even hardening as a biological boundary in the public imagination? And how does the biological model of race survive and indeed flourish in a nation that is increasingly multiracial? Given the diversification of our immigration stream as well as growing rates of interracial marriage over the last few decades, some scholars predict that racial mixture will bring about the demise of race (Daniel 2002) or at least a meaningful softening of color lines (J. Lee and Bean 2004). More generally, sociological research in recent years has come to emphasize the fluid and contextual nature of racial identity, whether in terms of individuals' self-description or group classifications. As a result, sociologists have perhaps inadvertently contributed to the "postracial" idea that race is less powerful or real than it once was. Yet despite these public conversations about the disappearance of race as a barrier to advancement, and academic treatises on the situational and constructed nature of race, the long-standing belief that race is etched on the human body and has far-reaching physical, social, economic, and political consequences has given up little ground. As I will discuss in the concluding chapter, the cohabitation of these perspectives on race—that is, the faith in physical race in the midst of an ostensibly postracial era in a multiracial society—offers insight into the contemporary forms that American racial conceptualization has taken.

Another major contention of this book is that there is no consensus among experts from any scientific background about what race is; disagreement flourishes not just between specialists in different fields, but within disciplines as well. Without greater agreement on—and a more concerted effort to promote—the constructionist understanding of race, it decidedly ranks as a minority viewpoint among the public that is most directly exposed to scientists' views: namely, undergraduate students. Those I interviewed were much more likely to define race in what I call "culturalist" terms—that is, to equate race with the ancestry-based cultural communities that sociologists call ethnic groups.

Why does the biological model of race hold such sway? It is not due merely to historical inertia, for the biological race concept met with considerable criticism in the twentieth century. Nor do biological accounts prevail simply because they are "true"; not only are they hotly contested by academics across the disciplinary spectrum, but history makes amply clear that in the past, various biological frameworks for race endured despite having had the empirical legs kicked out from under them. Instead, social changes—particularly demographic and political developments—have made biological views of race more appealing than they were a generation ago. Or, to put it more precisely, societal shifts have "redeemed" the biological race concept, stripping away its morally dubious connotations (for example, with eugenics) and associating it instead with benevolence and progress.

OVERVIEW OF THE BOOK

The Nature of Race is organized symmetrically. At its center are three chapters that present the findings from each of the data sets I described above: the textbooks, faculty interviews, and student interviews. The first of these is Chapter 3, which opens our inquiry into scientific communication about race by examining its presentation from the 1950s to the present in high-school biology textbooks, with comparisons to social science texts. Focusing on high-school texts targets scientific education that is more widespread than college training (as considerably more Americans graduate from high school than go on to college), and that underpins the toolkit of scientific knowledge undergraduates bring with them when they arrive at college. Chapter 4 picks up the story on university campuses, describing the definitions of race that emerged from interviews with anthropology and biology professors. Chapter 5 turns to their students, reporting on how those majoring in anthropology, biology, and other disciplines expressed their understandings of racial difference.

These three chapters are book-ended by two that place the transmission of race concepts through education in a broader perspective. Chapter 2 considers racial conceptualization as a topic of social scientific inquiry. It brings together disparate bodies of literature from varied disciplines that have touched on the question of how individuals define and think about racial difference. Chapter 6, which immediately follows the suite of empirical chapters, looks at institutional rather than individual conceptualizations of race. It situates formal education alongside other key institutions that embody and convey scientific ideas of race. And it offers an original typology by distinguishing key U.S. institutions that claim in some way to discern or identify individuals' racial membership based on scientific knowledge: the census, the law, the criminal-justice system, and the firms that sell DNA ancestry tests. I also look at the medical establishment as a primary institution through which scientific notions of racial difference are conveyed to the public.

Turning finally to the first and the last chapters of this book, the former provides a comprehensive overview of the book's questions and arguments, while the latter summarizes and then moves beyond them. Specifically, this final chapter poses the fundamental question of *why* American race concepts take the form they do today. This important question calls for sociological consideration of how notions of race reflect their times.

RACIAL CONCEPTUALIZATION AND ITS SIGNIFICANCE

What is racial conceptualization?

I use the term *racial conceptualization* to refer to the web of beliefs that an individual may hold about what race is. Our concepts of race are not limited to abstract definitions but rather incorporate a wide range of notions of what a race is, what distinguishes one race from another, how many and which races there are, how we can discern an individual's race, and how or why races emerge. In short, racial concepts are working models of what race is, how it operates, and why it matters.

Why do I contend that race concepts are more than simple definitions? A "definition" carries the connotation of a formal, abstract, and explicit summary statement, one that is articulated in a clear and thorough manner. Dictionaries readily provide definitions of race, such as "a group of people sharing the same culture, history, language, etc" (Jewell and Abate 2001, 1402), while a psychology textbook asserts, "Race refers to a set of hereditary physical characteristics that distinguish one major group of people from another" (McMahon and Romano 2000, 595). Formal definitions, however, cannot capture ideas that are inchoate, unexamined, or unexpressed. Nor do they easily extend to the body of ideas about human difference that might not fit neatly in a concise dictionary passage, but which are dimensions of how people understand race. A "definition" of race given in response to the question, "What is race?" (or "What is a race?") might not explain what distinguishes one race from another, how many races there are, or where races come from. Yet whether we examine them consciously or not, our answers to these questions and others make up the complex of our understandings about what race is. These notions contribute to a multifaceted model of race that helps us navigate a social world populated by races. How to determine a person's race; which races exist in the world; what it means to belong to a certain race—these are issues that life in a racialized society raises, and to address them we draw on our personal (yet deeply social) beliefs about the nature of race (Morning 2009). The term racial *conceptualization*— rather than the narrower word *definition*—captures this wider range of thinking.

Psychological perspectives on conceptualization

Psychological research lends support to this broad view of race conceptualization. In his pathbreaking book, *Race in the Making: Cognition, Culture and the Child's Construction of Human Kinds*, Lawrence Hirschfeld (1996, 1) argues that "[r]acial thinking is not simply a catalogue of human difference; it also encompasses beliefs about the very *nature* of difference." In

other words, it involves "a theory (or a theory-like constellation of beliefs) about human variation, its meaning, its scope, and its social significance" (80). The choice of the word *theory*—akin to the "working model"
I described above—is not accidental; it ties Hirschfeld's argument to a
broader psychological literature that investigates the formation of concepts
and categories in general, not just with respect to race. An influential
early article in the field, "The Role of Theories in Conceptual Coherence"
(Murphy and Medin 1985), posited that people's concepts "are organized
by theories" (290), that is, ideas about what kinds of things "go together"
and why. These "underlying principles" (297) of categorization or correlation determine what characteristics of an object become salient to us,
or what kind of relationship we presume it to have with other entities.
Similarly, David Schneider (2004, 120) uses the term *schemas* to describe
"theories we have about categories, . . . [which] function as frameworks
for understanding what we see and hear." These theories serve many
functions; they "aid in the recognition, interpretation, and labeling of
stimuli; affect memory for information; provide default values for missing information; and generally lead to efficient processing of schema-
related material" (122).

It is important to keep in mind, however, that the term *theory* does not
imply "a complete, organized, scientific account"; instead, it is better understood as "a mental 'explanation'" (Murphy and Medin 1985, 290), an
informal way of accounting for one's perceptions that may be uncon-
scious or unexamined.

> These theories provide subjective explanations that structure the social
> environment and define the partitions the perceiver imposes upon it.
> They explain what a given group of people is like, what attributes the
> group members share, and, more importantly, why they share these
> attributes. (Wittenbrink, Hilton, and Gist 1998, 49)

Psychologists' insights suggest that concepts of race are not simply
stock definitions or lists of racial features but ways of making sense of
the world; they embody implicit theories about human properties, social
relationships, and their determinants.

Key race concepts: "essentialism" and "constructivism"

If "racial conceptualization" refers to a cognitive process of meaning-making, what are the beliefs—that is, the "race concepts"—to emerge from this process? Scholars usually identify two types: the "essentialist" view of race and the "constructivist" (or "constructionist") perspective. In an early study of the race debate, for example, Leonard Lieberman (1968) distinguished essentialist "splitters"—academics who saw the human species as being naturally divided into races—from constructionist "lumpers," scientists who did not believe such racial subdivisions exist in our species. This stark essentialist-constructivist dichotomy may be too restrictive to adequately describe the range of beliefs about human difference that Americans hold today; it does not easily accommodate, for example, the "culturalist" concept that equates races with groupings of people who maintain shared values, norms, and practices. Yet essentialism and constructivism remain the key poles of academic debate on racial conceptualization, and all participants must contend with them. Moreover, they are not exclusively academic concepts: essentialist and constructivist accounts also appear in media coverage and everyday discussion, often dubbed the "race is real" versus "race is not real" camps. Given the centrality of essentialism and constructivism to both scientific and lay discourse about the nature of race, it is important to take a closer look at these two schools of thought.

ESSENTIALISM

Essentialism suggests that the members of a given group share one or more defining qualities—"essence(s)"—that are inherent, innate, or otherwise fixed. Haslam, Rothschild, and Ernst (2000) associate it more specifically with beliefs that a given social category is discrete, uniform, informative (that is, knowing a person is a member of the category gives us additional information about that individual), natural, immutable, stable, inherent, exclusive, and necessary (i.e., reflecting members' shared possession of a necessary condition or set of conditions). In the context of race, essentialism implies an inherited, immutable physical or psychological difference between racial groups, which are believed to be "natural kinds" (Quine 1977). Essentialist beliefs need not revolve around biology; they can be rooted in ideas about the soul, psyche, etc.—that is, whatever we believe to be the essence of human beings (Nelkin and Lindee 1995). In the United States today, however, this usually translates into discourse about biological (and particularly genetic) characteristics. An example of an essentialist account comes from zoologist Ernst Mayr (2002, 90), who has defined "a geographic race or subspecies" as "an aggregate of phenotypically similar populations of a species inhabiting a geographic subdivision of the range of that species and differing taxonomically from other populations of that species."

By all accounts, essentialism holds a prominent place in American concepts of race. Even scholars who do not personally subscribe to an essentialist viewpoint recognize that historically, notions of racial difference have been so tightly intertwined with beliefs about physical (or other essential) difference that today they can hardly be disentangled. In Hirschfeld's (1996, 42) definition of race, for example:

> Race theory is the recurrently encountered folk belief that humans can be partitioned into distinct types on the basis of their concrete, observable constitution. The notion of observable constitution captures the following features of racial thinking: racial differences are thought to be embodied, natural, and enduring, and are thought to encompass nonobvious or inner qualities (including moral and mental ones) as well as outward physical ones.

Although Hirschfeld does not support this vision of human difference, he cannot define race without including its references to biology. For this reason, scholars often speak as if there were only one view of race: "*the* race concept," one that is inevitably essentialist.

CONSTRUCTIVISM

Constructivism is fundamentally a theory about knowledge and how it arises. It maintains that what we know is not necessarily a reflection of what is really "out there" independent of human action, but is instead a product of social life. If essentialism posits that social categories simply reflect natural, stable differences between human groups, then constructivism counters that such categories are artificial or "man-made" through a process of "social construction." In his influential book, *The Social Construction of What?*, Ian Hacking (1999) describes the central argument for the social construction of some phenomenon X as: "X need not have existed, or need not be at all as it is. X, or X as it is at present, is not determined by the nature of things; it is not inevitable" (6). Kukla (2000, 3) adds to this argument the claim that X is "produced by intentional human activity," but the heart of the conflict between essentialism and constructivism lies in the determination of whether X—for example, race—is in "the nature of things" or is "a social invention" (American Sociological Association 2003, 7).

The dispute has frequently been translated as a question of whether race is "real," with the understanding that biology represents reality and social facts denote fiction. For this reason, some critics see constructivism as denying important truths about (biological) "reality," or as undermining valued scientific principles such as objectivity and positivism (Frank forthcoming; Gergen 1998; for examples of such accusations, see P. Gross and Levitt 1998; Sarich and Miele 2004). Yet constructivists do not see social groups as being any less real just because they are not rooted in biology. As Thomas and Thomas (1928) famously put it, "If men define situations as real, they are real in their consequences" (571–72). Religious communities, for example, are "real" features of our societies that wield enormous influence in world events, but we do not generally believe their membership is dictated by biological traits. The equation of "real" with "biological" then is not only unnecessary, but it obfuscates a debate whose outlines can be traced more clearly.

A more accurate way to contrast constructivism with essentialism is to recognize that the former proposes an alternative to the latter's explanation for what race is and how it is that races populate our social world. Where essentialists see racial categories stemming from largely fixed, inherited physical differences between human groups (and thus being enduring and universal features of our species), constructivists see the same categories as having been invented by human beings, and more specifically, as being the historical product of particular times and

places. Although different writers emphasize different historical ante-
cedents, constructivist narratives of the emergence of the race idea tend
to converge on fifteenth- through eighteenth-century European encounters with "others" as having given rise to belief in distinct, essential
races. Catholic Spain's treatment of converts of Jewish and Muslim origin, as well as European colonization and slavery in Africa, Asia, and
the Americas, are among the chief historical developments that constructivist scholars view as having fostered the notion of races (Fredrickson 2002; Smedley 2007). As this time line suggests, power and inequality play major roles in constructivist explanations for the formation
of social categories (Velody and Williams 1998). Omi and Winant (1994,
55), for example, define race as "a concept which signifies and symbolizes social conflicts and interests by referring to different types of human bodies." In the constructivist view, racial classification is at its root
an instrument of power, meant to establish social hierarchy and thus
elevate some people—economically, socially, and politically—at the ex-
pense of others.

The importance of racial conceptualization

The constructivist association of race beliefs with societal outcomes takes
us to the heart of why racial conceptualization matters. Simply put, our
ideas about the nature of race influence our racial attitudes and shape
social practices and policies.

What makes the contemporary debate about the nature of race such a
heated one is largely the connection that its participants draw between
race concepts and race attitudes, or more specifically, prejudice. For many,
the essentialist view of race is part and parcel of racism. Consider for
example geneticists Cavalli-Sforza, Menozzi, and Piazza's (1994, 19) definition of racism as "the belief that some races are biologically superior to
the others and that they have therefore an inherent right to dominate."
In this view, racism departs from the presumption of biological difference between races, and adds an inegalitarian or hierarchical interpretation of that difference. This linkage between racial concepts and attitudes is further supported by the historical observation that explicitly

oppressive projects such as eugenics and slavery were grounded in an essentialist vision of inherited, fixed, and far-reaching racial difference (Fredrickson 2002; Kevles 1995/1985; Nobles 2000). Contemporary individual-level research, moreover, has largely borne out this connection. In *The Anatomy of Racial Attitudes*, for example, Apostle et al. concluded that "how white people explain their perceptions of racial differences significantly influences what they are willing to support by way both of social policy and individual action to bring about greater racial equality in the society" (1983, 147; see also Sigelman and Welch 1991).

Yet there are also reasons to question any simple mappings of racial essentialism to racism. One is that empirical research has not always corroborated this relationship, a finding I discuss in greater detail in Chapter 2. Another is the theoretical possibility that essentialist belief in biologically distinct "natural" races need not be accompanied by racist belief in a hierarchy of races. Some proponents of the essentialist model of race believe it would be a disservice to historically oppressed minority groups to deny what they consider to be the important biological reality of racial groupings in humankind. They believe that race contains information that can help better address individuals' health needs; see for example Satel's (2002) article, "I Am a Racially Profiling Doctor," or "The Importance of Race and Ethnic Background in Biomedical Research and Clinical Practice" by geneticists Burchard et al. (2003).

Both the likelihood that individuals' racial conceptualization influences their racial attitudes and the current empirical uncertainty about just how particular race concepts are related to prejudicial attitudes are important reasons for pursuing—and improving—social scientific study of our notions of race. Perhaps an even more compelling motive, however, stems from the clearer observation that particular race concepts inform specific practices and policies.

Looking at the historical record of the United States, it is not hard to see how certain models of racial difference underpinned varied measures and activities. Slavery, Indian removal, immigration restrictions, intermarriage bans, and eugenic programs were all fueled by specific ideas of indelible racial difference. It is always harder to see how the present is shaped by our taken-for-granted beliefs. Still, there is ample evidence that our contemporary models of race affect how we do things, both as individuals and collectively as a society. For example, the foren-sic practice of attempting to racially label human specimens (such as skeletal fragments or other remains from disaster or crime sites) would make no sense unless it were undergirded by the belief that one's race is anchored in the body (Sauer 1992). In the United Kingdom, the same belief that race—as well as ethnicity—is genetically encoded has led to public authorities' use of DNA testing to assign children to foster-care families[3] and to verify the ethnic (and thus ostensibly national) identity of asylum applicants (Travis 2009). More broadly, research suggests that the belief that people of other races are very different from us dampens our willingness to engage with our neighbors (Putnam 2007) and to sup-port more generous social policies (Alesina and Glaeser 2004).

The contemporary link between concepts of race and models of gov-ernance has been vividly illustrated by several controversies. In 2007, Nobel prize winner James Watson drew on his conviction that Africans are innately less intelligent than Europeans to publicly question the util-ity of foreign aid to African nations, reasoning that their populations were incapable of improving their circumstances (Nugent 2007). This pronouncement echoed Arthur Jensen's widely publicized (1969) sug-gestion that public spending on the education of black children was fu-tile, given the natural limits of their intelligence. And in 2005, commen-tator Andrew Sullivan extended the relevance of racial difference from social policies to more fundamental rights. As he saw it, "one of liberal-ism's great contemporary problems" was

> how to reconcile the moral equality of human beings and the political
> equality of citizens with increasingly accurate scientific discoveries of
> aspects of human life that reflect our innate, biological inequality. The
> problem is intractable; and the more we try and solve this problem, the
> worse it can get. The better we get at improving the educational or
> social environment, or enlarging opportunity, the more tenacious and
> obvious our genetic differences will seem. That goes from individual to
> individual, but it also might apply to groups in certain categories.

Although Sullivan (2005) does not explicitly mention races (only ge-neric "groups"), in the United States the idea of "innate, biological ine-quality" has traditionally been closely tied to beliefs about race. In his view, essentialism is a key to good governance: it is only by an honest reckoning with individual and group inequalities that we can design realistic and effective social policy—or come to a satisfactory understanding of the moral and political status of our neighbors and compatriots.

In summary, our racial concepts—that is, the way we think about what race is and how racial difference is demarcated—have the potential to shape our evaluations of others and the courses of action we take with respect to them. This means that racial conceptualization merits much more than the limited attention that I will argue is all it has received from social scientists. This book is intended then to be both a call for greater empirical investigation of how Americans think about race and a response to that appeal.

AUTHOR'S CONCEPTUALIZATION OF RACE

After describing diverse concepts of race, it seems only fair to let readers know where I stand in the debate. I consider myself a constructivist, partial to definitions of race such as the ones by Omi and Winant (1994) and Hirschfeld (1996) quoted above. Specifically, I share with constructivists the belief that racial categories are the intellectual product of a particular (albeit enduring) cultural moment and setting, and that human biological variation does not naturally and unquestionably sort itself into the "black," "white," "yellow," and "red" groups that the Swedish naturalist Linnaeus outlined in the mid-eighteenth century (Hannaford 1996). Perhaps most fundamentally, I agree with Zuberi (2001) that as "a social invention" (American Sociological Association 2003), race is not an individual trait but rather a characteristic of a relationship or social setting. In other words, individuals do not carry race within them; instead, race is a label that is imposed on them (or a container into which they are put) depending on the society in which they find themselves. President Barack Obama nicely illustrates the contextual dependence of race: although he could be classified as "multiracial" or "white"—and would be in different societies or historical moments—he is usually referred to as "black" in the United States today. None of these labels is more "correct" than the other; there is no ultimate truth that resides in his body. Instead, the accuracy of each descriptor is a function of the culture in which he is classified.

These convictions about race stem from my studies in diverse disciplines, including demography, which shows that racial classification systems vary dramatically by time and place (S. M. Lee 1993; Morning 2008a); sociology and history, which reveal the arbitrariness with which the American "one-drop" rule assigns people of mixed-race heritage to a single race (F. Davis 1991; Wolfe 2001); and physical anthropology and biology, which report that human biological variation is gradual (or clinal) across geography rather than marked by sharp boundaries or disjunctures between one group of people and their neighbors.

My view of race is also undoubtedly colored by personal experience, and especially by the many instances in which I have encountered conflicts between different societies' approaches to racial classification. As a child, I knew that at home in Harlem, my parents, their friends, our relatives, our neighbors—we were all black. But that identity never held much water with my classmates downtown at the United Nations International School. Asian, European, and especially African students were amazed that I called myself black. "You're not black," they would say in reaction to my light brown skin. "You're tan!" Years later, as a student in Paris, I would get the same reaction from French friends. "You're not black," they would say. "You're *métisse*!" And as a Foreign Service Officer posted in Tegucigalpa, I even heard my Honduran colleagues say, "You're not *mulata*. You're white!" For years I only thought of these cross-national exchanges as funny anecdotes, but over time they began to pique my curiosity. How was it that something that seemed so obvious to people—my racial identity—could differ so much depending on where in the world I found myself? If my race was as real as everybody thought it was—something written on my face—then why didn't everybody come to the same conclusion?

When as a graduate student I was exposed to the argument that "race is a social construct," it seemed an immensely useful tool for explaining the variability in racial classification systems that I had encountered. But one thing bothered me about the constructivist school of thought: if this claim were really true, then why was it not more widely known? From Ashley Montagu's 1942 book, *Man's Most Dangerous Myth: The Fallacy of Race*, I learned that essentialist beliefs in fixed, physical racial characteristics had been challenged for at least sixty years. But why then did doctors still collect information about their patients' race? Why did people still debate whether black athletes have a racial advantage over their competitors? How did *The Bell Curve* (Herrnstein and Murray 1994), a book that argued races differed in intelligence, find such a wide audience? And why, for that matter, did my demography professors teach us to calculate life expectancies separately for whites and blacks? Was the "social construct" idea just a utopian myth, the product of sociologists' wishful thinking?

Reading Montagu's work half a century later opened up a historical perspective on the career of racial constructivism that prodded me to consider how ideas are disseminated over time, and—drawing on the sociology of knowledge—to think about that process in terms of stages. What if some scientists in the 1940s or even earlier had come to the conclusion that race was socially constructed, but the idea never won over a large segment of the academy? Then the lack of lay familiarity with racial constructionism could be attributed to its languishing in the "knowledge production" stage.[4] What if instead, scientists across the disciplinary spectrum had reached a consensus that race was socially constructed, but they were not successful at getting the message out to the wider public? That would constitute a blockage in the "knowledge transmission" stage. Finally, what if scientists did make a concerted effort to circulate the idea that race is a social construct, but the public was not persuaded? Then the lack of popular constructionism could be chalked up to a failure in the "knowledge reception" stage. In short, with the historical time line that *Man's Most Dangerous Myth* opened up, many different paths could have led to twenty-first-century Americans' retaining essentialist beliefs about race—if indeed they did. Answering the question of whether racial constructionism had any public purchase in the contemporary United States, and trying to account for that answer, led to this book.

Although I have presented my own perspectives on race in the interest of transparency, it should be clear that the objective of this book is not to proselytize for the constructivist point of view. Its aim instead is descriptive and analytical: to trace the ideas about human difference that are transmitted today from the academy to the public, and reflect on why these are the ideas that emerge and spread. My hope is to accurately report the many arguments that scientists and laypeople bring to the question, "What is race?," and not to judge them.

Accordingly, I propose a working definition of race that I believe both essentialists and constructivists could find acceptable. Specifically, I submit that race is a system for classifying human beings that is grounded in the belief that they embody inherited and fixed biological characteristics that identify them as members of racial groups. Where essentialists and constructionists would differ is on whether the belief in biological racial difference is accurate. But this definition is in itself agnostic on that matter, and so I offer it as a starting point for wading into the debate on the nature of race.

TWO What Do We Know about Scientific and Popular Concepts of Race?

> All but a very few individuals take it completely for granted
> that scientists have established the "facts" about "race" and
> that they have long ago recognized and classified the "races"
> of mankind. Scientists do little to discourage this view, and,
> indeed, many of them are quite as deluded as most laymen
> are about the subject. It is not difficult to see, therefore, why
> most of us continue to believe that "race" really corresponds
> to something which exists.
>
> —Ashley Montagu (1945), *Man's Most Dangerous Myth: The
> Fallacy of Race*

In a few trenchant lines, anthropologist Ashley Montagu captured the social nature of race as both object of expert scientific inquiry and stock item of everyday folk knowledge. His comment illustrates the close links— indeed, the complicity—between the two. In Montagu's view, popular belief in racial difference rests on the faith that science has penetrated its mysteries, while at the same time, scientists' understanding of race is thoroughly suffused with lay notions. This intertwined, mutually reinforcing structure underpins the widespread conviction that " 'race' really corresponds to something which exists."

Despite their interrelationship, making a distinction between scientific and lay concepts is a useful strategy when exploring American understandings of race. On one hand, historians, anthropologists, and sociologists have provided rich accounts of "race science" and its practitioners, past and present. Fairly separate from these scientist-focused studies, however, are the attempts psychologists, communications scholars, and sociologists have made to get at how ordinary people think (or thought) about race. This chapter brings together both bodies of literature in order to acquaint readers with the state of contemporary research on American race notions. The resulting overview illustrates how sparse the literature on racial conceptualization is, and it identifies important shortfalls that my study tries to—and future research should—address. First, however, a short history of American thinking about race from the eighteenth to the twentieth centuries sets the stage for the subsequent discussion of modern-day conceptualization. It was over the course of that period that the distinction between "scientific" and "folk" notions of racial difference emerged in the United States.

A BRIEF HISTORY OF RACE CONCEPTS IN THE UNITED STATES

As with any historical endeavor, taking stock of previous generations' ideas of race involves certain limitations.[1] Without the benefit of nation-wide, individual-level datasets—for example, there was no General Social Survey in the nineteenth century—historians, anthropologists, and others have investigated race concepts of the past by exploring scientific publications, newspaper articles, legal documents, census schedules, cartoons, novels, and other records of public discourse. One consequence is that such studies tend to privilege the viewpoints of elites—of published writers, government officials, or university professors—and leave the ideas of ordinary people unrecorded (Conner 2005; Ginzburg 1992). It is hard to know, moreover, how similar or dissimilar these elite views were to those of the broader public.

It seems likely that in the early years of the Republic, there was not much of a divide between scientific and lay notions of race, for the simple reason that the social distinction between scientist and layperson was once less sharp (Conner 2005). Certainly, the institutional landscape that we associate with science today—for example, universities, laboratories, government research institutes, private-sector research and development, etc.—is a fairly recent one. There were few colleges and universities in the United States until the 1862 Land Grant Act spurred their growth (Ben-David 1962), and even then, at least one historian has suggested that a fundamental "indifference to basic science" characterized our nation until the twentieth century (Shryock 1962). To further complicate the question of when it makes sense to talk about scientific versus popular views, what was considered scientific knowledge before the twentieth century would not be easily recognized as such today. Through much of the nineteenth century, knowledge of the world—the stuff of science—was equated with knowledge of God's creation, and thus American academics sought to reconcile their observations with theological doctrine (Clark 2006; Reuben 1996). As a result, both learned and lay notions of race were steeped in the same stream of religious thought. Biblical episodes such as Genesis, Noah and his three sons, or the Tower of Babel figured in popular and academic accounts of race in the United States (Sanders 1969; Smedley 2007).

Even when a recognizable class of scientific researchers arose in the Western Europe of the eighteenth century and the United States of the nineteenth, their thinking about race looked much like the public's simply because race science borrowed heavily from long-standing popular notions of difference (Hannaford 1996). As Smedley (2007, 27) puts it:

> Race, then, originated, not as a product of scientific investigations but as a folk concept; it initially had no basis, no point of origin, in science or the naturalistic studies of the times. The folk idea was subsequently embraced, beginning in the mid- to late eighteenth century, by naturalists and other learned people and given credence and legitimacy as a supposed product of scientific investigations.

The permeability of the scientific/lay boundary remains an important feature of American thinking about race. To be sure, such an interrelationship characterizes any area of scientific inquiry; as members of society, scientists always bring to their work ideas and assumptions that are shared with those outside the laboratory. But race—more than say quarks or microbes—was born as a concept before and therefore outside modern science, to be imported only later into a burgeoning scientific establishment. Given such wholesale incorporation, it is not surprising that scientists' views of race were largely elaborations of lay concepts. When we talk about "scientific" versus "popular" ideas of race over the course of U.S. history, we are describing sets of beliefs that are not necessarily very different in their content, but are labeled separately because they are voiced by people who came to be socially recognized as belonging to distinct classes. Indeed, it was only over time, with the twentieth-century crystallization of an academic constructivist perspective, that some scientific notions of race began to differ meaningfully from those held by everyday Americans.

"Race science" and folk race in the eighteenth and nineteenth centuries

The beginnings of "race science" can be traced to eighteenth-century Europe, when the forerunners of today's biologists and anthropologists sought to name, catalog, and describe the races of the world. Linnaeus (1707–78) is perhaps the best-known of the early taxonomists, but other influential human classification schemes were presented by François Bernier (1625–88), Georges-Louis Leclerc, Comte de Buffon (1707–88), and Johann Friedrich Blumenbach (1752–1840, "the father of anthropology"). These thinkers generally suggested that four to six races inhabited the earth, which in Linnaeus's case included *Homo sapiens monstrosus*, and in Buffon's outline, the "Polar Race" of Laplanders (Marks 1995; Smedley 2007). In addition to taxonomy, European scholars developed the first anthropometric measures of racial difference: Petrus Camper (1722–89) worked on "facial angles," Anders Retzius (1796–1860) introduced the cephalic index, and Paul Broca (1824–80) invented various instruments for the measurement of skulls and other human body parts (Hannaford 1996). Race played a prominent role in the early theoretical and methodological development of the sciences of humankind.

Eighteenth-century naturalists' taxonomies, which extended to all manner of flora and fauna, formed part of a broader "project of a general science of order" (Foucault 1973, 71) that was spurred in part by

Europeans' "discovery" of unfamiliar lands (Harding 1998). They epit-omize, moreover, the constructivist contention that race is an ideology that arose as a part of European attempts to make sense of—and dominate—others. The historian George Fredrickson (2002), for example, traced the emergence of racial essentialism to sixteenth-century Spain, particularly the belief that the descendants of Jewish and Muslim con-verts to Catholicism retained indelible markers of their ancestors' taint. According to this argument, such essentialist beliefs were then married to the color-coded social hierarchy that formed in the wake of European colonization in the Americas, Africa, and Asia. The end product was the essentialist and hierarchical black/white/yellow/red race concept that Linnaeus and other taxonomists formalized and that we recognize to-day. More generally, philosopher Ian Hacking sees race thinking as a fea-ture of all empires. "[T]he pervasive tendency to regard people of differ-ent races as essentially different kinds of people," he writes, "is produced by the imperial imperative, the instinct of empires to classify people in order to control, exploit, dominate, and enslave" (Hacking 2005, 114). The constructivist chronology of the rise of the race concept implies then that there existed a "pre-racial" Western world before the fifteenth or sixteenth centuries (Hannaford 1996; Snowden 1983)—but this claim is contested (see, e.g., Isaac 2004).

By any account, however, the United States occupies a striking his-torical position in that it never inhabited a West that was free of race thinking. Indeed, the founding of the United States coincided with the rise of race science, and so—unlike the states of Western Europe and their predecessors—our nation has always been part of a world where race also existed. As our foundational governing texts, such as the U.S. Constitution, the Naturalization Law of 1790, and the first census attest (not to mention writings such as Thomas Jefferson's (1784) *Notes on the State of Virginia*), the United States was steeped in racial ideology from the outset. We do not have an earlier history of significant experience with alternative bases for social and political stratification, such as the civic versus barbaric distinction that Hannaford (1996) attributes to the ancient Greeks and Romans, or the Christian versus non-Christian (i.e., infidel or pagan) distinction of medieval Europe (Fredrickson 2002).

Although American racial thought is rooted in European beliefs about human difference, its specific political, economic, and social organization has left a deep imprint on beliefs about race. First and foremost, the centrality of slavery in a society founded upon the principles of liberty and equality gave racial ideology in the United States a unique character. At its inception, race was a fundamental political organizing principle of the republic, enshrined in law as a determinant of who could enjoy the rights of citizenship. The equation of European ancestry with full citizenship and African heritage with slavery gave the American race concept its enduring preoccupation with a black/white binary. In addition, the nation's economic reliance on slave labor reinforced essentialist beliefs about Africans and their descendants. Other putatively inferior races were simply barred from national life: American Indians were not considered citizens of the early United States for the most part, and later, Asians faced immigration restrictions that either barred them from entry or denied them citizenship (DeGenova 2006). Black slaves, however, could not be dispensed with; to benefit from their labor, Americans had to keep them squarely within the national boundaries. To mark African Americans' degraded status then, even as they inhabited the heart of American society, beliefs about deep-seated, intrinsic, and unchanging racial characteristics—in other words, essentialist beliefs—flourished. The economics of slavery also had a hand in what is perhaps the most distinctive feature of racial conceptualization in the United States: the "one-drop" belief that blackness so thoroughly taints whiteness that even a person with just "one drop of black blood" is black. This system of hypodescent ensured that the offspring of slave and slave-owner would be counted as the latter's added slave property, and later, after Emancipation, that blacks' social status would be clearly demarcated against that of whites (F. Davis 1991). The associated refusal to recognize intermediate, mixed-race status—to see gray in addition to black and white—is another hallmark of racial conceptualization in the United States (Forbes 1993).

The importance of the institution of slavery in shaping American ideas about racial difference is also evinced by the fact that early scientific debates about race in this country were invariably linked to political clashes between pro- and anti-slavery factions (Nobles 2000). Before the Civil War, American scientists were embroiled in a dispute between "polygenists" and "monogenists" that they and others interpreted as having direct implications for the maintenance of slavery. Polygenists believed that each race descended from separate origins or acts of creation; monogenists adhered to the received theological wisdom about God's single creation of mankind and the resultant unity of the human species. Monogenists were not necessarily egalitarians or abolitionists— they accounted for the existence of races and racial inequality by referring either to the Great Chain of Being, which posited inequality as part of God's plan, or to the biblical stories of degeneration such as Adam and Eve's fall from grace, the destruction of the Tower of Babel, or the disparate fates of Noah's three sons (Sanders 1969)—but unlike the polygenists, they envisaged all races as members of the same human family.

When the monogenist/polygenist debate flared up in the 1830s in the wake of heightened abolitionist activity, it not only caught the public eye but, just as significantly, introduced science for the first time as a major authority on the nature of race. This prestige increased over the course of the nineteenth century as polygenists consolidated their expert status by marshaling empirical evidence of racial differences in skeletal structure, muscles, genitalia, brain size, sweat, speech, and intelligence, and by establishing the scientific fields of anthropology, craniometry, and anthropometry. Internationally recognized scholars such as Samuel Morton (founder of the first American school of anthropology), Josiah Nott and George Gliddon (authors of the extremely popular 1854 volume, *Types of Mankind*), and Harvard professor Louis Agassiz championed polygenist theory through their publications, their training of the first generation of the professoriate in their fields, and their pressure on the U.S. Census Office[2] to gather racial statistics that could be applied toward their research (Nobles 2000). In sum, their activities ensured that racial difference would become the province of science.

By the end of the nineteenth century, American attitudes toward slavery (and increasingly, immigration) had shaped a recognizable constellation of beliefs about racial difference. According to anthropologist

Audrey Smedley (2007, 28), Americans' understandings of race crystallized around the following tenets:

1. "a universal classification of human groups as exclusive and discrete biological entities"

2. "imposition of an inegalitarian ethos that required the ranking of these groups vis-à-vis one another"

3. "the belief that the outer physical characteristics of different human populations were but surface manifestations of inner realities, for example the cognitive linking of physical features with behavioral, intellectual, temperamental, moral, and other qualities"

4. "the notion that all of these qualities were inheritable—the biophysical characteristics, the cultural or behavioral features and capabilities, and the social rank allocated to each group by the belief system itself"

5. "the belief that each exclusive group (race), so differentiated, was created unique and distinct by nature or by God, so that the imputed differences, believed fixed and unalterable, could never be bridged or transcended."

Although we cannot say for sure how widespread these ideas were among either laypeople or scholars, there is little evidence of a divide between the two when it came to race. Instead, the twentieth century would usher in academic perspectives on race that were expressly conceived as correctives to popular notions of human difference.

Twentieth-century divergence of scientific and popular race concepts

The early years of the twentieth century hardly signaled a new scientific race concept on the horizon. The eugenics movement was in full swing in the United States, fueled by white Americans' anxiety over their race's survival. According to the eugenicist interpretation of Darwin's nineteenth-century evolutionary theories, the world's races were locked in a battle for the "survival of the fittest" (the term coined by sociologist Herbert Spencer), and the weaker ones were doomed to extinction. Widely read works such as *The Passing of the Great Race* (Grant 1916), *Foundations of the*

Nineteenth Century (Chamberlain 1911), and *Applied Eugenics* (Popenoe and Johnson 1918) stoked such fears through their predictions of "denordicization," racial impurity, and group conflict. The eugenics movement seemed to offer a solution with its calls for policy measures to boost the fertility rates of the white, Protestant, Anglo-Saxon middle and upper classes, and to suppress the reproduction of others. Moreover, the new field of genetics (the term was coined in the early twentieth century) also took up these concerns: in 1910, a Eugenics Record Office was established on the same site as the Cold Spring Harbor biology laboratories (Kevles 1995/1985). Eugenics had a large following in several Western nations, and its scientific proponents were part of an international network that linked the U.S. Eugenics Records Office to Germany's Society for Race Hygiene, the British Eugenics Education Society, and institutes in Sweden and Russia devoted to *Rassenbiologie*. Eugenicist tracts would go on to play a direct role in the genocidal policies of the Third Reich, and indeed in Adolf Hitler's writing of *Mein Kampf* (Hannaford 1996).

But if the Holocaust was the apogee of eugenic thinking in the West, it also brought on the collapse of that movement and a powerful alternative to the essentialist model of race. In the wake of World War II, international revulsion at the Nazi regime's experiments and murders demolished the legitimacy of eugenic science, even tarnishing the image of associated disciplines such as genetics and demography (Hodgson 1991; Kevles 1995/1985). Although scientific dissent from eugenics and racial essentialism had materialized well before World War II—for example, G.K. Chesterton published *Eugenics and Other Evils* in 1922—growing awareness of the Nazis' eugenic atrocities accelerated academics' movement toward rethinking the race concept and communicating their newfound views to the public. Julian Huxley and A.C. Haddon's 1935 *We Europeans* exposed race as "unscientific," Jacques Barzun published *Race: A Study in Modern Superstition* in 1937, Ashley Montagu inveighed against *Man's Most Dangerous Myth: The Fallacy of Race* (1942), and Ralph J. Bunche denounced race as "the great American shibboleth" (quoted in Hannaford 1996).[3] The anthropologist Franz Boas and his students made the revolutionary contributions of divorcing culture from biology (i.e., explaining that culture was not inherited "in the blood"), demonstrating the malleability of human measurement, and refuting assumptions about the superiority of certain groups with respect to others. Anthropologists Ruth Benedict and Gene Weltfish published an educational pamphlet in 1943 entitled *The Races of Mankind* that circulated widely in American schools, churches, press, and other organizations. And beginning in 1950, the United Nations Educational, Scientific and Cultural Organization (UNESCO) convened panels of biologists, anthropologists, and others to draft a series of official Statements on Race (Montagu 1972).[4]

The new, anti-essentialist concept of race to culminate from this scientific activity has been described by Lieberman (1968) as encompassing the following tenets:

- Human biological variation cannot be neatly divided into discrete categories.
- Racial characteristics are not transmitted together as complexes.
- Populations have always interbred, making the emergence of distinct races impossible.
- Racial boundaries are drawn arbitrarily, depending on the tastes of the classifier.

This set of claims directly opposed the elements of traditional American racial thinking that Smedley (2007) described. It is thus fair to say that around the middle of the twentieth century, social and biological scientists had developed a new outlook on race that was radically different from the long-standing lay notion. Lieberman called it the "lumper" view (as opposed to those who saw humans as "split" into biological races), and it has also been associated with constructivism due to its claim that the boundaries of racial groupings are invented by the classifier. It might be more accurate though to label it the "anti-essentialist" concept of race, one that aims to directly refute the biological claims advanced by racial essentialists.

The development and consolidation of the anti-essentialist perspective on race is extremely important in the history of American racial conceptualization because it marks the first major divergence between popular and scientific beliefs on the nature of race. This does not mean, however, that anti-essentialism became the norm or even widespread among social and biological scientists. Hannaford (1996) argues that Benedict—unlike Montagu—did not dispute the biological reality of race; instead, she endeavored to teach that racism was unjustified because races could not be arrayed along a hierarchy of superiority and inferiority. Similarly, Reardon (2005) has carefully traced the diverse views held by the authors of the UNESCO series of statements on race. Finally, Lieberman (1968) argued that although "lumpers" such as Ashley Montagu, Frank Livingstone, C. Loring Brace, Jean Hiernaux, and Lancelot Hogben argued race to be a fiction, there were also "splitters" such as Theodosius Dobzhansky, Stanley Garn, and Ernst Mayr who believed that biological races exist as a subspecies taxonomic unit that may range from a population differing in only a few gene frequencies to one that is on the verge of becoming a separate species. In other words, the fact that some academics began to embrace a new understanding of race did not mean that most or even many scientists' notions came to differ substantially from laypeople's. The extent to which "expert" opinion as a whole on race diverges from that of the public is an open question that existing research has not attempted to answer.

THE STATE OF RESEARCH ON CONTEMPORARY RACIAL CONCEPTUALIZATION

Sociologists today are strong supporters of the constructivist perspective on race. The view that race is "a social invention that changes as political, economic, and historical contexts change" has not only been promulgated in official statements of the American Sociological Association (2003, 7), but has become a central tenet of sociological teaching and writing. For example, the long-running *Sociology* textbook series defines race as "a socially constructed category" (Macionis 2001, 652).

But despite their emphatic insistence on the artificial nature of race, sociologists have made surprisingly little effort to learn how widespread this or any other concept of race is among individuals in the United States. Although race in general has been a major concern of American sociology since its inception (McKee 1993; Morris 2007; Winant 2007), racial conceptualization in particular has been overshadowed by other preoccupations. Early sociologists, most notably Robert E. Park (1864–1944), focused on race relations, paving the way for theories of racism in the civil rights era that drew new attention to institutional structures of racial oppression (Winant 2000). Since the 1940s (and especially the 1950s), national surveys have tracked Americans' opinions about issues such as school and workplace segregation, interracial marriage, and residential choice, investigating attitudes toward groups and policies that might pose obstacles to achieving racial equality (Schuman et al. 1997). And since the 1960s, diversifying immigration inflows and rising intermarriage rates have prompted scholars to revisit long-standing assumptions about racial identity and classification, launching new research on the categorization of mixed-race people and immigrant groups (J. Lee and Bean 2004). By the end of the twentieth century, American sociology had acquired a significant body of knowledge on race relations, stratification, discrimination, classification, and identity—but not on racial conceptualization. We know a great deal about whether people in different regions, educational cohorts, or income classes have similar or diverse attitudes toward interracial marriage or racial classification of their children. In contrast, we know virtually nothing about how Americans in different parts of the country or from different walks of life conceive of what race is in the first place. Are certain models of race more prevalent in some settings than others? What is the range of race conceptualizations we might find in the public today? Do young people envision race differently than older ones, or the foreign-born differently from the native-born? Such empirical questions have not even been broached, let alone answered.

Instead, sociologists, along with anthropologists, historians, political scientists, and legal and literary scholars have been interested in "public representations of and doctrines about race" (Hirschfeld 1996, 10)—in other words, the cultural manifestations of widely shared notions of race. Their analyses have illustrated how commonly held beliefs about race influence and are influenced by public discourse in countless areas, including advertising (Blanchard and Bancel 1998; Dávila 2001), film

(Rodríguez 2004; Vera and Gordon 2002), census enumeration (Nobles 2000; Wolfe 2001), beauty pageants (King-O'Riain 2006), immigration law (DeGenova 2006; Haney López 1996), white supremacist literature (Ferber 1999), and public health regulation (Molina 2006) to name just a few. These social researchers look to both historical and contemporary media and texts to describe prevailing representations of racial difference, and to investigate the relationship between these diffuse images of race and their social, political, and economic contexts. Important studies of the race concept in general include those by Gossett (1997/1963), Hannaford (1996), and Smedley (2007), and several works have concentrated more specifically on race ideas in science (e.g., Barkan 1992; Marks 1995; Nobles 2000; Reardon 2005). Although these studies provide important indicators of public racial ideology, however, their data do not permit individual-level analyses of how people see race or how different concepts of race are distributed in the population.

In recent years, psychology has been the discipline to most directly examine individuals' racial conceptualization. Lawrence Hirschfeld's pioneering work (see Hirschfeld 1996, 1997, 1998), which draws not only on experimental methods but on his anthropological training, has attracted considerable attention to the topic of race concepts. To be sure, his central argument—namely, that the human brain has a natural facility for categorizing human kinds, which makes socially created race taxonomy particularly easy for us to learn[5]—has not been unanimously accepted by psychologists. Still, his work has been a catalyst for new investigations of racial conceptualization that include the development of a Race Conceptions Scale (Williams and Eberhardt 2008), the finding that the salience of race in an individual's perception depends on his or her context (Cosmides, Tooby, and Kurzban 2003), and the research on essentialist beliefs concerning race and other social categories (e.g., Bastian and Haslam 2007; Demoulin, Leyens, and Yzerbyt 2006). Psychologists' study of conceptualization has been tightly linked to their interest in prejudice, which is not always limited to the area of race. As Hirschfeld (1996, 23) put it:

> The fact is, psychologists have not really developed theories about race. Instead they have elaborated theories about mental processes that

produce beliefs about categories of things that include, but are not restricted to, race. Psychologists do not theorize race; they theorize operations (e.g., prejudice, stereotypy, ingroup bias) that act on racial and other categories.

In the psychological approach to conceptualization, race is just one of many forms of social categorization of cognitive interest.

Psychologists and social historians come to the phenomenon of race conceptualization from opposite directions. Although sociologists and historians have focused so consistently on mass depictions of race that the individual is invisible, psychologists have trained their lens so intently on the private individual that she hardly seems to be part of a broader society. Sociologists have seen the forest of society-wide racial imagery, but not individual trees, whereas psychologists see individual trees very clearly without connecting them to a larger forest. The psychological emphasis on the mental construction of race does not tell us whether or how individuals' membership in particular social groups is related to the kinds of race concepts they hold. From this body of work, we cannot know which notions of race are most prevalent in a given population or how they vary according to people's economic, educational, geographical, religious, political, or other characteristics. These questions might be considered the domain of sociologists, but our discipline has done little to link race concepts to individuals at all.

Given the gaps between diverse disciplinary efforts to understand Americans' concepts of race, four fundamental questions have yet to be decisively answered. First, what concepts of race do individuals hold in the United States? Second, how prevalent is each? Third, how do Americans' concepts of race vary with their social, economic, or other status? And fourth, how have Americans' racial concepts varied over time, if at all? In this chapter I explore the limited body of empirical research that has taken up these questions, beginning with studies of social and biological scientists' race ideas, and then turning to explorations of laypeople's views. Empirical research on racial conceptualization has tended to focus on either scientific or popular views, not both simultaneously. This organizational separation, however, does not presume that scientists' concepts of race are markedly different from those of nonscientists; that is an open question to be explored.

CONTEMPORARY SCIENTISTS' CONCEPTS OF RACE

No single agreed-upon portrayal exists of the state of contemporary thinking about race in the biological and social sciences at the start of the twenty-first century. Observers' reports range all over the spectrum, from the perception that academics are uniformly constructivists to the claim that scientists are largely racial essentialists, including the opinion that scientists' racial concepts vary significantly.

Impressions of the state of scientific race conceptualization

Social science literature often gives the impression that academics across the disciplinary spectrum have concluded that race has no biological underpinning, only social origins. Political scientist Melissa Nobles (2000, 11) has written, for example, that "[t]he intellectual consensus today is that race has no objective existence." This depiction is not limited to the social sciences, however. Evolutionary biologist Joseph Graves (2001, 5) claims, "Today, the majority of geneticists, evolutionary biologists, and anthropologists agree that there are no biological races in the human species," and reports that two American Association for the Advancement of Science (AAAS) panels of philosophers, biologists, and social scientists have reached the same conclusion (156).

Other observers see a fundamental lack of agreement among academics on the nature of race (Angier 2000; Cooper 2003; Jackson 2008; Ossorio and Duster 2005; Sankar and Cho 2002; Wade 2004; Wadman 2004). Some point to a disciplinary divide between social scientists who share a constructionist outlook and biologists and physical anthropologists who hold a range of opinions or largely maintain an essentialist approach (Cartmill 1999; Duster 2003b; Keita and Kittles 1997; Krieger and Bassett 1993; S. S. J. Lee, Mountain, and Koenig 2001; Odocha 2000). Describing geneticists, Foster and Sharp (2002) write that "although the simplistic biological understanding of race and ethnicity associated with the eugenics movement may be dead, the far more subtle presumption that racial and ethnic distinctions nonetheless capture 'some' meaningful biological differences is alive and flourishing" (844). But many find conflict within disciplinary fields (Jackson 2008). Braun (2002, 165) emphasizes the variety of biological scientists' views: "Multiple, frequently conflicting, and generally implicit understandings of the concepts of race and ethnicity circulate in biomedical circles, with some researchers proposing that race has no genetic meaning, others arguing that the estimated 5 to 6 percent genetic difference is sufficiently meaningful biologically to justify an intensive research program, and still others arguing that the whole controversy can be circumvented by substituting ethnicity for race." In her subsequent analysis of biomedical literature on race published from 2000 to 2004, Braun identifies five different viewpoints in circulation (Braun 2006; see also McCann-Mortimer, Augoustinos, and Lecouteur 2004). Goodman (1997, 21–22) offers the following panorama:

> A crude typology of world views goes something like this. At one end of the spectrum are the true believers . . . for example, the psychologist J. Philippe Rushton asserts that there are three main races—Mongoloid, Negroid and Caucasoid—and he ranks them according to intelligence and procreative ability . . .
>
> At the other end of the spectrum are two groups who agree that races are a myth, but draw radically different conclusions from that premise. The politically conservative group, known for proclaiming a "color-free society," argues that if races do not exist, sociopolitical policies such as affirmative action ought not to be based on race. Social constructionists, on the other hand, realize that race-as-bad-biology has nothing to do with race-as-lived-experience . . .
>
> A fourth group, the confused, occupies the middle ground. Some do not understand why race biology is such bad science, yet they avoid any appeal to race because they do not want to be politically incorrect. Others apply race as a quasi-biological, quasi-genetic category and cannot figure out what is wrong with it. Still others think the stance against racial biology is political rather than scientific.
>
> That middle category of the confused is huge. It includes nearly all public health and medical professionals, as well as most physical

anthropologists. Moreover, the continued "soft" use of race by that well-meaning group acts to legitimize the "hard" use by true believers and scientific racists.

Thus many observers see uncertainty and conflict as characterizing the use of race in biology, medicine, and physical anthropology. As these assessments suggest, debate about the nature of race is likely to be not only interdisciplinary, but intradisciplinary as well.

Finally, some scholars see essentialism as the dominant racial concept in academia. A growing sociological and anthropological literature on the "geneticization" (Lippman 1993) or "molecularization" of race suggests that essentialist visions remain powerful in the academy (Fausto-Sterling 2004; Fullwiley 2007a; Outram and Ellison 2006c; Pálsson 2007). Related to re-search on molecularization in the life sciences (Shostak 2005) and genetic determinism in American social and political life more generally (Condit 2004; Duster 2006; Nelkin and Lindee 1995; Nerlich, Dingwall, and Martin 2004), this body of work argues that race is being "reinscribed" or "refash-ioned" today in terms of DNA (Abu El-Haj 2007). In this view, there is a continuity between contemporary scientific depictions of race and the es-sentialism of the past; as Duster (2003b) memorably put it, earlier race no-tions have simply been "buried alive" in today's sciences.[6]

Empirical research on scientists' race conceptualization

In summary, recent literature contains a wide range of opinions about the state of scientific racial conceptualization today. But what empirical evidence is out there to indicate which views actually prevail?

QUALITATIVE RESEARCH

One relevant body of research is made up by researchers' in-depth, qualitative assessments of the racial concepts that circulate in particular domains or sites of scientific activity. Anthropologist Duana Fullwiley, for example, uses interviews and ethnographic observation to trace the ways in which geneticists at particular laboratories think about race (Fullwiley 2007a, 2007b, 2008). Although her subjects often have difficulty defining exactly what they mean when they refer to "race," Fullwiley finds that traditional essentialist concepts of races—for example, as originally "pure," or as corresponding to Linnaean categories—routinely informed her subjects' interpretation of their genetic data. Montoya (2007) reported similar findings in his ethnographic study of diabetes researchers and their thinking about what Mexican ethnicity represented in their research. In a special issue of *Social Studies of Science* (volume 38, issue 5), Warwick Anderson (2008) chronicles a medical-school class where the instructors sought to convey a constructivist sensibility regarding race only to find their students skeptical and more accepting of biomedical perspectives closer to essentialism, and Epstein (2008) reports on the concepts of race held by personnel involved in recruiting subjects for clinical drug trials. The same issue also contains content analyses: Kahn (2008) explores media and journal discourse about BiDil, the nation's first race-targeted pharmaceutical drug, while Fausto-Sterling (2008) studies claims made about racial difference in the literature on bone density. Elsewhere, Braun (2006) examines the rhetoric used in selected "key texts" in the debate on race and genetics, and Shields et al. (2005) study the inclusion of race as a variable in research on smoking. In addition to these interview studies, ethnographies, and content analyses, historical projects such as Jenny Reardon's (2005) *Race to the Finish* and Wailoo and Pemberton's (2006) *The Troubled Dream of Genetic Medicine* describe ideas of race over a broader sweep of time. All of these works find that long-standing essentialist ideas of racial difference play a role in varied sectors of contemporary biomedical science.

Such rich and detailed analyses provide crucial insights into the kinds of race concepts that circulate among social and biological scientists in the United States. But they are rarely generalizable studies that offer an overarching view of how widely held particular views are in an entire profession or field of specialization. For a barometer of racial conceptualization in a discipline overall, two types of quantitative study have been conducted: surveys of scientists, and content analysis of scientific journal or textbook literature. I will concentrate on textbooks in the next chapter, but report here on a few analyses of journal discourse.

Cartmill (1999) calculated the shares of physical anthropology articles utilizing racial taxonomy over the 1965–96 period, putting them at about 40 percent annually on average. Finding no discernible trend over time, he concluded that "neither the proponents nor the opponents of racial classification have any grounds for thinking that history is on their side" (656). Gissis (2008) studied the use of race in American and British journals of genetics, epidemiology, and medicine from 1946–2003, discovering that it went through a period of decline before subsequently re-emerging. (See also Ahdied and Hahn's 1996 investigation of references to race, ethnicity, and national origin in the *American Journal of Public Health*.) Catherine Lee (2009, 1189) analyzed over two hundred articles appearing in biomedical journals since 1990, and found that although "scientists sensed the importance of race or ethnicity in biomedical research and thus used these concepts . . . they rarely defined them or articulated how race or ethnicity operated in their models. When racial or ethnic variation was found, most researchers did not provide an explanation for how and why such findings resulted or their medical significance."

In a related vein, Outram and Ellison (2006a) interviewed the editors of nineteen genetics journals in order to learn "how and why race/ ethnicity comes to be used in the context of genetic research," despite "continuing critiques from anthropology and related human sciences that focus on the social construction, structural correlates and limited genetic validity of racial/ethnic categories" (83; see also Ellison et al. 2008b). Their results showed "how these critiques have failed to engage geneticists, and how geneticists use a range of essentially cultural devices to protect and separate their use of race/ethnicity as a genetic construct from its use as a societal and social science resource" (Outram and Ellison 2006a, 83).

Journals in the biomedical and social sciences make up a complex, multifaceted body of scientific discourse that offers many potential avenues to investigate. There are special issues devoted to debate about the nature of race, such as those published in *Nature Genetics* (2004), *American Psychologist* (2005), *Patterns of Prejudice* (2006), *Biosocieties* (2006 and

2007), and *Social Studies of Science* (2008), not to mention those in science popularization magazines such as *Discover* (1994) and *Scientific American* (Bamshad and Olson 2003). There are editorials, such as *The New England Journal of Medicine*'s "Racial Profiling in Medical Research" (Schwartz 2001), and guidelines to potential authors about the use of race and ethnicity in research reports (Outram and Ellison 2006b). Scientific journals also publish professional associations' official statements regarding race—such as the American Association of Physical Anthropologists' (1996) "Statement on Biological Aspects of Race" and the American Anthropological Association's (1999) "Statement on Race"—as well as panel recommendations such as "The Use of Racial, Ethnic, and Ancestral Categories in Human Genetics Research" (2005) from the National Human Genome Research Institute's Race, Ethnicity, and Genetics Working Group, or "The Ethics of Characterizing Difference: Guiding Principles on Using Racial Categories in Human Genetics" by a Stanford University working group (S. S. J. Lee et al. 2008).

In addition to the articles described above, where editorial boards or professional organizations make their cases for one perspective or another, there is a wealth of journal contributions that raise questions about the use of race in biological and social science, or take up positions in the controversy. In medical literature in particular, many authors aim to answer practical questions about the applications or concrete implications of the debate on race. Examples include: "Is Research into Ethnicity and Health Racist, Unsound, or Important Science?" (Bhopal 1997 in *British Medical Journal*); "Genetic Influences on Health: Does Race Matter?" (Bamshad 2005 in *Journal of the American Medical Association*); "The Practitioner's Dilemma: Can We Use a Patient's Race to Predict Genetics, Ancestry, and the Expected Outcomes of Treatment?" (Barr 2005 in *Annals of Internal Medicine*); "'Population Profiling' and Public Health Risk: When and How Should We Use Race/Ethnicity?" (Ellison 2005 in *Critical Public Health*); and "Racial Categories in Medical Practice: How Useful Are They?" (Braun et al. 2007 in *PLoS Medicine*).

The "position pieces" that explicitly argue for a particular conceptualization of race frequently target the twin issues of the biological reality and utility of the race concept. To give readers a sense of their orientation,

I reproduce article titles here. Publications that argue in favor of a biological race concept include: "Racial Differences in the Response to Drugs—Pointers to Genetic Differences" (Wood 2001); Mayr's (2002) "The Biology of Race and the Concept of Equality"; "Categorization of Humans in Biomedical Research: Genes, Race and Disease" (Risch et al. 2002); Burchard et al.'s (2003) "The Importance of Race and Ethnic Background in Biomedical Research and Clinical Practice"; "Under the Skin: On the Impartial Treatment of Genetic and Environmental Hypotheses of Racial Differences" (Rowe and Rodgers 2005); and Rushton and Jensen's (2008) "James Watson's Most Inconvenient Truth: Race Realism and the Moralistic Fallacy." On the other side of the fence, articles that argue against a biological concept of race include: "Race and Genomics" (Cooper, Kaufman, and Ward 2003); "Race and Reification in Science" (Duster 2005); "Race and Genetics: Controversies in Biomedical, Behavioral, and Forensic Sciences" (Ossorio and Duster 2005); "Racial Categories in Medicine: A Failure of Evidence-Based Practice?" (Ellison et al. 2007); "Reviving 'Racial Medicine'? The Use of Race/Ethnicity in Genetics and Biomedical Research, and the Implications for Science and Healthcare" (P. Martin et al. 2007); "Genomics, Divination, 'Racecraft'" (Palmié 2007); and "Individual Genomes Instead of Race for Personalized Medicine" (Ng et al. 2008). This literature leaves out scientists' publications in book format or in the news media, such as Cavalli-Sforza's (2000) *Genes, Peoples, and Languages*, Leroi's (2005) op-ed piece in the *New York Times*, or Chowkwanyun's (2007) essay "Why Genes Don't Determine Race" in *TNR Online*. Still, journal articles that explore the relationship among race, genetics, and health make up a sizable corpus; Gissis (2008) put the number of such articles published since 2002 at around two thousand.

Finally, there is another body of journal literature that also reveals something of scientists' visions of racial difference: the vast repertory of research articles that refer to race (or "ethnicity") without entering into the debate about its relevance or indeed, necessarily reflecting on what racial difference represents in the analysis (M. Anderson and Moscou 1998; Fausto-Sterling 2008; Happe 2006; S. S. J. Lee, Mountain, and Koenig 2001; J. Martin and Yeung 2003; Root 2007; Webster 1994–95). Such articles can be found throughout the social and biological sciences, where race is routinely included as a variable in data analysis, but the meaning of race is not an area of inquiry. Thus a study of black/white differences in heart disease—or in college-graduation rates—may rely significantly on race as a variable without defining what the concept means or what its group categories represent. Although these publications do not address race directly, however, they may provide the most accurate depiction of how race is conceptualized in their respective fields. Journal editorials and position pieces, after all, convey the views of the minority of scientists who actively reflect on the topic. Most social and biological scientists do not focus on race, however, and even among those who use it considerably in their research, many work with standard categories without considering their origins or significance. For this reason, content analysis of scientific literature that explicitly engages the race debate is likely to overrepresent the views of specialists in the area (including both those who argue for and against a biological model of race).

SURVEYS OF SOCIAL AND BIOLOGICAL SCIENTISTS

Given the limitations of content analyses and small-scale qualitative studies, surveys of randomly sampled individuals offer an indispensable tool for learning how scientists understand race.[7] Yet this is the least frequent research strategy taken to gauge the state of scientific thought about race. Research that directly asks scientists about their definitions of race has been conducted almost entirely by anthropologist Leonard Lieberman and his colleagues. In particular, he led a 1984–85 survey of 725 professors in PhD-granting biology and anthropology departments that asked for their opinion of the statement, "There are biological races in the species *Homo sapiens*." The results support the contention that scientists' concepts of race are far from unified and that they vary according to their academic discipline. Seventy-four percent of the biologists surveyed agreed that biological races exist in our species, compared to 49 percent of the physical anthropologists and only 31 percent of the cultural anthropologists. Lieberman (1997, 550) attributed these differences to "the concepts, traditions, and data of each discipline," citing anthropologists' awareness of ongoing debate concerning the nature of race and their exposure to data on clinal (i.e., graded, rather than discrete) patterns of human phenotypic and genetic variation. Moreover, anthropologists in all four traditional subfields—cultural anthropology, linguistic anthropology, archaeology, and physical (or biological) anthropology—are likely influenced by cultural anthropologists' study of variation in classification practices across societies and time periods. In contrast, biologists are accustomed to the application of taxonomic categories to both plant and animal life and might see subspecies nomenclature such as "race" as a useful and unremarkable tool for identification.

Lieberman's work makes two pathbreaking contributions to the empirical study of scientific racial conceptualization. Not only does he provide the only large-scale survey of individual scientists' beliefs about race, but he and his colleagues examined the relationships between those beliefs and their adherents' socio-demographic and institutional characteristics. In other words, he did not provide just a snapshot of scientific racial conceptualization, but linked those concepts to particular characteristics. Exploring the patterns of variation in racial conceptualization is especially important when it comes to scientists' views because they cannot be simply explained away as a matter of disciplinary differences; there is too much disagreement within academic fields to support that conclusion. As Stark, Reynolds, and Lieberman (1979, 90) put it, "We have, among authorities in the same discipline who employ similar techniques to analyze similar bodies of facts, different patterns of discovery and interpretation." Among colleagues in the same academic field, then, what factors contribute to their diverse conceptualizations of race?

Lieberman and his colleagues examined variation in scientists' racial conceptualization according to six factors: gender, minority status, age, political orientation, geography, and institutional setting. With respect to the first, Lieberman (1997) found that across disciplines, women were consistently more likely than their male colleagues to reject the notion of biological races. Among biologists, 21 percent of female respondents rejected the race concept versus 9 percent of males; among physical anthropologists, 50 percent of the women did so versus 40 percent of the men; and among cultural anthropologists, 56 percent of the women disagreed compared to 52 percent of the men.[8]

These findings about gendered racial conceptualization suggest a hypothesis that has been applied to a broader class of variables: the idea that marginalized social status is associated with the tendency to challenge biological determinism. Minority status, for example, has been mentioned as a factor in racial conceptualization (Lieberman 1997; Littlefield, Lieberman, and Reynolds 1982; Shanklin 2000). Littlefield et al. (1982, 646) concluded, "Anthropologists who teach in [nonelite] institutions, and whose social origins are relatively less privileged, tend to be more receptive to the no-race position than their colleagues in the elite institutions." Similarly, Stark et al. (1979) found that faculty interviewees who believed that races exist were more likely to come from a higher socioeconomic class as determined by the income and education levels of their families of origin. They also cited others' research indicating that individuals from families of recent immigrant origin or Jewish background were more likely to maintain that "No races exist now or ever did." Stark et al.'s explanation could be applied equally to the findings on gender and minority status: "those who have benefited more from the extant structure of social relationships will tend to grant more legitimacy to the use of a concept reflecting and supporting that structure" (97).

For similar reasons, it is often suggested that political orientation colors individuals' views on the social construction of race and other classifications (e.g., Cartmill 1999, 652). Specifically, conservatives are linked to essentialist views, seen as justifying the status quo, while liberals are associated with constructionism and its implication that social structures are ultimately flexible. In one example, Harrison (1999, 614) argues that "neoconservative foundations" such as the Pioneer Fund actively "promote research that seeks genetic determinants for upward mobility, IQ, and violence." Political attitudes might explain some of the difference between social and biological scientists, if, as Ladd and Lipset (1975) argued, biologists are more conservative on the whole. They may also be associated with the regional differences that characterize "splitters" versus no-race "lumpers." Stark et al. (1979, 93) discovered that splitters were more than twice as likely as lumpers to live in the South or Midwest of the United States (43 percent versus 17 percent), which they referred to as "the conservative heartland."

Age cohort appears to shape racial conceptualization because it influences exposure to particular understandings of race. In 1982, Littlefield et al. related historical changes in anthropologists' views of race to time trends in the demographics of the discipline and in national politics. In a similar vein, Lieberman and Jackson (1995, 239) predicted that contemporary graduate students, "unexposed to the sensitizing experiences of the social movements of the 1960s and 1970s" (not to mention the postwar condemnation of mid-century race science), would become more likely to accept race as a biological given. Stark et al. (1979) pointed to the same in explaining why they found younger faculty more likely than older professors to adopt a splitters' "race exists" position.

The foregoing discussion of factors influencing scientists' racial conceptualization has emphasized individual socio-demographic characteristics. However, status characteristics of the institutions in which these individuals operate may play a role as well. The empirical evidence to date is inconclusive. The results shown in Lieberman et al. (1992) demonstrate only minor differences in racial conceptualization between faculty in PhD- , BA/MA- and AA-granting biology and physical anthropology departments. But research conducted in the 1970s and reported in Littlefield et al. (1982, 646) found larger differences, where only 32 percent of the faculty in PhD-granting physical anthropology departments were no-race "lumpers" as compared with 48 percent and 53 percent of the faculty interviewed in BA/MA-level departments and AA-granting departments, respectively. Littlefield et al. also noted that socioeconomic privilege was more closely correlated with racial concept among the higher-level departments, and hypothesized that in the two-year colleges, the sociocultural characteristics of the students (who were from less privileged backgrounds than those in PhD- and BA-granting departments) might play a larger role in influencing their professors' outlook on race. This exploration raises the possibility that institutions of higher education are important not just for what they impart to students, but for the influence they exercise on their faculty members' understandings of racial difference.

The research of Lieberman and colleagues, conducted nearly thirty years ago, is too outdated to offer a portrait of scientists' race views in the early twenty-first century. It predates major advances in genetic research that have influenced the terms of scientific debate about race. This body of empirical work nonetheless offers a rich starting point for hypotheses about the individual and institutional characteristics that may shape scientists' race thinking. Equally important, it highlights how large a gap exists in our knowledge of contemporary racial conceptualization. Small-scale interview studies, local ethnographies, and topic-specific content analyses contribute important and nuanced insights into the intricacies of racial beliefs, but are not broad enough to convey a sense of how large sectors of the scientific community think. Conversely, the large-scale survey studies conducted by Lieberman and colleagues offer a much-needed overview of scientific practitioners' racial conceptualization, but their work is now so badly outdated as to provide more of a historical than a current vantage point.

Discussion of literature on scientists' race concepts

In the absence of empirical data that can offer a definitive statement regarding racial conceptualization among today's scientists, a wide range of scholarly opinions flourish. Some observers believe that scientists have overwhelmingly rejected a biological concept of race, while others are persuaded that scientists have largely retained such essentialist views. The empirical data that have been gathered on the topic, however, do seem to largely rule out one scenario: that scientists across the spectrum have reached a consensus that race is a purely social construct without biological underpinning. Surveys, interviews, content analyses, and ethnographies have not pointed to cross-disciplinary rejection of the biological vision of race. Instead, the empirical question outstanding seems to be whether the academy is divided when it comes to thinking about the nature of race, or whether scientists are fairly unified in their essentialist, biological conceptualization of race. The survey studies fielded by Lieberman and colleagues suggest the former (as do many observers—see for example Braun 2006; Gissis 2008; Goodman 1997; Olson 2001; Wadman 2004), while the ethnographic and small interview studies described above that point to the traditional race notions embedded in scientists' research and analysis could be taken on the whole to suggest the latter.

POPULAR CONCEPTS OF RACE TODAY

When it comes to the lay public, empirical research on individuals' race concepts—as opposed to diffuse beliefs about race that are manifest in cultural artifacts such as films and novels—has analyzed roughly three types of data: (1) in-depth interviews or focus group discussions, (2) large-scale surveys, and (3) psychological experiments. Each has different strengths and weaknesses. While discourse analysis of interviews and focus groups permits the identification of important themes and their description in rich detail, it tends not to lend itself to generalization about the public at large. Instead, national random surveys offer a portrait of how racial concepts are distributed in the population and with what factors they are associated. But the question approach usually used in these surveys is problematic, for reasons that will be discussed below. Finally, psychologists' study of racial conceptualization has focused on exploring the link between conceptualization and prejudice, but pays little attention to how racial conceptualization varies with individuals' socio-demographic characteristics.

Focus groups and interviews

In-depth interviews might seem like a natural way to examine people's beliefs about what race is, since their flexible structure permits the kind of initial exploration of new ideas that is particularly productive in understudied areas such as racial conceptualization. Yet this is perhaps the least-used tool of social research when it comes to studying race concepts, and the findings about conceptualization that have emerged from interview research have usually been minor elements of a scholarly agenda focused on other questions. For example, in her study of "long-distance nationalism" among Haitian-origin youth, Glick Schiller (2005) finds that her subjects' ideas about the nation are inextricably bound up with ideas about race through essentialist metaphors such as that of "blood." And in her research on working-class men in the United States and France, Lamont (2000) contends that her American interviewees' notions of race can be classified as biological, historical, psychological, or cultural. However, this finding, though of real relevance to the question of how Americans conceptualize race, is not a central concern for Lamont's study of moral boundary-marking.

The focus-group research conducted by communication scholar Celeste Condit and colleagues has made a large and direct contribution to the empirical study of popular beliefs about genetics, race, and the relationship between the two. In the article "Lay Understandings of the Relationship between Race and Genetics," Condit, Parrott, and Harris (2002) reported the results of a focus group in the southeastern United States where participants were asked "Do persons of different races have the same genes?" In related studies the researchers asked respondents to "list some races" (Condit et al. 2003), and posed the questions, "What do you think is generally meant when people use the term 'race'?" and "Is race defined by culture? Geography? Heredity or genetics? Color? Religion?" (Dubriwny, Bates, and Bevan 2004). They also conducted a random-digit-dial telephone survey in Georgia in 2002–3. Sixty-one percent of the survey's 644 respondents agreed that "Genetics plays a primary role in determining an individual's race"; in fact, the most frequent response, given by 42 percent, was to "strongly agree" with the statement (Condit et al. 2004b, 260).

Based on this series of projects, Condit et al. (2004b, 253) drew the following conclusions:

1. lay people identify race primarily by physical features, but these identifications are categorized into a variety of groupings that may be regional, national, or linguistic;
2. they believe that physical appearance is caused largely by genetics, and therefore that race has a genetic basis;
3. lay people believe that perceived differences in traits thought of as "non-physical" are caused by factors other than genes, so that;
4. while lay people do perceive races as hierarchically arrayed, they do not necessarily attribute the basis of these hierarchies to genetics.

In other words, Condit et al. concluded that "[l]ay people understand race as a multifactorial concept" (Dubriwny, Bates, and Bevan 2004, 193). More specifically, they interpreted their data as pointing to "three inter-dependent factors in the lay understanding of race: genetic variation and physical characteristics, cultural factors (including cultural attributes, religious beliefs and socioeconomic status) and socially constructed factors (including history of discrimination, use of race to separate and segregate and a general awareness that race is a social construct)" (ibid.).

The Condit studies are innovative and insightful, contributing a com-pelling answer to the question of how people conceptualize racial differ-ence. Their local scale, however, means they are not easily generalizable to a national portrait of racial conceptualization. Moreover, their focus-group methodology is not intended to provide descriptive statistics about individual race concepts. As the authors recognize, their project "studies how public discourse about genetics and race evolves, rather than pro-viding a secret window to individual attitudes" (Condit, Parrott, and Harris 2002, 385). Indeed, they argue against an individual-level analysis of racial conceptualization:

> This study clearly suggests that the social resources for the understand-ing and application of science are not best conceptualized solely in terms of individual knowledge and attitudes. The knowledge of a social group is a product of the *interaction* of the disparate knowledge of its several members. (Condit, Parrott, and Harris 2002, 385)

These scholars' work serves to remind other researchers of what may be missed or overlooked in the kind of individual-level analyses to be described next.

Large-scale surveys

Perhaps the most extensive body of empirical research to offer insight into individuals' racial concepts comes from large surveys of randomly sampled respondents. The survey items from which race concepts are inferred, however, are almost uniformly questions that were designed to measure racial attitudes—that is, "favorable or unfavorable evaluation[s]"

(Schuman et al. 1997, 1) of "racial and ethnic groups and their attributes, aspects of relations between groups, public policies relevant to race, contact between those groups, and assessments of the character of intergroup relations" (Bobo 2001, 267). In other words, most of the relevant survey questions available were not developed to capture racial concepts per se, but rather to reflect prejudice and other racial attitudes. As a result, for the most part large-scale surveys have constituted only a blunt tool with which to trace contemporary beliefs about the nature of race.

The survey approach to measuring racial conceptualization centers on what I call the "outcome explanation" approach. This strategy is exemplified by the question on the National Opinion Research Center's General Social Survey (GSS) that asks respondents to choose from among four explanations for why blacks on average "have worse jobs, income, and housing than white people" (Schuman et al. 1997). One response option on this telephone survey is that blacks have "less in-born ability to learn" than whites; an individual's selection of this item has been interpreted as indicating that he or she holds an essentialist race concept (see, e.g., Bobo, Kluegel, and Smith 1997). In a variation of the "outcome explanation" approach, Jayaratne et al. (2002, 2006) conducted telephone surveys in which they put the following question to a representative sample of six hundred white Americans: "Some people think whites tend to differ from blacks in intelligence. Do you think their genes have anything to do with this difference?" Moreover, the researchers then varied the question to also ask whether respondents believe genes explained black/white differences in athleticism, "drive to succeed," math performance, and tendency toward violence.

An early and especially detailed use of this explanation approach was presented in Apostle et al.'s (1983) *The Anatomy of Racial Attitudes*. In 1973, they asked over five hundred whites in the San Francisco Bay area to evaluate possible reasons why "white people get more of the good things in life in America than black people," why whites have higher IQ test scores than blacks, why a hypothetical black John Smith had achieved career success, and why "the average black person is less well off than the average white person." In their respondents' ensuing explanations for black/white differences, Apostle et al. discerned six "explanatory modes":

1. *supernatural*: God made the races different
2. *genetic*: races are different by nature/according to the laws of nature
3. *individualistic*: blacks have failed to "use their free will to better themselves"
4. *radical*: whites in power are the conscious perpetrators of black oppression
5. *environmental*: impersonal social forces are at work
6. *cultural*: cultural dissimilarities are at work

The researchers noted, moreover, that the same individual may draw on more than one mode in offering an account of racial difference. In particular, the genetic mode seemed to be especially prevalent in combination rather than alone. Apostle's team categorized only 12 percent of their survey respondents as either "pure" geneticists or supernaturalists (i.e., holding essentialist beliefs in innate and immutable racial difference), but the researchers determined that an additional 24 percent held genetic or supernatural views in combination with others (83).

The results of such surveys have led some observers to conclude that racial essentialism is on the decline in the United States (Bobo, Kluegel, and Smith 1997; Harrison 1999; Hutchinson 1997). In 1973, 36 percent of Apostle et al.'s (1983) white respondents espoused racial essentialism, but four years later, the GSS estimated that only 26 percent of whites believed "most blacks have less in-born ability to learn" (Schuman et al. 1997, 154–55; see also Sniderman and Piazza 1993). In 1996, almost twenty years later, only 10 percent of white GSS respondents agreed that blacks had less ability than whites, and by 2004, this figure had dropped to 7 percent. Taken together, these figures appear to point to a steady and significant decrease over time in the extent to which Americans believe that race reflects fixed, essential differences. As early as the 1980s, Apostle et al. concluded that "we are well past the era in which genetic explanations were dominant" (229).

Yet other survey evidence complicates the depiction of essentialist notions of race growing rarer with time. When Apostle et al. (1983) posed their questions differently, they obtained different results. In response to the question, "How do you feel about the idea that, for reasons which we cannot know, God made the races different?", 16 percent of their white survey respondents reported "they were convinced this was true," 16 percent "leaned in that direction," 25 percent were doubtful but left the possibility open, and 42 percent were "disbelievers" (78). And when asked, "How about the genetic arguments that the forces of nature have created the differences between races that we find today?", 9 percent believed it to be true, 32 percent "leaned" that way, 31 percent doubted it, and 29 percent did not believe (78). Though not necessarily inconsistent with Apostle et al.'s other findings, these results could also be interpreted to mean that 57 percent of the whites they surveyed thought it was possible that God created racial differences, and that 72 percent thought it possible that genes dictated racial difference. Jayaratne et al.'s (2002; 2006) results also challenge the assertion that racial essentialism is on its way to extinction in the American public. For one thing, Jayaratne et al. have estimated that at least one-third of whites now believe that genetics lie behind racial differences. For another, they found that this figure jumps sharply depending on what type of difference is at issue; for example, 70 percent of their respondents believed that genes explain black/white differences in athletics. Similarly, a 1995 survey of 686 people in Connecticut found that almost half believed in at least one biological difference (other than skin color) that distinguished whites from blacks (Plous and Williams 1995). Thirty-one percent of the respondents believed that white skin is thinner, 24 percent that blacks have longer arms, and 14 percent that whites are more sensitive to pain (cited in D. Schneider 2004, 458).

In short, it is hard to come to any firm conclusions about Americans' racial concepts based on the empirical survey data that are currently available. Different survey questions, methods, dates, sample sizes, locations, and interviewee characteristics all pose a challenge to distilling clear-cut results. For example, Bobo and Smith (1998, 199–200) have shown that question format can have a large impact on how people characterize racial differences. For one thing, whites' likelihood of claiming significant differences between themselves and blacks rise noticeably when they are asked to address specifically the areas that have been the mainstays of American belief in racial biology: athletic ability, sexual drive, and intelligence (Apostle et al. 1983, 210). For another, socially desirable responses may be more likely to arise in some data-collection situations than others. D. Davis (1997) and Condit, Parrott, and Harris (2002) point to the effect that an interviewer's race has on respondents, and Brückner, Morning, and Nelson (2005) show that telephone versus Internet surveys produce different degrees of socially desirable response to questions about race and genetics.

The likelihood of social desirability effects on interviewee responses poses a real challenge to the drawing of any conclusion about trends in American race conceptualization over time. Actual beliefs about race may have changed much less than have language norms concerning their expression. In this connection, it is worth noting that even the analysts who point to statistical declines in essentialist racial thinking recognize that whites' diminished willingness to voice beliefs in innate racial difference does not necessarily imply a lessened adherence to such views. Apostle et al. (1983) noted that some of the decrease was likely due to the fact that "it was no longer as socially acceptable as it once was for a white American to admit openly that he or she believed that blacks are inferior" (150), and their study provides considerable support for this idea. Not only did their white respondents frequently mention considering what they should or should not say for fear of being labeled a racist (ostensibly unfairly), but they were much more likely to say that other whites claimed significant differences between themselves and blacks than they were to affirm such differences themselves.[9]

Most fundamentally, the "outcome explanation" (or "explanatory mode"—see Apostle et al. 1983) approach often used on surveys was not designed to measure racial conceptualization, and so is a flawed indicator of everyday notions of race. By asking whether genetic difference accounts for socioeconomic race differentials, these questions confound opinions about the existence of genetic race differences, the existence of socioeconomic race differentials, and the relationship between the two.

When asked to explain "why white people get more of the good things in life" (Apostle et al. 1983), interviewees must draw on their views of whether (1) whites are in fact better off than blacks; (2) genes have anything to do with race in general; and (3) genes have anything to do with the specific outcomes that the survey presents, such as income differentials or differences in intelligence. A person who declines to identify differences in "in-born ability" as the cause for the black/white wage gap could be someone who believes that there are no racial differences in "in-born ability," or someone who believes that there are race differences in ability, but that these are not the cause of racial wage differentials. The difference is enormous when it comes to trying to identify the racial concepts held by that person, but it cannot be detected from this General Social Survey item. Because such "outcome explanation" questions do not ask directly how respondents define race or explore other facets of racial conceptualization (for example, which groups are races and what the principal differences between races are), they are not suited for the measurement of individual racial conceptualization.

In short, any instrument to gauge racial conceptualization must be designed for that purpose, multifaceted, and able to cope with complexity. Apostle et al.'s (1983) work raises the real possibility that individuals hold multiple concepts of race simultaneously, making it difficult to discern distinct conceptual approaches when they so often emerge in combination, or when one does not seem to exclude the coexistence of another. In particular, the "individualist" account for racial inequality, which is the most frequent among whites today (Schuman et al. 1997, 156–58), makes no reference to biology yet may be driven by essentialist beliefs. As Apostle's team acknowledges, the individualist belief that blacks have failed to exercise the options open to them often contains a genetic rationale at its core, as revealed by further probing of respondents (26–27). Although Bobo, Kluegel, and Smith (1997, 16) interpret contemporary data on racial attitudes as indicating that whites "prefer a more volitional and cultural, as opposed to inherent and biological, interpretation of blacks' disadvantaged status," the work of Apostle and colleagues suggests that the line between the two outlooks is blurred.

A final shortcoming of the attitudinal surveys is their tendency to re-duce racial conceptualization to a matter of whites' perceptions of blacks. By concentrating their efforts on interviewing whites about blacks, re-searchers overlook the possibility that whites' definitions of race might vary if they were prompted to consider other racial groups besides blacks, and the researchers ignore the understandings of race that nonwhites hold (but for exceptions see Hunt 2007; Sigelman and Welch 1991). This is a serious omission: in a nation where whites' share of the total popula-tion is projected to drop below 50 percent before 2050 (S. Roberts 2008), such an approach sets the stage for explorations of racial conceptualiza-tion to take place in less than half the nation.

Variation in racial conceptualization

Despite the serious shortcomings of survey data to date as a tool for mea-suring racial conceptualization, large-scale survey research has the po-tential to produce broadly generalizable results and to permit the study of variation in racial conceptualization over time, across place, and by socio-demographic grouping. Although the age, local scope, and imper-fect measures of existing survey data are limiting, it is nonetheless worth considering the patterns of variation in racial conceptualization they suggest. Below I present the socio-demographic characteristics that re-searchers have investigated in connection with racial conceptualization along with their results. Where relevant, I also remind readers of the role such factors appear to play in scientists' understandings of race.

RACE OR MINORITY STATUS

This is perhaps the characteristic to which empirical research on racial conceptualization has paid the greatest attention. In studies of scientists, several scholars suggested that race or other forms of minority status (e.g., immigrant origins, Jewish identity) were negatively associated with essentialist concepts of race (Lieberman 1997; Littlefield, Lieberman, and Reynolds 1982; Shanklin 2000; Stark, Reynolds, and Lieberman 1979). However, recent research on the lay public paints a more complicated picture. On one hand, Jayaratne (2002) found persistent differences in whites' and blacks' likelihood of accepting genetics as a basis for racial difference. Across different realms (intelligence, drive to succeed, math performance, and tendency toward violence), roughly 30 to 35 percent of whites saw genetics as an underlying cause, whereas approximately only 20 to 25 percent of blacks did so. Similarly, Dubriwny, Bates, and Bevan (2004, 194) found that

> African-Americans have a fluid definition of race that is not fully dependent on genetics or physical characteristics. Specifically, African-Americans are more likely to see culture as a part of race, deny color as a part of race and recognize the constructed nature of race through discussions of discrimination, segregation and self-definition . . .
>
> [European-Americans'] emphasis on color, other physical characteristics, genetics and geography as important to the definition of race combined with the general denial of culture and self-definition combine to create a definition of race that is based in large part on physical characteristics and heredity.

Research by social psychologists Williams and Eberhardt, however, cautions against a simple white/majority versus nonwhite/minority dichotomy when it comes to racial conceptualization. In a sample of college students where 63 percent of the nonwhite respondents were Asian, 13 percent identified themselves as Latino and 11 percent as multiracial or other race, and 3 percent were black,[10] the researchers found their nonwhite respondents to be more likely than whites to conceptualize race in biological terms. Moreover, Condit, Parrott, and Harris (2002, 383) found that in their focus groups, African American men were more likely than others "to use body build, strength, and athleticism as measures of racial distinctiveness than any other group." The researchers noted moreover that "when made by the Black participants, these comments were made with a sense of pride and seem to be used as positive markers of racial identity, which runs counter to widely expressed fears that linking athletic performance with racial identity might have a demeaning effect."

GENDER

Despite the expectation that female gender would function like a minority status and predispose women to reject racial essentialism (Lieberman

1997), empirical analyses have shown the association between gender and racial conceptualization to be weak to nonexistent (Apostle et al. 1983; Condit, Parrott and Harris 2002; Jayaratne et al. 2006).

AGE AND COHORT

In the 1970s, Apostle et al. (1983) found that older Americans were more likely than younger ones to espouse what they called the "traditional" explanatory modes for racial difference (supernatural, genetic, and individualistic) as opposed to the "modern" environmentalist and radical modes. (Note however that among academics, Stark et al. (1979) found that younger faculty were more likely than older professors to adopt a splitters' "race exists" position.) Roughly thirty years later, Jayaratne et al. (2006) found a significant and positive correlation between age and the belief that genes determine racial difference. The fact that age seems to remain positively associated with racial essentialism in the general population regardless of time period may mean that period effects have less impact on race concepts than a general "life course" trend whereby individuals become more likely to embrace biological race notions as they grow older. However, it may also indicate that the cohorts alive in the 1970s and the first decade of the twenty-first century have both lived through a continuing trend over time where society has consistently turned further and further away from essentialist beliefs about race so that the period effect has reinforced the age effect.

EDUCATION AND OCCUPATION

Conflating their analysis with age somewhat, Apostle et al. (1983) also found that white Americans with less education and at lower occupational levels were more likely than others to adopt the "traditional" supernatural, genetic, or individualistic accounts for race differentials. In particular, college students were more likely than adults in any other occupation to espouse a "modern" environmentalist or radical explanatory mode: 42 percent did so compared with 36 percent of professionals and 21 percent of blue-collar workers (171). In their survey of white Americans, Jayaratne et al. (2006) also found that education was negatively associated with essentialist race conceptualization. These findings run counter to Stark et al.'s (1979) conclusions based on their survey of college professors: they determined that faculty from a higher socioeconomic class (as determined by the income and education levels of their families of origin) were more likely to believe that biological races exist (see also Littlefield, Lieberman, and Reynolds 1982).

POLITICS, RELIGION, AND REGION

Both Apostle et al. (1983) and Jayaratne et al. (2006) found religiosity to be positively associated with racial essentialism among white Americans. Moreover, the latter group of researchers also found the positive correlation between political conservatism and racial essentialism that many scholars have claimed exists (e.g., Duster 2003a; Longino 1990; Shakespeare 1998). Stark et al. (1979, 93) linked both social and political conservatism to region in their study of academics, noting that the U.S. "conservative heartland"—the South and Midwest—was home to a disproportionate share of essentialist race "splitters." Among laypeople however, Jayaratne et al. found no correlation between Southern residence and racial concept.

Racial concepts and attitudes

More than any link to socio-demographic characteristics, empirical research on racial conceptualization has overwhelmingly pursued the relationship between race concepts and racial prejudice. Scholarly interest in this link goes back over fifty years to Gordon Allport's (1954) groundbreaking work *The Nature of Prejudice* (Haslam, Rothschild, and Ernst 2002). Apostle et al. (1983) tied concepts and attitudes together by positing that racial attitudes comprise three elements: perception, explanation (i.e., conceptualization), and prescription regarding racial difference. Among these, they stressed the importance of explanation over perception, maintaining "the ways people respond to an out-group are less dependent on perceived differences than on how the perceived differences are explained" (15). Moreover, the belief that essentialist race concepts in particular are a fundamental ingredient in prejudice is widespread enough to figure in many definitions of racism. See and Wilson (1989, 227), for example, describe racism as a "complex belief system" based on claims that an out-group "is either biogenetically or culturally inferior."[11]

A considerable amount of empirical evidence supports the linkage of essentialism to prejudice, not just in the realm of race but with respect to other social categories. Apostle et al. (1983, 34) found that interviewees who believed race differences to be physical and inborn were most prejudiced and least willing to support policy solutions to racial socioeconomic inequality (see also Kluegel 1990). Jayaratne et al. (2002, 2006) also report that whites' belief in genetic racial differences is positively associated with negative attitudes toward blacks. In an experimental setting, Johannes Keller (2005) was able to elicit greater levels of prejudice by making essentialist ideas more salient for his subjects. Similarly, Condit et al. (2004a) found that subjects who were exposed to public service announcements on genetics and heart disease that mentioned "blacks" and "whites" exhibited greater levels of prejudice than those who heard the same messages without any races specified. Finally, psychologists Nick Haslam, Brock Bastian, and others have conducted a series of studies that systematically explore the relationship between essentialist thinking and prejudice. They have found that not only are individuals who hold essentialist beliefs (about varied kinds of social categories) more likely to endorse stereotypes (Bastian and Haslam 2006; see also Yzerbyt, Rogier, and Fiske 1998), but they also have a stronger preference for stereotype-consistent information rather than stereotype-inconsistent information (Bastian and Haslam 2007).

Prentice and Miller (2007) argue, moreover, that essentialist thinking has consequences beyond prejudice and stereotypes. As they put it, psychological essentialism—that is, "the belief that all members of a category share a common underlying essence and that this essence causes many of their observable features"—has an impact on "the way members of essentialized categories are perceived, approached, and evaluated" (203; see also Medin and Ortony 1989). In this vein, Williams and Eberhardt (2008) created a Race Conceptions Scale spanning social to biological concepts of race, finding that individuals scoring near the latter end were not only more likely to endorse racial stereotypes, but had less diverse friendship networks and expressed more pessimism about the possibility of redressing racial inequality. Similarly, No et al. (2008) developed a Lay Theory of Race Scale to administer to Asian American students, and found that essentialist concepts of race were associated with less desire to assimilate to what they perceived as "white" American culture. Bastian and Haslam (2008) report that immigrants to Australia who held relatively essentialist beliefs were less likely to adopt an Australian identity in their process of acculturation.

Yet despite the empirical evidence linking essentialism to prejudice, there are also several findings that prevent drawing any simple conclusion. As Prentice and Miller (2007, 204) put it, "the relationship between essentialism and social evaluation is not entirely straightforward." In their article "Are Essentialist Beliefs Associated with Prejudice?", Haslam, Rothschild, and Ernst (2002) discovered that essentialism was strongly associated with anti-gay sentiment, but not with racism or sexism.[12] Moreover, they learned that subjects essentialized gay men differently than they did blacks or women. Whereas research subjects saw blacks and women as constituting groups that were natural, discrete, immutable, and stable over time, the subjects associated gay men with other essentialist aspects: category uniformity, inherence, and informativeness. As a result, the researchers emphasized that their findings did not demonstrate that "essence-related beliefs play a causal role in prejudice" (98).

The relationship between essentialism and prejudice is further complicated when the beliefs of nonwhites are taken into consideration. On the 2004 General Social Survey, blacks were actually more likely than whites to claim that racial differences in socioeconomic status were due to blacks' lesser in-born ability: 13 percent of black respondents agreed compared to 7 percent of whites (see also Hunt 2007; Sigelman and Welch 1991). Although Jayaratne's (2002) data do not put blacks ahead of whites in terms of the proportion espousing racial essentialism, they suggest that fully a quarter of black respondents believed genes caused blacks to be less intelligent than whites.

Moving beyond the level of individuals' beliefs, moreover, any scholar wishing to establish that essentialism is intertwined with racism must reckon with what can be called the "strategic" use of essentialism by minority or stigmatized groups. According to Harrison (1999, 616; see also Shakespeare 1998), some groups may wish to benefit from "the political usefulness of reified racial categories" as they press for egalitarian social change. Some Afrocentric scholars for example are proponents of highly essentialist theories (Morning 2009). Another example might come from multiracial activists who see themselves as "challenging" or "undermining" racism, yet whose understanding of multiracial identity is an essentialist one that rests on some notion of "pure" races being mixed through biological reproduction (Spencer 1999, 2006). Conversely, Harrison (1999), Sundstrom (2008), and Visweswaran (1998) contend that some conservative politicians deny the existence of race for racist purposes, namely to eliminate social policies targeting racism and racial inequality. (This stance does not constitute a social constructionist position, however—even if it does appear to abandon essentialism—since it denies the social reality of race.) Epstein (2007) finds an example of strategic essentialism in the efforts of female policy makers to attract attention for women's health concerns; for these largely white and middle-class women, "whose relative social equality has been affirmed, conceptions of essential or biological difference appear to pose no substantial political risk. Instead, such essentialism serves as a foundation for their professional agendas." In the Netherlands, Verkuyten (2003, 373) found that members of both the native Dutch majority and diverse ethnic minorities drew on essentialist arguments, leading her to conclude, "Essentialism is not by definition oppressive, just as anti-essentialism is not by definition liberating."

Verkuyten's comment raises a philosophical question that is independent of observed patterns of belief: Is a nonracist essentialism possible? Consider for example the Association of Black Cardiologists' support for the race-targeted pharmaceutical BiDil, extended in the belief that it held the promise of improved medical care for African Americans, or the Latino geneticist motivated to better understand the mechanics of health problems that disproportionately afflict people of color in the United States (Fullwiley 2007a). Though we might consider their assumptions to be essentialist, can we say they are racist as well? It clearly seems possible that belief in natural, biological divisions in humankind need not be yoked to a hierarchical worldview that ranks races above or below each other. Difference need not mean inequality. Yet whether such bias-free essentialism actually exists in our society to a significant extent is another question.

Discussion of literature on popular race concepts

One of the most striking findings to emerge from the existing literature on lay concepts of race is that their range does not seem to be confined to the essentialist/constructionist dichotomy that characterizes scientific debate on the topic. In some of the most nuanced research on this issue, communications scholars found that ideas about physical difference, cultural practices, and social construction all simultaneously informed their subjects' understandings of race (Condit et al. 2004b; Dubriwny, Bates, and Bevan 2004). And Apostle et al. (1983) identified six different modes for explaining socioeconomic race differentials that might translate to distinct concepts of race, such as the vision of races as creations of a divine power, the work of racist whites, or the logical outcome of neutral social forces. Each of these explanatory accounts can be understood as facets of a larger model of race, which includes ideas about what races are, how they originate, and what differentiates them.

Within these expanded typologies of racial conceptualization, essentialist views of race may not be as dominant as scholars have assumed. Although current measurement instruments are far from ideal and socially desirable reporting is a serious concern, the shares of survey respondents who now subscribe to essentialist beliefs about racial differences in ability are quite small. At first glance, such findings might undercut "new racism" theories that maintain racial prejudice continues to be widespread in American society. But on further examination, the apparent move away from racial essentialism over time may merely reflect a shift to more veiled discourse—for example, about minorities' not choosing to "better one's self" (Apostle et al. 1983) or "catch the vision" (Emerson, Smith, and Sikkink 1999). Moreover, empirical research on the relationship between racial conceptualization and racial prejudice has offered puzzling results. Some scholars report a clear-cut association between racial essentialism and

prejudice while others dispute it. Just as race concepts themselves constitute an area of inquiry that remains largely unexplored, the link between
concepts and attitudes would benefit from empirical research that does not
shy away from challenging long-standing assumptions.

CONCLUSION

The study of racial conceptualization as a society-wide phenomenon has
yet to find a real home in any one discipline. At present, different fields
have contributed diverse elements to this research agenda. From sociology and history we have an idea of public discourse on race that speaks
to the concepts that both everyday people and elites have held. Anthropologists have taken a close look at scientific practices past and present
and the notions of racial difference they betrayed. Recently, communications scholars have explored how groups make meaning out of discourse on race and biology. And psychologists have brought powerful
theoretical tools and experimental methods to the investigation of racial
conceptualization.

Researchers in these diverse fields of endeavor have not collaborated,
however, to produce a body of knowledge that describes or analyzes the
race concepts held either by Americans in general or scientists in particular. As a result, we have little data with which to answer basic questions such as: What share of the U.S. population holds essentialist concepts of race? How many subscribe instead to a constructivist vision? Do
these percentages vary depending on factors such as gender or educational attainment? Do they vary by region or religious affiliation? And
how have they changed over time (if at all)?

The patchwork of research that has been conducted on these questions is quite suggestive. Contrary to what many sociologists seem to
assume, essentialist beliefs about inherited, intrinsic racial differences
appear to be far from dead in academia. Conversely, essentialist thinking
may not be as total in the lay public as scholars have presumed. Another
intriguing set of findings pertains to variation in racial conceptualization
in the population. Racial essentialism seems to be more prevalent among

older people, the less-educated, those who are more religious, the politically conservative, and whites. These claims, however, are based on a very thin layer of empirical research—often no more than one study, possibly conducted decades ago—and are often contradicted by another study's findings.

Considering the limitations of the data on which they are based, these research results offer little more than hypotheses. Some of the most broad-based studies are simply too old by now to offer much guidance, while others use research instruments that are not well-suited to the measurement of racial conceptualization. And without a better understanding of social desirability effects, it is especially difficult to make a statement about any changing concepts of race over time. It may very well be the case that the tenets of racial conceptualization that Smedley (2007) attributed to the early years of the twentieth century are still in force today.

THREE **Textbook Race**

LESSONS ON HUMAN DIFFERENCE

A study of some of the methods and systems of classification not only is fascinating but gives you an excellent opportunity to make use of the scientific attitude and method in coming to fair conclusions.

—Arthur O. Baker, Lewis H. Mills, and Julius Tanczos Jr. (1959), *New Dynamic Biology*

High-school textbooks such as *New Dynamic Biology* have had a lot to say to young Americans about race. Over the course of the twentieth century, they have introduced their readers to "the races of man" and provided detailed charts of our species' racial diversity. They have warned against the dangers of racism and informed pupils of the race-specific risks for particular diseases. They have narrated vivid historical accounts of racial origins and homelands. And occasionally, they have presented race as a socially constructed classification scheme. With their colorful illustrations and straightforward prose, textbooks have been a major channel for disseminating scientists' views of race to the public.

The impact of high-school textbooks is both wide and deep. In a nation where education through secondary school is nearly universal and textbooks are a major element of the curriculum, high-school texts reach an extraordinarily large audience.[1] According to the National Center for Education Statistics (2009), U.S. high schools enroll roughly sixteen million students annually, and it has been estimated that those students spend 75 percent of their classroom time and 90 percent of their homework time using textbooks (Keith 1985). Textbooks also shape the thinking of the teachers who study them while preparing lesson plans (Klein 1985). Furthermore, these texts have the potential to have an especially profound influence because we treat them as authoritative sources of meaningful, accurate, and uncontested information about the world. Indeed, social analysts of science such as Fleck (1979/1935) and Kuhn (1996/1962) used the term *textbook science* to refer to the fundamental knowledge that experts in a field agree upon. According to Foshay (1990, 33), the textbook is a modern-day descendant of the earliest religious and philosophical scriptures, and it retains an aura of infallibility. As he put it, "A school textbook carries with it the assumption that it contains the uncontroverted truth."

Since the early twentieth century, a variety of scientists, educators, and public officials have recognized the enormous potential for education in general, and textbooks in particular, to shape popular thinking about race. In 1939, the American Committee for Democracy and Intellectual Freedom, chaired by renowned anthropologist Franz Boas, called on "scientists, school administrators, teachers, and publishers" to "clarify the whole race question in the minds of the young," mostly by ridding textbooks of references to race as a hierarchy of nations or cultures (614). Similarly, in its 1967 Statement on Race (the fourth in the series launched in 1950), the United Nations Educational, Scientific, and Cultural Organization (UNESCO) proclaimed, "The schools should ensure that their curricula contain scientific understandings about race and human unity, and that invidious distinctions about peoples are not made in texts and classrooms" (Montagu 1972, 161). In the wake of the civil rights movement, the problem of racism in textbooks—especially in the humanities—received special attention. In 1977, the Council on Interracial Books for Children published *Stereotypes, Distortions and Omissions in U.S. History Textbooks*, which was soon followed by investigations such as *The Slant of the Pen* (Preiswerk 1980b), *Ethnic Groups in History Textbooks*

(Glazer and Ueda 1983), and *Reading into Racism* (Klein 1985). That concern over what schoolbooks teach about race endures today in works such as Nash, Crabtree, and Dunn's (1997) *History Trials: Culture Wars and the Teaching of the Past*, Selden's (1999) *Inheriting Shame*, and Zimmerman's (2002) *Whose America? Culture Wars in the Public Schools*.

This chapter takes a look at contemporary high-school textbooks and the messages they convey about the nature of race. It aims to address one of this book's central research questions: what concepts of race do scientists transmit to the public through formal education? Additional responses to this question, however, will come in the next two chapters, which describe professors' and students' views of college teaching.

This study of textbooks differs from previous research on the topic in two important respects. First, I investigate the broad concepts or definitions of race that textbooks present, rather than evaluating whether the texts display racial prejudice. Second, I examine biology and social science texts, taking on a wider range of disciplinary fields than the previous studies that focused on history instruction. Specifically, I analyze over twenty contemporary textbooks in the biological and social sciences and put them in historical perspective by comparing them to a sample of nearly seventy biology textbooks that were published between 1952 and 1994.

As I will show, textbooks in different disciplines approach the topic of race from different angles. Psychology books tend to mention race in connection with racism, while biology texts insert it in lessons on human genetics. Nonetheless, a few common features cross disciplinary boundaries; for example, formal definitions of the term *race* can be found in both social- and biological-science texts. More importantly for my purposes, textbooks in different subjects can all be evaluated in terms of their orientation toward essentialist or constructivist notions of race. In response to the question, "What kinds of concepts of race do high-school textbooks convey?" I find that U.S. texts are much more likely to expose students to essentialist understandings of race than to promote the idea that race is socially constructed.

Before turning to the empirical findings, it is worth elaborating on the relationships among textbooks, scientific expertise, and popular knowledge. Although it is probably easier to see how textbooks reflect scientific rather than lay views, it is important to realize that they are indeed shaped by popular beliefs about race. Despite the use of phrases such as "textbook science," textbooks today are not simply the direct output of scientific committees. The "real writer" of a textbook, according to Keith (1991, 48), "is most likely to be the publisher's in-house editor and not the identified editor on the book's title page." Moreover, primary and secondary textbooks in the United States are molded by commercial and political pressures (Skoog 1992; Tyson-Bernstein 1988). The textbook industry is dominated by a handful of conglomerates that compete fiercely to sell their wares. Not only must publishers consider how individual consumers (whether students or teachers) will react to their products, but they must navigate a politicized process where state and local officials select texts for use in their districts, at times with input from public hearings. The most highly publicized examples of this process come from various states' scrutiny of evolutionary theory in biology textbooks. But scientific texts are vetted by lay people on an ongoing, everyday basis. As a result, textbooks are not only scientific publications: they are also consumer goods for market purchase and government-regulated treatises. They are tailored to scientists' specifications, political currents, and popular tastes, all at the same time.

Consequently, textbooks occupy a position at the intersection of academic science and the lay public where they offer a clear vantage point on the relationship of mutual influence that exists between scientific and popular beliefs. Textbooks reflect—albeit imperfectly—the scientific views of their era, and they reveal what ideas are presented to the public as "scientific" and thus worthy of attention. At the same time, textbooks also illustrate how much lay thinking informs scientific models. In their colorful pages, we see for example how widely shared popular beliefs about pure races or which groups constitute races serve as basic premises for scientists' research on human biological diversity and history. Scholars of science use the term *co-production* (Jasanoff 2004) to describe this two-way relationship where scientists' categories shape social order, and at the same time, "societal arrangements affect the kinds of categories that scientists can use to characterize human diversity" (Reardon

2005, 9). In textbooks we can see both how scientists' ideas are made popular and how lay ideas become scientific.

RESEARCH ON RACE IN TEXTBOOKS

Previous research

As mentioned above, studies of race in educational curricula usually focus on racism, particularly in history textbooks.[2] They do not generally take up the question of how textbooks define the race concept, nor have they extended the scope of their inquiry to include science education. Indeed, my research is the first to examine how American science education of the genomic age handles race.

Previously, the question of how textbooks conceptualize race has been researched most extensively by anthropologists Leonard Lieberman, Alice Littlefield, and their colleagues. They examined college texts in biology and in physical anthropology that were published from 1932 to 1989, focusing on biology and anthropology because (1) "the concept of race was developed by members of these disciplines"; (2) "its validity, definition, and social consequences have recurrently been debated by biologists and physical anthropologists"; and (3) "teaching about this concept falls within the overlapping domains of these disciplines" (Lieberman et al. 1992, 301). Based on the analysis of sixty-nine physical anthropology textbooks, the researchers identified the 1970s as a decade of change when the anthropology texts abandoned the essentialist "races exist" view that had dominated earlier. By the late 1970s, the opposite "races do not exist" view became the most frequent position held by the physical anthropology textbooks (301; Littlefield, Lieberman, and Reynolds 1982).[3]

In contrast to the anthropology texts' straight-line trend over time, the seventy-seven biology textbooks that Lieberman et al. sampled exhibited a more puzzling outcome. As late as the 1975–83 period, more than half of the biology texts still accepted the essentialist "race exists" view, which moreover had gone unchallenged prior to 1965. (In contrast, a small number of physical anthropology texts had already rejected the "race exists" view in the 1932–64 period.) When the researchers updated these findings by adding a small 1987–89 sample of eight college biology texts, they were surprised to discover that none even mentioned race. In short, while both the anthropology and biology texts had begun to move away from the "race exists" position in the late 1960s and early 1970s, only the physical anthropology texts went on to switch sides entirely and embrace the opposite "race does not exist" view. Biology textbooks, on the other hand, appear to have moved from affirming the existence of race to simply omitting mention of it. Lieberman et al. (1992, 310) write, "We view this as preferable to presenting race as if it were an accepted concept, but not as informative as presenting both the newer information and the issues that have been debated."

These findings from twenty years ago leave open the question of how today's textbooks handle the concept of race. Moreover, Lieberman's methodology calls into question even the results from the 1932–89 period he studied. In response, I have tried to extend—and improve upon—Lieberman's research approach. Like Lieberman and his colleagues, I study the racial content of textbooks and its variation by academic discipline and time period, but with key differences in sample and technique. First, I analyze high-school instead of college textbooks to get at scientific communication that reaches a wider public. Only half of the American population twenty-five and over has been exposed to some college education, whereas over 90 percent have attended (if not completed) high school (National Center for Education Statistics 2002). Furthermore, by reaching students at a younger age than college texts do, high-school textbooks offer an earlier—and thus particularly influential—introduction to scientific thought about the human body. Second, I study a wider range of disciplines, moving beyond biology and anthropology to incorporate textbooks in psychology, sociology, and world cultures and geography. Third, this project brings a badly needed update to Lieberman's work, extending the sampling time frame to 2002 and thus covering a period in which knowledge of human genetic diversity and evolutionary history has increased tremendously.

This chapter's most important innovation over previous research however lies in its broader and deeper analysis of what textbooks say about race. The Lieberman studies simply assigned textbooks to one of two categories: either the "(biological) race exists" or the "no race" position, without going into explanation of why or how a book might be classified that way. In contrast, I ask a wider array of questions about the texts. Do the textbooks explicitly define the term *race*? Are races catalogued or described? Do the textbooks account for the development of races? What do their illustrations convey? This more detailed approach recognizes that there are myriad ways in which texts convey concepts of race. They may teach that race is anchored in biology (for example, in discussing genetic disorders) or that it is socially contingent (for example, by contrasting national racial classification schemes). Analyzing textbooks' content along multiple dimensions is indispensable for a clear picture of what they have to say about the nature of race.

A study of contemporary high-school textbooks

To describe the concepts of race transmitted through textbooks, in 2002 I selected twenty-three of the most widely used current high-school texts in anthropology, biology, psychology, sociology, and world culture and geography.[4] The social science fields were chosen as those most likely to discuss the nature of human difference (unlike economics or political science) and to be offered in high school (unlike demography). Eleven of the books were biology texts, and twelve were from the social sciences, distributed as follows: one anthropology textbook, three psychology books, three sociology texts, and five textbooks of world culture or geography. These books were all published in the period from 1994 to 2002. In addition, I compiled a historical sample of sixty-nine high-school biology textbooks published in the United States between 1952 and 1994, which I use to throw some of the characteristics of the contemporary textbooks into sharper relief. Appendix A describes how the textbooks were selected and lists all ninety-two of them.

My analysis focused on three types of race-related material found in textbooks. First are what I call "direct" discussions of race: passages that focus explicitly on race (for example, when defining the term). Second are "indirect" discussions, where race is mentioned but is not the focal topic (for example, when racial groups are linked to particular genetic disorders). Finally, I also examined "implicit" discussions of race, where neither race nor racial labels are overtly mentioned, yet the text or illustrations could be interpreted as drawing on ideas of race. An example I frequently encountered, especially in older texts, was the linkage of varied non-European groups to "primitive" or "Stone Age" peoples. As Smallwood and Green (1968, 697) reassured students, "One does not necessarily have to study fossil bones or cave paintings to learn about man's primitive ancestors. There are several primitive societies within man's present-day population that can yield invaluable information."

WHAT CURRENT BIOLOGY AND SOCIAL-SCIENCE TEXTBOOKS TEACH ABOUT RACE

Imagine a seventeen-year-old high-school student taking classes in biology, world geography, and psychology among other subjects. In her backpack are likely to be textbooks that take very different slants on the nature of race. For one thing, not all—and perhaps none—will mention the word *race* explicitly. The geography text may refer to "ethnic groups" and the biology book to "populations," even if they are referring to the same groups with labels such as "white" and "black." Almost certainly, the textbooks will link race to different topics: the psychology book may define the term in the course of a discussion on prejudice, while the biology book will probably bring it up in a passage on genetic disorders, and the geography text may recount the origins of contemporary groups in ancestral homelands. Most importantly, these distinct academic disciplines are likely to send students very mixed signals about what race is: it may be associated with cultural difference in the geography book, with phenotypic diversity in the psychology text, and with genetic variation—and occasionally social construction—in biology. Moreover, the conflicting messages are not the result of disciplinary differences alone; within the same academic field, different textbooks may conceptualize race differently, and sometimes even the same textbook conveys contradictory messages about what race is.

In the midst of this confusion, the constructivist vision of race as reflecting man-made categories is rarely depicted with clarity and consistency. In my small sample, the exception is the sole anthropology book, and I will begin by describing it in order to set it apart from the others as a useful point of comparison. In contrast, the psychology textbooks took an essentialist stance, geography books sidestepped the issue of race for the most part, and both sociology and biology textbooks presented a curious blend of essentialist and constructivist elements.

Constructivist teaching in an anthropology textbook

Only one textbook of anthropology—*Anthropology* (2002) by Carol R. Ember, Melvin Ember, and Peter N. Peregrine—appeared on the high-school curriculum adoption lists from which my textbook sample is largely drawn. (See Appendix A for a description of the sampling procedure and the list of textbooks studied.) It is nonetheless an important comparative element of the sample because it is by far the contemporary textbook that discusses the concept of race at the greatest length and that makes the greatest effort to convey a constructionist viewpoint of race. *Anthropology* also provides a useful starting point for discussion because it presents many of the critiques of the biological race concept that are found in other texts. Of the twenty-three current textbooks I studied, six included some such criticism: the anthropology text, all three sociology books, and two of the eleven biology textbooks.

Anthropology (Ember et al. 2002) concentrates its critique of the race concept in a chapter entitled "Human Variation and Adaptation," which takes up three broad areas of direct racial discussion: (1) definition and explanation of the race concept; (2) comparison of the race and ethnicity concepts; and (3) challenges to "the myths of racism" (210) concerning civilization, behavior, and intelligence. Together, these passages reject the utility of the race concept for understanding human biological variation. First and foremost, the authors argue that "different populations are not neatly classified into discrete groups that can be defined in terms of the presence or absence of particular biological traits" (209). Interbreeding is one reason given for these fuzzy boundaries; the other is that traits usually vary in a smooth pattern across space—in "clines" or gradients—rather than along abrupt and sharply delineated boundary lines. Moreover, the geographic reach of two traits that might be considered racial markers are not necessarily aligned with each other—they do not "co-vary"—so "the gradient for skin color would not be the same as the gradient for nose shape" (210). For example, if skin color were chosen as the appropriate measure of race, the authors argue it would be a poor indicator: Africans and native Australians who share similar skin color are quite dissimilar in genetic terms. In short, the authors base much of their objection to race as a biological tool on evidence drawn from biology and physical anthropology; that is, they use "anti-essentialist" arguments (Morning 2007).

In addition to the claim that racial classification is objectionable because of its factual invalidity, the authors of *Anthropology* (Ember et al. 2002) also oppose its use on the grounds that it has been an instrument of racism. In particular, racial groupings "are largely social constructions that have been used to justify discrimination, exploitation, and even the extermination of certain categories of people." Consequently, "[t]he misuse and misunderstanding of the term race and its association with racist thinking is one reason why many biological anthropologists and others have suggested that the term should not be applied to human biological differences" (209). In this way, Ember et al. introduce an ethical dimension to the conceptualization of race that can be found in other texts as well.

Despite the authors' assertion that race is a social construct, however, *Anthropology* (Ember et al. 2002) provides little in the way of explanation of what that means. It does not chronicle the historical process of construction, but rather leaves unexamined the questions of when the race concept formed and under what social circumstances. Instead, in a later section entitled "Race as a Social Category" (318–19), *Anthropology* argues that racial groups should more accurately be considered ethnic groups, which "emerge as part of a social and political process" (320). Here race is a particular version of ethnicity. But the specifics of the social construction of race per se are ignored. For example, the textbook's definition of ethnicity, which the authors would apply to race, emphasizes cultural difference and ignores the beliefs about biological difference that under-pin racial classification:

> The process of defining ethnicity usually involves a group of people emphasizing common origins and language, shared history, and selected cultural differences such as difference in religion. Those doing the defining can be outside or inside the ethnic group. (320)

The overall effect is that *Anthropology* (Ember et al. 2002) challenges essentialist beliefs about race primarily by presenting anti-essentialist arguments that draw on biological research. Its (pro-) constructivist arguments, on the other hand, while adamant, are not as fully developed or supported. Nonetheless, the attempt to use both anti-essentialist and constructivist arguments is notable because they are not always used in combination (Morning 2007).

Essentialism in contemporary sociology, psychology, geography, and biology textbooks

Although the authors of *Anthropology* (2002) may have made some arguments more fully or convincingly than others, they are consistent in their rejection of an essentialism that views races as coherent or distinct groups of individuals sharing common characteristics. In contrast, the textbooks in biology, psychology, sociology, and world cultures/geography that are described below tend to convey some essentialist notions of race, to differing degrees.

Below I analyze the concepts of race found in each disciplinary grouping of texts, paying particular attention to the books' definitions of the term *race*. Across disciplines, textbook definitions reveal a common approach to race as involving a calculus of difference and sameness (Box 1). Departing from this basic premise, however, the disciplines emphasize different aspects of racial classification, and the two broad groupings of social science and biology each introduce perspectives that the other ignores. It is important to note, moreover, that not all disciplines were equally likely to take up these topics. Definitions of race appeared in all three sociology texts, but came up in only four

---

Box 1.   Definitions of Race by Discipline, Selected Textbooks

---

Anthropology: "[R]acial classifications are largely social constructions that have been used to justify discrimination, exploitation, and even the extermination of certain categories of people." (Ember et al. 2002, 209)

Sociology: "[R]ace denotes a category of people who perceive themselves and are perceived by others as distinctive on the basis of certain biologically inherited traits. Race is a social and cultural category, not simply a biological one. A race exists primarily in the perceptions and beliefs of its beholders." (Calhoun et al. 2001, 241)

Psychology: "Race refers to a set of hereditary physical characteristics that distinguish one major group of people from another." (McMahon and Romano 2000, 595)

Biology: "Ecological races are populations of the same species that differ genetically because they have adapted to different living conditions. Members of ecological races are not yet different enough to belong to different species, but they have taken the first step." (Johnson 1998, 184–85)

---

of the eleven biology textbooks,[5] one of the three psychology books, and none of the world geography texts. Similarly, critiques of the race concept appeared in all of the sociology texts, but in only two of the biology books and none of the psychology or geography texts.

SOCIOLOGY

As with the anthropology textbook, the three sociology texts examined here seek to impart to students an understanding of the social basis of race. It is only in these two disciplines that textbooks teach the idea that racial classification is a matter of perception, and that racial perception is a social activity involving both self and others. In *Understanding Sociology*, Calhoun et al. (2001, 241) explain that "race denotes a category of people who perceive themselves and are perceived by others as distinctive." Macionis's (2001) *Sociology* describes race as "socially constructed" since "racial categories only come into being because a society considers some physical traits important" (354–55).

However, the sociology textbooks do not dissociate race from biological difference as completely as the anthropology book did. For one thing, they make a weaker case against essentialism than the anthropology book does because they offer less comprehensive arguments against the biological utility of racial categorization. Although all three sociology books point to the difficulty of assigning individuals to races based on superficial characteristics (due either to racial intermixture or the great variety of phenotypes within so-called racial groups), they do not mention the "no covariation" idea, introduced in *Anthropology* (Ember et al. 2002), of clinal transition in one trait following a different pattern than the gradient for another trait.

The sociology textbooks also send mixed messages about the validity of the traditional Caucasoid/Mongoloid/Negroid tripartite racial scheme. While Macionis (2001) criticizes this product of eighteenth-century Linnaean taxonomy, Thomas (1995) upholds it in several ways. He presents it as "one of the best-known" racial classification systems, illustrates it with photographs of three men representing each race (Figure 1), reinforces familiarity with it through review questions (e.g., "Into what three racial categories does one of the best-known classification systems attempt to place people?" [235]), and uses its white/yellow/black framework to describe the physical features of certain groups:

> In some instances, a group's characteristics cut across racial categories, making classification extremely difficult. How, for example, should the people of southern India, with their white facial features, black skin color, and straight hair, be classified? Or, how should the Ainu people of Japan, who have oriental features and almost white skin, be categorized? To which category do the Bushmen of Africa, with their yellowish skin and oriental eyes, belong? And what racial group should be chosen for the Australian aborigines, who have dark skin and blond woolly hair? (232)

Ironically, even as the passage attempts to question the validity of the tripartite racial scheme, it resorts to the terminology of that framework to characterize the issue at hand, thus suggesting to students that human variation can in fact be profitably understood as a matter of "white facial features" or "oriental eyes."

The sociology textbooks' efforts to convey a social constructionist idea of race are similarly undercut by their simultaneous grounding of

Figure 1. "Caucasoid, Negroid, and Mongoloid Groups," 1995. The textbook's caption reads, "One well-known racial classification system sorts individuals into Caucasoid (left), Negroid (center), and Mongoloid (right) groups. Within each of these groups, however, identifying features such as hair texture and skin color can vary a great deal."

SOURCE: W. LaVerne Thomas, *Sociology: The Study of Human Relationships* (Austin, TX: Holt, Rinehart and Winston, 1995), 233. Photo credits: (l) Will & Deni McIntyre/Photo Researchers; (c) Richard Hutchings; (r) David R. Frazier Photolibrary.

racial difference in biology. The three books offer the following definitions of the term *race*:

- Calhoun et al. (2001): "a category of people who perceive themselves and are perceived by others as distinctive on the basis of certain biologically inherited traits. Race is a social and cultural category, not simply a biological one." (241)
- Thomas (1995): "category of people who share inherited physical characteristics and who are perceived by others as being a distinct group." (232–33)
- Macionis (2001): "a socially constructed category composed of people who share biologically transmitted traits that members of a society consider important." (354)

Although each definition points to the role of perception (on the part of self and others) in constructing racial categories, they also suggest that racial groups are indeed characterized by "inherited," "biological" traits their members share in common.

The message that race corresponds to biological variation is further reinforced by the texts' depiction of race as a matter of physical difference in contrast to the cultural differences reflected in ethnicity. "Race and ethnicity, then, are quite different," Macionis (2001, 356) writes. "One involves traits that are biological; the other, cultural . . . People can fairly easily modify their ethnicity . . . Assuming people mate with others like themselves, however, racial distinctiveness persists over generations." This juxtaposition is hardly new: in *Economy and Society*, Weber (1978/1956) defined ethnic groups as those that "entertain a subjective belief in their common descent . . . it does not matter whether or not an objective blood relationship exists" (389), whereas "race identity" involved "common inherited and inheritable traits that actually derive from common descent" (385). However, the implication in Macionis (2001) that racial affiliation is a matter of genetic heredity and not cultural practice is striking because on the previous page, the author stresses the social construction of race by dating the emergence of the concept to the nineteenth century, accounting for its spread in terms of sociopolitical objectives and informing readers of the variation in racial classificatory systems by time and place. Indeed, this is the only sociology textbook to use historical information to support the constructionist viewpoint.

On the whole, the three sociology textbooks suggest to students that race is a reflection, albeit unfaithful, of real underlying physical difference. Discernible innate differences do exist, even if social life and cultural conventions color how we interpret them. This approach not only confuses the constructionist message simultaneously conveyed, but it also leaves students ill-equipped to understand how groups and individuals can be assigned to racial categories regardless of their physiology. The traditional "one-drop" rule in the United States does not require any particular phenotype in order to designate an individual as black, only the reputation of black ancestry. But this well-known facet of our social organization—namely, that one can "look" white but "be" black— cannot be explained by the textbooks' equation of racial classification with phenotype. In short, the sociology books' definitions fail to distinguish between the invocation of biological difference and its actual existence. Winant (2001) helps clarify the discrepancy; in his account, race is "a concept that signifies and symbolizes sociopolitical conflicts and interests *in reference to* different types of human bodies," and it *"appeals to* biologically based human characteristics (so-called phenotypes)" (317, italics mine). In other words, race need not correspond to actual biological difference even if it claims to do so; this is the distinction that is confounded in the sociology textbooks studied here.

PSYCHOLOGY

In the one psychology textbook in this sample that offers a definition of race, racial difference is a purely biological phenomenon, unmediated by social perception. "Race refers to a set of hereditary physical characteristics that distinguish one major group of people from another," Mc-Mahon and Romano (2000, 595) write in *Psychology and You*. Nor is race context-dependent, for "racial problems and disharmony" are "as old as the human race itself" (595).[6] Instead, race is simply a given: "The more contact we have with people of other races, . . . the more aware we become that these groups are made up of individuals who are not only different from one another but also similar to ourselves in many ways" (Rathus 1998, *Psychology: Principles in Practice,* 469). Moreover, its principal importance lies in the complications it poses for interpersonal or group relations (Kasschau 2001, *Understanding Psychology*; McMahon and Romano 2000).

This interest in race relations is perhaps the only type of racial discussion that is shared by textbooks in all the social sciences studied here. In particular, racism, ethnocentrism, and/or prejudice all receive some mention in anthropology, psychology, sociology, and world-cultures texts. However, their discussions differ according to whether they place the blame for these phenomena on individual beliefs and actions versus social structures and cultural norms. While all three sociology textbooks teach that racism and discrimination have a societal dimension, the psychology texts diagnose them as individual attitudinal shortcomings. If blacks and whites in the United States inhabit separate "worlds," it is because of (inexplicably) "persistent attitudes of prejudice" (Rathus 1998, 467). As Bonilla-Silva (1996) has pointed out, the treatment of racism as an individual psychological phenomenon precludes analysis of racism as a dynamic force that is sustained by social institutions. Moreover, as I have argued is too often the case in academic sociology, attention to racial *attitudes* such as prejudice seems to displace attention to racial *conceptualization*. Or to put it more accurately, the conceptual question of what race is often appears to be taken for granted or considered a given, so that it is not necessary to explain what race is, only to discuss the phenomenon of racism.

Although the analysis of racism is not the same as the conceptualization of race, explanatory approaches to racial antagonism have repercussions for social constructivist arguments. Constructivism involves the claim that our comprehension of the world is a product of collaboration between culturally transmitted beliefs and reinforcing social institutions, whereas the psychological interpretation of racism traces that outlook to personal experiences and motivations such as "victimization" and "scapegoating" (Rathus 1998). Thus the societal dimension that is fundamental for a constructivist perspective is missing in the psychology textbooks.

WORLD CULTURES AND GEOGRAPHY

Race is rarely mentioned explicitly in the world-cultures and geography textbooks studied in this sample. Instead, the term *ethnicity* is frequently used, even when the groups in question are labeled with traditionally racial identifiers such as "white," "black," "mulatto," "mestizo," "Caucasoid," or "Mongoloid"—all terms appearing at least once in my world-studies sample. In *Global Insights: People and Cultures*, for example, the authors chart the "ethnic" composition of Latin America by reporting the population shares of "mulattos," "mestizos," "Africans," "Indians," and "Europeans," among others (Farah et al. 1994, 454). The label "ethnic" makes little sense here however. Not only are the groups the authors list traditionally defined as either principal races or mixtures of them, but they are too large to correspond to particular cultures, which the textbooks insist elsewhere is the underpinning of ethnic groups. For example, according to *Geography: People and Places in a Changing World*, "An ethnic group (1) shares common beliefs, language, and culture; (2) often lives in a particular territory; and (3) is tied together by a strong sense of national unity" (English 1997, 192). Africans, Europeans, and Native Americans do not fit this description. In short, then, the world-cultures and geography books seem to have simply borrowed the term *ethnicity* to replace the word *race*. This substitution is exemplified in *World Geography Today*'s discussion of South Africa, one of the few countries where the textbooks locate race and racism: "After the 1948 elections, South Africa's white-run government formally established the separation of the country's many ethnic groups" (Helgren and Sager 2000, 479). The "ethnic" groups named are "Whites," "Coloureds," and "Blacks." But today, "public facilities are being integrated, and people of different races meet each other socially more often." (480) In other words, the concepts of ethnicity and race are interchangeable.

By eliding race and ethnicity, the world-studies books remove any point of entry for a discussion of what races are. Ethnicity refers to cultural groupings, and races are the same as ethnic groups, so there is nothing left to explain. Moreover, without races there is no racism to discuss. Yet many of the events described in these textbooks, such as colonization and slavery, would be illuminated by inquiry into race and racism. Equally important, an engagement of the race concept would be relevant to questions that students might have about the content and structure of the textbooks themselves. Why, for example, is ethnicity something that is ostensibly discernible in human physical features if it is a matter of culture? Farah et al. (1994, 451) refer to "Indian influence" remaining in "the burnished skin tones and high cheekbones" of the inhabitants of Salvador, Brazil, and Iftikhar et al. (2001, 446) present a photograph of three similarly dressed Puerto Rican students with the caption, "Their faces suggest Latin America's ethnic diversity. The facial features and skin color of the population reflect Native American, European, and African backgrounds" (Figure 2).

An explicit engagement with the meaning and consequences of the race concept might also help students understand why the textbooks give pride of place to the arrival of Europeans in their histories of each

Figure 2. "Latin America's Ethnic Diversity," 2001. The textbook's caption begins, "Lunch Break at Ponce. Students in Ponce, Puerto Rico's third-largest city, pose for their picture. Their faces suggest Latin America's ethnic diversity. The facial features and skin color of the population reflect Native American, European, and African backgrounds."

SOURCE: Ahmad Iftikhar, Herbert Brodsky, Marylee Susan Crofts, and Elisabeth Gaynor Ellis, *World Cultures: A Global Mosaic* (Upper Saddle River, NJ: Prentice Hall, 2001), 446. Photo credit: Porterfield-Chickering, Photo Researchers.

region of the world. In fact, the world-studies textbooks examined here demonstrate every form of "ethnocentric distortion" that Preiswerk (1980a) detected in his research on history textbooks (interpreted here by Klein 1985, 58–59):

- "The ambiguity of the concepts of culture, civilization and race"
- "Linear evolutionism" (i.e., "other peoples need to 'catch up' to us [Europeans]")
- "Contacts with us are the foundation of their historicity"
- "Glorified self-presentation"
- "Unilateral legitimation of European action" (e.g., colonial exploitation benefited the colonies)
- "Intercultural and intertemporal transfers of concepts," as in, "They still live in the Stone Age."

Box 2.   Selected Accounts of Racial Ancestry in World Geography Textbooks

---

Boehm, Glencoe World Geography *(2000):*

"The blending of peoples can be seen throughout Latin America. In some countries, such as Mexico, Honduras, and El Salvador, mestizos—people of mixed Native American and European descent—make up the biggest part of the population. In other countries, such as Cuba and the Dominican Republic, mulattoes—people of mixed African and European descent—form a large percentage of the population." (176)

"The term Iran means 'land of the Aryans,' and many Iranians believe they are descendants of the Aryans, Indo-Europeans who migrated into the region from southern Russia about 1000 B.C." (373)

English, Geography *(1997):*

"Originally populated by seafarers from Southeast Asia, Micronesia today has 380,000 people, who differ in race and culture from their Melanesian neighbors." (377)

"Hinduism began when Indo-European (Aryan) tribes invaded India from the northwest between 1500 and 1000 B.C . . . The Aryans conquered the original inhabitants of India, the Dravidians, and drove them southward." (620)

Helgren and Sager, World Geography Today *(2000):*

"The Chinese culture has the longest continuous history of any on Earth. By 5000 B.C., the first rice farmers worked the land near the Chang River. One thousand years later, to the north along the Huang He, an organized society of people lived in small agricultural villages. These Mongoloid people occupied much of northern China for thousands of years." (507)

"Japan's first inhabitants were the Ainu, who probably arrived from Central Asia several thousand years ago. The Ainu were driven farther and farther north by Mongoloid invaders from Asia who arrived in Japan around 300 B.C." (520)

These similarities in ethnocentrism between history books and world-studies texts are likely due to the latter generally incorporating a considerable amount of historical narrative.

Indeed, unlike the other social science textbooks, world-culture and geography books present a particular form of racial subtext that is embedded in historical accounts: the genealogy of modern-day human populations. Through their references to patterns of migration and admixture, world-studies textbooks often build a racial framework for understanding human history. As the examples in Box 2 show, peoples from around the world are frequently depicted as descendants of earlier groups who are described with racial terminology. More precisely, their putative ancestors may be described as "races" or as having particular physical appearances, or they may be described with long-standing racial labels such as "Mongoloid" or debated racial designations such as "Aryan" and "Dravidian." In this way, the world-culture and geography textbooks lay the foundation for the cataloguing of ethnic diversity—and the confounding of race with ethnicity—that is such a prominent feature of their instruction.

BIOLOGY

Like the geography books, contemporary biology textbooks also speculate about the origins of various human groups. However, they do so with more direct references to race than the geography texts use, and they push the period of speculation even further back, beyond the earliest recorded human history and even before the beginnings of the species *Homo sapiens*.

Six of the eleven biology textbooks in this sample present the "multi-regional hypothesis" concerning the origins of human races. This model proposes that each race in our species *Homo sapiens* descends from a different population of the extinct species *Homo erectus*, now generally thought to have emerged 1.5 million years ago. Each separate group of *H. erectus* would then have evolved independently into *H. sapiens*. This model is usually contrasted with the "Out of Africa" theory that *Homo sapiens* evolved once, in Africa, and thus all living human beings today can be traced back to that original African group. Although polygenism—the belief in the separate origins of human races—has appealed to American scientists since the nineteenth century, this particular version rooting racial difference in *Homo erectus* dispersion is an outgrowth of the mid-twentieth century work of anthropologist Carleton S. Coon. As a 1965 biology textbook summarized:

The anthropologist, Dr. Carleton S. Coon, has recently suggested that *Homo sapiens*, or modern man, evolved independently from five different races or subspecies *of Homo erectus* in five different areas or territories of the world. This is in sharp contrast to the generally accepted idea that *Homo sapiens* originated only once and then distributed himself around the world east and west and north and south. According to Coon's view the five principal geographical races of *Homo erectus* evolved from *Australopithecus*-like ancestors which had spread from Africa to various parts of the world. Coon contends that the evolutionary transition from *Homo erectus* to *Homo sapiens* occurred independently in Java some 40,000 years ago, in two places in China to yield the Mongoloid race (about 350,000 years ago) and the ancestors of the American Indian (about 150,000 years ago), in western Europe some 250,000 years ago to yield the Caucasoid race, and in Africa some 5000 to 8000 years ago to yield the Negroid race by a blending of four different racial lines. (Nason 1965, 775)

Although the contemporary biology textbooks have discarded the chronological aspect of Coon's theory—according to which blacks would only recently have made the transition to human status—and generally favor the "Out of Africa" view, their presentation of the general outlines of the multiregional model suggests to students that racial differences are so long-standing that the human species has always been split along biological racial divisions.

The biology textbooks also convey a powerful essentialist message to students about present-day racial difference through their instruction on human genetics. Ten out of the eleven texts use racial categories when describing the mechanisms of genetic disorders such as sickle-cell anemia and cystic fibrosis. Sickle cell is now routinely linked to "African Americans" or "blacks," and cystic fibrosis to "whites" or "Caucasians" (e.g., Biggs et al. 2002; Biological Sciences Curriculum Study 2002). Alongside these groupings, "Jews of Eastern and Central Europe" (Raven and Johnson 2002) appear in connection with Tay-Sachs disease. Sometimes geographic indicators are used instead ("The PKU allele is most common among people whose ancestors came from Norway or Sweden," Biggs et al. 2002, 318), but sometimes racial nomenclature is imposed on geographic markers as well, for good measure: "Sickle-cell anemia . . . is most common in black Americans whose families originated in Africa and in white Americans whose families originated in the countries surrounding the Mediterranean Sea" (Biggs et al. 2002, 329). And although sickle cell is regularly described as an adaptation to malaria prevalence, the textbooks only occasionally note that it has evolved in malarial areas outside Africa as well (Figure 3) and generally choose instead to present it as contained within racial boundaries (Figure 4). The consistent linkage of race with genetics in this manner suggests to students that not only is race a useful concept for biologists, but it is one with grave and far-reaching consequences.

Finally, biology textbooks present definitions of race that are decidedly essentialist. In *Biology: The Web of Life* (2000), Strauss and Lisowski explain, "Race is a biological term that describes genetic groupings of animals, including humans" (292). Johnson (1998, 184–85) elaborates, "Ecological races are populations of the same species that differ genetically because they have adapted to different living conditions. Members of ecological races are not yet different enough to belong to different species, but they have taken the first step."

Social construction does not enter these definitions for several reasons. First, the biology texts ground difference firmly at the genetic level; neither human perception nor social processes play a role. Even the ostensibly outward "physical characteristics" or phenotype that influence others' perceptions in the social science accounts (e.g., Macionis 2001; McMahon and Romano 2000) are barely mentioned. Second, the biology books' definitions of race are intended to be as applicable to other species as they are to humans. Although perception and bias can also come into play as scientists define nonhumans (Hey 2001), the question of social and cultural construction of categories by the members of that species is eliminated. More importantly, the equal application of race to all living things defuses the sensitivity of race; for example, the categorization of honeybees is not likely to raise our concerns about the sociopolitical abuses of race. Finally, the suggestion that there are races throughout the animal kingdom, just as there are races of human beings, effectively "naturalizes" the category of race. Race is not in the eye of the beholder, it is just "out there," as true for penguins as it is for us. In short, in their definitions of race the biology textbooks do not raise any doubt that living

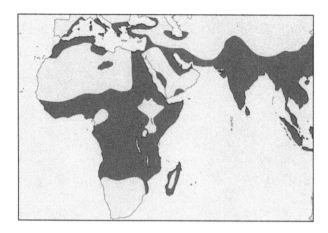

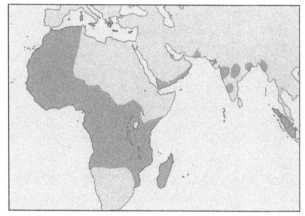

Figure 3.   Malaria and Sickle-Cell Anemia in Africa,
Europe, and Asia, 2002

NOTE: The prevalence of malaria is shown on the map above,
that of sickle-cell anemia on the map below.

SOURCE: Kenneth R. Miller and Joseph Levine, *Prentice Hall
Biology* (Upper Saddle River, NJ: Pearson Prentice Hall, 2002), 348.
Map by Mapping Specialists.

things can be decisively grouped as races according to their genetic
characteristics.

The biology textbooks also take their definitions of race in an essentialist direction completely foreign to the social sciences. By noting that
race is "the first step" toward speciation (Johnson 1998, Johnson and

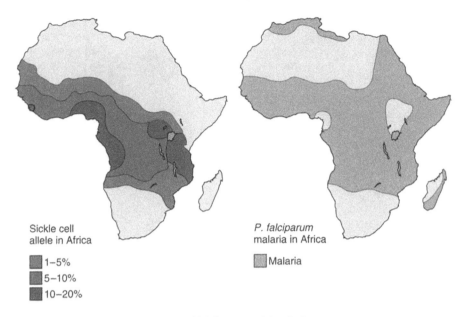

Figure 4.   Sickle-Cell Anemia and Malaria in Africa Only, 2002

NOTE: The prevalence of sickle-cell anemia is shown on the map at left, that of malaria on the map at right.

SOURCE: Peter H. Raven and George B. Johnson, *Biology* (Boston: McGraw-Hill, 2002), 260.

Raven 2001), the biology texts raise the possibility that racial difference is a precursor to much greater difference—that is, species difference, which implies the inability to interbreed and produce fertile offspring. In this way, race is not only a matter of cross-sectional difference at a given point in time, but it raises the specter of an over-time process that will result in much wider gulfs between the descendants of today's races.

However, just as the sociology textbooks seem to dilute their constructivism with some essentialist precepts, biology texts occasionally make statements about race that could be interpreted as anti-essentialist if not constructivist. For example, Raven and Johnson (2002, 492) state, "Human races do not reflect significant patterns of underlying biological differentiation." And Johnson (1998, 226) notes, "Scientists disagree about how and when different racial groups . . . evolved." But the fact

that the same textbooks also define race with respect to physical difference, use racial identifiers in their treatment of human genetics, and/or
present the multiregional hypothesis of distinct racial origins undercut the reservations they express about the biological utility of the race
concept.

Biology textbooks in historical perspective

One of the things that struck me most when I first began to review contemporary high-school biology textbooks was how little they mentioned
race. Only four of the eleven biology texts I sampled presented a definition of the term *race*, and more generally, they seemed to have little
to say on the topic. Had I been mistaken to think that biologists might
consider race to be a subject that fell within the scope of their high-
school curricula? I wondered. Out of curiosity, I went to Columbia University's Teachers College library to take a look at a few textbooks from
the 1950s and 1960s, and to my surprise, I discovered that they contained
lengthy discussions of race. Chapters and sections devoted to the "the
races of man," taxonomic charts of races, photographic collages of the
world's races, and even quiz items on race were quite common. What
had happened since then? To find out, I began to analyze in a systematic
fashion high-school biology textbooks published prior to the 1990s. The
more I learned about post–World War II biology texts, the more I realized that my recent sample of books published in the 1990s and the first
few years of the twenty-first century reflected a real departure from
earlier pedagogical approaches to race instruction. As a result, the characteristics of contemporary biology textbooks were thrown into sharp
relief when compared to their predecessors. In the following pages I will
briefly describe the aspects of contemporary biology textbooks that
stand out most when contrasted with earlier generations. For a fuller account of the evolution of biology textbooks in the last fifty years, readers
may wish to consult Morning (2008b).

Over the second half of the twentieth century, U.S. high-school biology textbooks retreated in many ways from explicit engagement with
the topic of race. They have become less likely to define the term, to list

the races that purportedly exist, and to describe the signature character-istics of specific races. When they do discuss race directly, moreover, they do so in passages that have steadily grown briefer over time. Finally, the visual illustrations of racial taxonomy that were once so common have now largely disappeared; see Figure 5 for an example from 1952. Such photographs and drawings depicting "the races of man" appeared in 92 percent of the textbooks I sampled from the period 1952 to 1962, but in only 7 percent of those published between 1993 and 2002. In short, race is much less prominent a feature of high-school biology textbook lessons than it used to be. The texts of the past demonstrate, however, that race was once considered to be an integral element of biology instruction for young people.

However, close examination of biology textbooks over a fifty-year span reveals that race has not so much disappeared from their pages as it has become redefined, linked to different topics, and referenced in less direct ways. Three transformations in the textbook treatment of race are particularly notable. First, race has become an integral element of discussions of genetic disorders. Second, discussion of the origins of races has increased. Third, race has gone from being presented as largely a phenotypic phenomenon—that is, having to do with surface physical traits such as skin and eye color—to being one that is overwhelmingly portrayed as a matter of genetic difference.

The linkage of race to genetic disorders such as cystic fibrosis, which I described previously, has climbed sharply over time. In the 1963–72 period, only 15 percent of the textbooks sampled used racial categories in their explanations of the genetic roots of disease. By the 1983–92 decade, the share of textbooks doing so had increased to 47 percent, and then it nearly doubled, reaching 90 percent in the 1993–2002 period. Of course, such genetic disorders were not as well-investigated in the 1950s and 1960s, and high-school textbooks had less to say about them. Still, it is worth noting that as genetic diseases have become better understood, racial classification has consistently been an integral feature of their textbook exposition (and scholarly investigation—see Kevles 1995/1985; Wailoo and Pemberton 2006)—even though these diseases are no respecters of racial boundaries.

Figure 177. THE RACES OF MEN

Nordic

Alpine

CAUCASIAN

Mediterranean

Hindu

Indian

Asiatic

Malay

MONGOLIAN

African

Oceanic

Pigmy

ETHIOPIAN

Figure 5. "The Races of Men," 1952

SOURCE: William M. Smallwood, Ida L. Reveley, Guy A. Bailey, and Ruth A. Dodge, *Elements of Biology* (Boston: Allyn and Bacon, 1952), 264.

The second area in which textbooks have reintroduced race over time is through their inclusion of the multiregional hypothesis in their accounts of human evolutionary history. The theory that today's races descend from separate groups of prehuman ancestors has gained a striking predominance in today's textbooks. Almost two-thirds of the biology textbooks published from 1992 to 2002 introduced the multiregional hypothesis, although a smaller number—43 percent—explicitly presented it as an explanation for the existence of today's races. Still, this represented an increase over the 1983–92 decade, when only 24 percent of the biology texts referred to the multiregional hypothesis to explain the existence of races. It is important to note that today's biology textbooks do not necessarily endorse the multiregional hypothesis. Raven and Johnson (2002, 489) for example conclude, "By both these sets of evidence [Y chromosome and mitochondrial DNA], the multiregional hypothesis is wrong. Our family tree has a single stem." Nevertheless, the fact that so many texts present the polygenetic theory means that high-school students are frequently exposed to the essentialist belief that racial differences are ancient and that they have divided our species, *Homo sapiens*, from its inception.

The third, and most fundamental, transformation in biology textbook coverage of race has been the marked shift from a phenotypic to a genotypic concept of racial difference. This movement is reflected in myriad smaller changes in textbook racial content that have occurred over time: increased references to genes in formal definitions of race, the decline of visual taxonomies and listings of surface traits of races, and the growing presence of race in passages on disease as they increasingly became catalogues of genetic disorders (as opposed to the infectious variety more prominent in older textbooks). Consider for example the contrast between the definitions of race found in two biology textbooks published nearly forty years apart. The 1960 textbook *Biology* explains that "race" denotes "a subdivision of a stock; composed of people who tend to have certain inborn physical characters in common, such as Nordic and Hindu races" (Kroeber, Wolff, and Weaver, 622). Although "inborn physical characters" could imply genes, in that context they would most likely bring to mind the traits such as skin and hair color that illustrated the visual taxonomies found in textbooks of the times. In contrast, Johnson's (1998) *Holt Biology* offers the following definition: "Ecological races are populations of the same species that differ genetically because they have adapted to different living conditions" (184). By this time, the fundamental boundaries of racial groups are presumed to be determined by differences in DNA, and surface phenotypic traits such as eye color are irrelevant.

These and other changes in biology textbooks' portrayal of race over time are no doubt due to varied forces: changes in the social and political climate of the United States, developments in scientific thinking, and restructuring of the textbook industry, to name just a few. However, it is worth noting one factor that does *not* seem to have played a role in the "geneticization" (Lippman 1993) of race in high-school curricula. Despite the newer textbooks' claim that genetic data offer a better, more accurate measure of human variation than the phenotypical taxonomies of the past, they have not led to clearer or more detailed descriptions of race in textbook pedagogy. In other words, race does not seem to have become genetic in high-school textbooks because this shift offered students a more thorough or empirically grounded account of racial difference.

On the contrary, the contention that genetic data offer an improved grasp of human variation has been accompanied by a paradoxical retreat from detailed explanation of the specific attributes of human groups. Although contemporary textbook definitions confidently explain races to be delineated by genetic difference, exactly what kind of genetic differences these are, or what the signature genotypes of specific races are, is left to the student's imagination. This ambiguity represents a real change from the old phenotypical typologies, which clearly laid out the main identifying characteristics of each race. Genetic accounts of race, in contrast, have yet to offer any such decision rules. For that matter, the genetically based "groupings" (Raven and Johnson 2002; Strauss and Lisowski 2001) or "ecological races" (Johnson 1998; Johnson and Raven 2001) to which textbooks now refer are not named or otherwise labeled, so it is impossible to ascertain how many there are, where they originate, or how they relate to the traditional phenotype taxonomy. Nor is it possible to judge the bases upon which genetic races are delineated:

what kinds of difference, and of what degree, signal the presence of a racial boundary? In moving from phenotypic to genetic race, the textbooks have effectively "black-boxed" (Latour 1987) the process of racial classification.

We can get an idea of the loss of detail that has accompanied textbooks' newer discussions of race by comparing the 1952 taxonomy shown in Figure 5 to two newer ones, from 1976 and 1998 (in Figures 6 and 7 respectively). The 1952 taxonomy reflects the fairly complex scheme popular then, which posited broad "stocks" of mankind that usually comprised about a dozen (sub)races. Second, it has a clear hierarchical order, with "Caucasians" at the top and "Ethiopians" at the bottom. Third, it includes a detailed typological chart (not shown) that permits identification of subraces by such phenotypical features as hair, eye, and skin color. Finally, it incorporates the cultural component of dress as a meaningful clue to racial difference; the Nordic's suit is juxtaposed with the head coverings, jewelry, and/or nudity of the lesser races. In short, these visuals attempt to convey a great deal of information to students in addition to the pages and pages of text that accompany the charts. In contrast, the taxonomy from 1976 is much briefer, cataloguing only five races, arrayed on two levels. Moreover, the claim to a comprehensive listing of races has become weaker: the 1952 image definitely included "*The* Races of Men," whereas the 1978 illustration purports only to include "Five Major Human Races," suggesting perhaps that other races exist but have been left out of this presentation.

Finally, the 1998 taxonomy found in *Holt Biology* (Johnson 1998) makes an even more limited attempt to provide a complete taxonomy of human races. Its graphic claims to portray only "different racial groups, some of which are represented by the people above." Not only does this illustration forgo the informational detail found in the 1950s (such as typological charts of phenotypical traits or reliance on clothing to indicate racial membership), but it does not even name the races depicted or tell the reader which have been excluded.

Even the textbooks' central assertion about the superiority of genetic versus phenotypic measurement of race is curiously unsupported by their empirical presentation. Today's textbooks often claim that genetic

Figure 29-12. Five major human races are Caucasoid (a), Negroid (b), Mongoloid (c), Australoid (d), and Amerind (e).

Figure 6. "Five Major Human Races," 1976. The textbook's caption reads, "Five major human races are Caucasoid (a), Negroid (b), Mongoloid (c), Australoid (d), and Amerind (e)."

SOURCE: Raymond F. Oram, Paul J. Hummer Jr., and Robert C. Smoot, *Biology: Living Systems* (Columbus, OH: Charles E. Merrill, 1976), 614. Photo credits: (a) Bruce Charlton, (b) Lavina Miller, (c) Editorial Photocolor Archives, (d) Photographic Library of Australia, and (e) Editorial Photocolor Archives.

data now offer a better, more accurate measure of human variation than the phenotypical taxonomies of the past. Raven and Johnson (2002, 491) write, "if one were to break the human species into subunits based on overall genetic similarity, the groupings would be very different than those based on skin color or other visual features." Similarly, the Biological Sciences Curriculum Study's 1990 textbook asserted that "classification by gene pools produces many times the number of human groups represented by traditional races" (397). Such statements could be interpreted as a strong challenge to the notion of race, perhaps seeking to replace traditional racial classification with new categories based on

Figure 7. "Different Racial Groups," 1998. The textbook's caption reads, "Scientists disagree about how and when different racial groups, some of which are represented by the people above, evolved."

SOURCE: George B. Johnson, *Holt Biology: Visualizing Life* (Austin, TX: Holt, Rinehart and Winston, 1998), 226. Photo credit: Sergio Purtell / Foca Co.

genotype instead of phenotype. Yet when we turn to the same text-books' exposition of topics from human evolution to heredity and disease, we find not the large number of "human groups" that supposedly result from modern genetic research, but instead the familiar racial groups of old. "Mongoloids," "Negroids," and "Caucasoids" (and their semantic descendants) still populate high-school biology textbooks, appearing in over 90 percent of the racial taxonomies found in this sample. Hardly new innovations, all three groupings are direct descendants of Linnae-us's 1740 edition of *Systema Naturae* (Marks 1995). Claims of new biological categories notwithstanding, contemporary instruction on human genetics largely reinforces, rather than replaces, the long-standing tripartite racial scheme that textbooks have promoted for decades.

Placing a black box around racial classification wards off one of the most important questions about the origins of the categories in question. Are the new races the products of research into population DNA patterns, or do they correspond to preexisting groupings that have subsequently been shown to embody genetic differences? At issue is the difference between *"extracting* basic divisions of the human species" from biological data versus *imposing* such divisions (Marks 1996, 353). In today's biology textbooks, the question is never raised. In passages on genetic disorders, for example, the texts imply that racial categories provide a meaningful framework for studying disease, yet there is no indication of whether the racial groupings used are the product of—or would be upheld by—a tabula rasa inquiry into human biological variation.

Textbooks' messages about the nature of race are not only obscured by the relative lack of discussion that characterizes the newer books relative to the older ones. In addition, the phenotype-to-genotype shift "buries" racial difference both literally and figuratively.[7] Literally, of course, the source of racial difference goes from being highly visible, an aspect of our surface appearance, to becoming a virtually invisible part of our internal makeup. Figuratively, by embedding race more deeply within the human body, it comes to seem more essential, closer to the core of who we are (Nelkin and Lindee 1995). Relocating racial essence from skin color to DNA also buries it—or shields it—by making it visible only to the expert, not the layman. The determinants of racial difference can be apprehended only by a trained few, armed with the most sophisticated equipment.

Textbooks' assertion that races are genetically determined groupings (without offering further elaboration) may result from several circumstances. With the human genome having been sequenced only recently, there may be a lack of data upon which to base authoritative pronouncements regarding racial difference. Yet this has not prevented textbook authors from teaching that races are in fact genetically distinct. Similarly, one might argue that the textbooks do not detail the genetic determinants of racial classification because new understandings of human variation as clinal or intergraded render such categories obsolete; this is contradicted however by the textbooks' liberal use of discrete racial categories to teach students about genetic disorders or human evolution. Thus the state of scientific knowledge does not seem to offer an explanation for the textbook treatment of race and genes. In this book's concluding chapter, I will consider potential explanations for the geneticization of race that move beyond developments in the life sciences.

Taking a long view of high-school biology textbooks' treatment of race over time allows a clearer understanding of the kinds of messages they convey today. A historical perspective suggests that biology textbooks have not come to reject racial essentialism over time so much as they have simply shifted the grounds upon which race is based, from phenotype to genotype. The new textbook definitions of races as gene-tically distinguishable still posit that racial difference is inscribed in the human body and not embedded in social relationships. Although many contemporary textbooks avoid directly engaging the topic—which might be considered an abandonment of essentialism in itself—their routine and/or unquestioned use of traditional racial groupings in discussing disease, heredity, and other topics contradicts such a conclusion.

CONCLUSION: ESSENTIALISM AND CONSTRUCTIVISM IN CONTEMPORARY HIGH-SCHOOL TEXTBOOKS

For an idea that many social scientists believe has vanquished older es-sentialist understandings of race, social constructivism has made few inroads in American secondary education today. The notion of race as a cultural product and not a biological one is disseminated only in a few social science curricula, and—to judge from the ordering lists of the states with centralized textbook adoption procedures—the least-taught social sciences at that. At the same time, material reinforcing an essen-tialist interpretation of race can be found in both biology and social sci-ence textbooks. So far, scientists' public calls for the educational system to promote new understandings of race that take both social history and human variation into account have had little impact. High-school stu-dents today are apparently more likely to be familiar with the attribu-tion of certain diseases to certain races than they are with the observa-tion that racial boundaries have changed markedly over time.

As shown above, the idea of race as a social construct appears only in the anthropology and sociology textbooks studied. However, the anthro-pology text marshals more extensive arguments in favor of constructiv-ism, likely due to its discipline's long engagement with questions of race and its input from both cultural and physical anthropologists to make a case supported by both social and biological research. One reflection of the process the discipline has already gone through to grapple with such issues can be found in the Statements on Race issued by the American

Association of Physical Anthropologists and the American Anthropological Association in 1996 and 1999 respectively. In comparison, the American Sociological Association issued such a Statement later (in 2003). Although the idea of social construction has deep roots in the discipline of sociology, the textbooks examined here expend less effort to apply it to the concept of race than the anthropology book does, and they are less likely to reconcile it with information about human biology. While the anthropology textbook makes a strong anti-essentialist case as well as something of a pro-constructionist case for race, the sociology textbooks demonstrate a less sustained constructivism and even some recourse to biological essentialism.

As do the sociology texts, the biology textbooks also seem to occupy an ambivalent position along the essentialist/constructionist spectrum. Their definitions of race and discussions of genetic disease reinforce the idea of race as an innate, biologically determined attribute. A few texts attempt to challenge the validity of phenotype-based racial classification. However, with the origins of race categories going unaddressed, the textbooks offer no starting point for a constructionist analysis of race; none of the biology textbooks put forth the argument that the racial boundaries drawn among human beings can be understood as social, political, and historical products. Similarly, the psychology and world-studies texts in this sample provide no foundation for a constructionist approach to race. Not only do the psychology textbooks promote the equation of race with biology, but their emphasis on the individual precludes consideration of the social dimension of ideology. In the case of the world-studies texts, it is their labeling of all difference as "ethnic" that leaves no room for examining the concept of "race."

As a result, it would be difficult to claim that social-science texts are more likely than biology books to promote constructivism. Even though only the social sciences of anthropology and sociology convey the constructionist message in this collection of textbooks, psychology and world culture do not and in fact are even less likely than biology to critique traditional essentialist notions of race.

Given the small size of this interdisciplinary sample, the results described above are more suggestive than generalizable. Yet they point to striking differences in the racial content of textbooks published for specific disciplines. Rather than indicating a widespread consensus on the nature of race, they show that high-school students may be exposed to conflicting interpretations depending on their course program. What is a social construct in one class is a fundamental division among *Homo sapiens* in another. Most important for the central concerns of this book, this analysis suggests that the notion of race as socially constructed is only rarely transmitted in American secondary education today. Educators appear to have foregone a prime opportunity to disseminate the view of race as socially constructed among a wide swath of young Americans, despite the support the idea ostensibly enjoys among scientists.

If high-school textbooks still regularly present race as a characteristic of the human body, what does this tell us about the scientific community whose knowledge informs those texts? Does the textbooks' frequently essentialist portrayal of race imply that biological and social scientists share this view? Or is there a "time lag," which means the texts are behind the curve when it comes to the latest scientific thinking? The rarity of constructionist thinking in U.S. textbooks may or may not reflect its popularity in the academy. The next chapter shifts the spotlight to anthropologists and biologists to consider just what ideas of racial difference prevail among contemporary scientists.

FOUR

Teaching Race

SCIENTISTS ON HUMAN DIFFERENCE

Question: How would you define "race" or explain what it is?

Answer 1: I think I would define race as a particular form of ethnicity which is extremely powerful by virtue of its—of the way it's naturalized through the body.

Answer 2: I guess a group of individuals that share at least one unique feature to them that is not shared by the rest of members of individuals they recognize as belonging to the same species.

The two definitions of race quoted above testify to the wide range of approaches and arguments that faculty interviewees used when I asked them to describe their understandings of race. Both answers come from colleagues in the same discipline—anthropology—and in the same department on the campus of a large public and urban university. Despite their shared training and pedagogical mission, the two anthropologists held very different perspectives on the nature of race. The first saw race as a system of classification that is *made to seem* natural—that is, "naturalized"—implying that in fact it is not. In contrast, the second interviewee saw race as determined by characteristics that members do in fact share (and others do not), making it natural indeed.

To explore the current state of thought on race among biological and social scientists, this chapter describes the interviews I conducted with forty-one professors of biology and anthropology at four research universities.[1] Its primary goal is to respond to the question "What concepts of race do scientists hold?" by describing the variety of views that respondents offered. In addition, I will identify some of the institutional and individual characteristics that may be related to such understandings of human difference.

Academic science is a crucial research site for any investigation of racial conceptualization because the ideas of biological and social scientists are central to what is considered expert, authoritative knowledge of racial difference. Scientists' views on race make their way to the public, moreover, through multiple channels: publication in specialist journals and coverage in the mainstream press, research products—such as pharmaceutical drugs—that are widely sold or distributed, and teaching (including textbook writing) that reaches millions of young Americans every year. In short, scientists' ideas of race have the potential to be enormously influential, and so this chapter investigates just what those ideas are.

As the opening quotes suggest, I found considerable variation in professors' concepts of race—variation that was not just interdisciplinary but *intra*disciplinary. Despite the smallness and the particularity of my sample, it clearly puts to rest the notion that academics across the disciplinary spectrum have come to an agreement on the nature of race. This study also soundly refutes the claim that constructivism is the consensus position at which all academics have arrived. As I show below, the view that "there are biological races in the species *Homo sapiens*" still holds an important place in contemporary social and biological science. What is much less clear, given the small scale of my sample, is whether this and other views of race are related to individuals' socio-demographic characteristics (such as age or gender) and institutional settings (e.g., disciplinary field, university eliteness) as other studies have suggested. In compensation, however, the rich detail of the qualitative interview data yields two important insights. One is that the traditional constructivist-versus-essentialist dichotomy is a poor framework for characterizing scientific debate about race because it overlooks what I call "anti-essentialism," a distinct discourse in itself. Second, the interviews emphasize the role of ethical judgment in scientists' grappling with race, and accordingly, this chapter concludes its empirical report with an examination of how interviewees sought to balance the moral imperatives of disavowing racism and embracing the "ethos of modern science" (Merton 1968, 607).

INTERVIEWING ACADEMICS ABOUT
THEIR CONCEPTS OF RACE

In the fall of 2001 and spring of 2002, I drove around the northeastern United States to interview college professors and their students about their definitions of race. In cramped professorial offices overflowing with yellowed paper, in labs that smelled of chemicals and musty bones, and in bare, impersonal conference rooms, I asked my interviewees how they would define or explain the term *race*. Over the school year, I talked with forty-one professors and fifty-two students at four universities, usually for one to two hours each.

The campuses I visited differ in important ways. The largest was the one I call "State University," which enrolled nearly thirty thousand undergraduates at the time and is its state's flagship public institution. State was also the most racially diverse college in my sample: whites made up only slightly more than 60 percent of the undergraduate body.[2] "City University" is another large public institution, one of the main attractions of the large urban area it inhabits. With two-thirds of its students coming from within the state, City enrolled roughly fifteen thousand undergraduates, and as with State, its admissions rate hovered around 60 percent. In sharp contrast to State, however, City was the least racially diverse university in my sample: more than 85 percent of its undergraduates were white. I also conducted interviews at two private universities that were similar in terms of their small student bodies (around five thousand undergraduates each), highly selective admissions rates near 10 percent, and tuitions above $25,000 per year. Again, however, they differed in their racial composition: less than 65 percent of the undergraduates at "Ivy University" identified themselves as white, compared to over 70 percent at "Pilot University" (so named because I conducted a relatively small number of initial test interviews there). In summary, I selected four institutions that would let me compare how faculty and students' race concepts might vary across campuses that differed in their eliteness and racial diversity. (Details of the sample selection process, both for universities and faculty interviewees, can be found in Appendix B.)

To get a sense of the race concepts that both biological and social scientists held, I interviewed a randomly selected sample of professors of biology and anthropology. I focused on these two disciplines following Lieberman et al.'s (1992) reasoning that they had traditionally been most involved in the elaboration and teaching of the race concept. The resulting sample of anthropologists and biologists differed in several ways from the U.S. population as a whole, and not just in terms of professional training. This group of interviewees was largely male (66 percent), mostly white (83 percent), and overwhelmingly left-leaning in political orientation (90 percent). The median age in the sample was forty-nine years. Three-quarters of the interviewees reported they had no current religious affiliation; the modal religion of Judaism was reported by only 16 percent of the faculty. Nearly half the interviewees were originally from the Mid-Atlantic states of New York, New Jersey, or Pennsylvania, but 17 percent were born outside the United States. In terms of socioeconomic background, 63 percent of the interviewees stated their father had held a managerial or professional occupation; 53 percent reported the same concerning their mother's occupation. Turning to their professional rank, the largest group was made up of full professors (39 percent), followed by associate professors (27 percent), non-tenure-track faculty (20 percent), and assistant professors (15 percent). Finally, the interviewees were fairly evenly divided by discipline: nineteen were anthropologists and twenty-two were biologists.

As an African American interviewing predominantly white respondents, a priority for me was to try to reduce as much as possible any interviewee discomfort that might arise given the sensitive nature of race discussion. My preoccupation was not simply a matter of courtesy; the most pressing problem was that in my presence, interviewees might offer only "socially desirable"—rather than honest—answers. To minimize the likelihood of such an "interviewer effect," I consulted the research literature on race-of-interviewer effects and found that they are not generalized or applicable to all interview topics, but rather that they come into play only under certain circumstances (Campbell 1981; Cotter, Cohen, and Coulter 1982; but see contradictory claims in D. Davis 1997). In particular, interviewees are most affected when asked to comment on the racial group of which their interviewer is a member. Given this finding, I avoided questions eliciting respondents' attitudes or opinions about specific racial groups.

I also informally tested the impact of my racial appearance on interviewees by recruiting a white female graduate student to conduct half of the pilot student interviews in my stead. Although we conducted only eight test interviews, the content of students' responses did not seem to vary based on interviewer race. This may simply indicate, however, that race is such a sensitive subject that it provokes self-censoring regardless of interviewer race; for example, both Frankenberg (1993) and Bonilla-Silva (2002) document extensive hesitation on the part of whites to discuss race even with white interviewers.

Finally, analysts of race-of-interviewer effects have rightly noted that it is the interviewer's *perceived* race, and not his or her personal self-identification, that influences interviewee responses. An excellent illustration comes from Deirdre Royster's experience as an interviewer; although she identifies herself as black, most of her white interviewees seemed to believe she was white based on her appearance (Royster 2003). In this connection it is worth noting that several respondents appeared unsure of my race and asked me at the end of the interview how I identified myself in racial terms, while others presumed I was multiracial. As it turned out, though, interviewees' racial classification of their interviewer did not map to any one conceptualization of race.

HOW DO SCIENTISTS CONCEPTUALIZE RACE?

A few of the instances in which faculty interviewees commented on my racial background offer a good starting point for delving into the range of arguments about human difference that I encountered. In particular, several scientists drew on their reading of me as a mixed-race person to bolster their cases about the nature of race. Here are three examples:

- At the conclusion of one of my very first interviews, a cultural anthropologist at City University asked me how I identified myself in racial terms, and concluded, "You're a perfect walking example of why [race] doesn't work." A few minutes later he reiterated, "I just wonder, looking at you, I wonder how anybody could maintain that there are these hard and fast races."

- A few weeks later, a biology professor at State University was explaining to me how race might come up in a lecture on genetics. Skin color, he suggested, "could be used as an example of quantitative genetics . . . the general thought is that by and large, although there are some environmental influences, there are four sets of genes which determine skin color." After considering a hypothetical example involving the offspring of "an African black" and "a Swedish Caucasian," he turned to me. "I take a look at you, and you might have—don't be offended—you have, if there are four . . . that means there are eight genes, and I would say you have three or four black genes and four or five white genes . . . Just on skin color." In this view, my multiracial appearance offered a textbook example of the genetic mechanics of race.

- Finally, one rainy afternoon a physical anthropologist at Ivy University was giving me a tour of his large laboratory, pointing out various human skeletons and the traits he felt reflected their racial heritage. Soon, however, the talk turned to sources of uncertainty in determining race from skeletal remains. "Environments have changed enormously," the anthropologist explained. "There's been more intermixing." At that point, he turned to me and said, "I mean, if you give me your skull and so forth, and I look at your nasal aperture, I'm not going to have a clue that you have any black ancestry." Shortly afterward, however, he amended, "Now I might, given your teeth, because they're large."

These three anecdotes provide a telling introduction to the presentation of biologists' and anthropologists' concepts of race because they highlight how scientists can and do arrive at very different conclusions even when confronted with exactly the same data—in this case, me. In each scenario, a scientific expert found in my physiognomy evidence for a radically different understanding of race. For the cultural anthropologist, my features were proof that it was impossible to draw neat boundaries around discrete races, and thus, biological race did not exist. But for the biology professor, my traits were a clear-cut expression of racial characteristics embedded in DNA: "white genes" and "black genes." Finally, the physical anthropologist allowed that racial identification was not always straightforward, but that ultimately, our bodies display the telltale marks of our racial heritage. The variety of conclusions about race that thoughtful and highly trained specialists can draw from the same source of data is the hallmark of contemporary debate on human difference.

Defining race

After a series of introductory questions about interviewees' professional background and the place of race in their discipline, I opened the conversation about racial conceptualization as follows. "I'd like to ask you a little more about how you define the term 'race,'" I would say. "For example, if a student in one of your classes asked you to give a definition of the term 'race,' what would you say?"

ESSENTIALISM: RACE IS BIOLOGICAL

When academic scientists were asked how they would define race, almost two-fifths (sixteen out of forty-one) described it as a biological phenomenon (see Table 1). In most cases, professors depicted race as the product of evolutionary processes acting on (more or less) genetically isolated human populations; the lack of intermixture conserves in each group genetic traits that have developed differently through separate processes of adaptation to the local environment, as well as through nonadaptive processes. For example, one biology professor at Pilot University described race as

> any useful and evolutionarily meaningful way of distinguishing two groups that do not interbreed at a high rate. If they interbreed at a high rate, then they can't possibly have any differences that are evolutionarily

or genetically important . . . When you have groups that are reproduc-
tively fairly isolated, or completely isolated, then you start wondering if
they're species. There's not a lot of gene flow and there are obvious
differences and they seem to have a genetic basis; heritability's an
important definition. Then to talk in terms of them being distinct
subspecies is probably useful.

Other evolution-related language that respondents used to define race
included: "limited gene pool," "open dynamic breeding groups which
display some restriction of gene flow," "species polymorphism," "regional
adaptations," and "relatively small homogeneous genetic group." As the
quotation above illustrates, some respondents equated "race" with "subspecies," often broadening its scope well beyond human beings to describe a phenomenon of "distinctive geographic variants" to be found in
any animal (or plant) species. The common element in the arguments I
label here as "essential" is the assertion that human biological variation
is patterned or clustered along racial lines, making races biologically
identifiable entities.

It is important to note, however, that about half the faculty who offered biological definitions for race also pointed out the limitations of racial classification schemes. One critique was that intermixture between
humans across the globe had precluded (or reversed) the formation of
racial groups. Another frequent criticism was that suites of human traits
do not covary in tandem as would be necessary for racial grouping. In
other words, the pattern of geographic variation in one human trait (such
as eye shape) might suggest a certain racial breakdown, but another
trait—say, lactose intolerance—was likely to follow a very different pattern of geographic variation, and therefore suggest an entirely different
racial classification framework. Basically, the biggest problem for biological race categories (according to their proponents) was the difficulty of
pinpointing racial boundaries. As a result, the proponents tried to allow
for "fuzzy" or imprecise boundaries in their essentialist models of race:

So what is race? Well, I think the textbook will say that there are three
major races—Negroid, Caucasian, and Asian or Mongoloid—and a
hundred years ago it was easier to see those particular designations. I

Table 1.   Faculty Race Concepts by Academic Discipline

	All		Anthropologists		Biologists	
Definitions of Race	N	%	N	%	N	%
Race is biological	16	39.0	6	31.5	10	45.5
Race is not biological	11	26.8	4	21.1	7	31.8
Race is social and not biological	5	12.2	1	5.3	4	18.2
Race is social	9	22.0	8	42.1	1	4.5
Total	41	100.0	19	100.0	22	100.0

	All		Anthropologists		Biologists	
Opinions of Statement on Biological Races[a]	N	%	N	%	N	%
Agree	8	23.5	3	23.1	5	23.8
Contingent agreement[b]	8	23.5	2	15.4	6	28.6
Neutral / Don't know	2	5.9	0	0.0	2	9.5
Disagree (biological argument only)	7	20.6	3	23.1	4	19.1
Disagree (biological and social arguments)	2	5.9	0	0.0	2	9.5
Disagree (social argument only)	7	20.6	5	38.5	2	9.5
Total[c]	34	100.0	13	100.1	21	100.0

NOTES:

[a]Statement read, "There are biological races in the species *Homo sapiens*" (Lieberman 1997).

[b]"Contingent Agreement" includes interviewees who said they would agree if the statement were altered somewhat.

[c]This question was asked of thirty-four professors rather than the full sample of forty-one because it was omitted when interviews were particularly lengthy.

think that's the official view of what race is, but you could always say historically it's not clear either when you start getting into the Middle East, even a thousand, five hundred years ago, what the racial distinctions were . . . So I guess in the old definition they're like you would imagine they are: the edges are a little blurred, but the old classical definition of race is a lot clearer. And don't we kind of look at people today, like when we first started here, I said you're part Caucasian and part black, so I'm taking two of the standard races, and I'm mixing them in some proportion, and that's probably the best I could do in terms of race: three races, classical definition, blurring at the edges, people at the blurred area define themselves probably more for political and religious reasons.—*Biologist, State University*

Given that so many faculty interviewees who espoused a biological perspective on race perceived fuzzy boundaries as a shortcoming, it is not surprising that many made an effort to reconcile the fluidity of racial categories with their reality and utility. After discussing the difficulty of determining what level of difference should be considered as corresponding to racial difference, a biology professor at Pilot University added, "but I think the concept of race is not completely artificial, because it does address the question of geographic origins and evolution of man." In other words, race might be an imperfect measure, yet it has some information value and provides a tool or set of labels to work with. (More than one interviewee pointed out that species and subspecies classification was not a straightforward matter either, yet this taxonomic approach is widely used despite the debates it provokes.) Perhaps the most adamant assertion that imprecise boundaries need not derail the biological race concept came from "Professor A.," a physical anthropologist who had given a great deal of thought to the question of racial classification, and who had come to reject the idea that clear-cut delimitation or distinctiveness was necessary or desirable for a system of racial categorization. In Professor A.'s view, racial groups should be considered inherently "fuzzy sets"[3] that are constantly undergoing change due to both ecological and sociocultural forces, but the fact that their boundaries and numbers are constantly in flux does not undermine their reality:

So many of the things I get back in terms of critique or something is, "but, you know, nothing is distinct." And I say, get rid of that word "distinct." Because that's—that's what is the problem with the interface between the biologists, the PCs, social cultural anthropologists and so forth—is they've got this concept of distinct . . . What would it take to have races? What would you need? And so forth. And very few really come up with total distinction. And this has been—I don't know how I can put this delicately. I don't think I can. The people who have tried to say that there is no such thing as racial groups or races or race and so forth usually point to the lack of distinctiveness. They, you know: "we have clines and so forth, so nothing is distinct as we go through here." That's not, to me, the issue. If you're looking for distinctiveness, for Christ's sake, look at molecules and look at elements, you know, where you can count the number of protons and neutrons and, you know, come up with distinctiveness. You're not going to find it in living biological populations, whether it's birds, whales, mongoose, or humans. But this concept of—in other words, distinctiveness has become the straw man around which you validate the concepts of race or racial variation or different populations. And that is a mistake, I think.

Professor A.'s depiction of the "distinctiveness" criterion for racial classification as a "straw man" ran counter to the sentiment among other essentialist researchers that the lack of clear boundaries was a real problem for the biological race concept. But his grappling with the issue of distinction meant that like many other proponents of an essentialist race model, his thinking about race was very much engaged with the arguments of his opponents and shaped to refute them. As we will see, essentialist and anti-essentialist claims are closely intertwined, taking form in opposition to each other.

ANTI-ESSENTIALISM: RACE IS NOT BIOLOGICAL

The remaining faculty interviewees—twenty-five, or just over 60 percent—rejected the biological race model, using two broad lines of attack. One was what I call the "anti-essentialist" perspective, where scientists depicted the biological race concept as factually incorrect, a "myth" or false belief. The other strategy I label as "constructivist," where interviewees portrayed race as an ideology, a way of seeing and naming human difference that is socially produced. Although these two outlooks are hardly mutually exclusive, they tended to not be used simultaneously. Eleven faculty members used exclusively biological information, making anti-essentialist claims about the race concept, whereas nine referred solely to historical, social, or political factors to characterize the constructed nature of race. Only five professors combined both anti-essentialist and constructionist arguments to refute the biological race idea. In the following comments on anti-essentialism, I limit discussion to the eleven interviewees who adopted this argument exclusively.

Anti-essentialist discourse is characterized by the use of biological evidence to demonstrate that race groupings do not reflect patterns of human biological variation, countering essentialist claims to the contrary. As do the proponents of biological race, anti-essentialists refer to human evolutionary history, but they arrive at very different conclusions. The anti-essentialist arguments that my interviewees presented can be roughly grouped into two interrelated types. On one hand were statements emphasizing the fundamental biological unity or similarity of human beings. In this vein, an anthropologist at City University stressed, "There are very, hardly any genetic difference between breeding populations of *Homo sapiens*, very, very tiny amount of genetic material." His comment alludes to the widely reported finding that human beings share 99.9 percent of their DNA in common. Another statistic that has often been quoted in the media and was repeated by the interviewees is the observation that there is greater genetic variation within racial groups than between them.

The second, complementary anti-essentialist approach was to highlight the difficulty, arbitrariness, and/or inaccuracy involved in drawing racial boundary lines. "I don't think that the phenotypic characteristics are distributed in a way that allows the recognition of distinct races," a physical anthropology professor at City University said. And a biologist at State University explained, "Human history, human variation is much more complex than any rough categorization can approximate." Calling the correspondence between racial categories and nature "very crude, very approximate," another State University professor of biology asked:

> Does a human race as a category correspond to a well-defined population of some sort in nature? Well they don't, they never do—not even close usually—so that's the ultimate justification for why I don't use them; that's why I try to stick to geography.

Several respondents noted that human traits vary in a clinal (i.e., gradual) way, rather than in a discrete fashion that would lend itself to racial boundary-marking.

Anti-essentialist scientists offered several explanations for why racial genetic distinctiveness had not emerged among human beings.[4] Referring to the evolutionary model of isolated groups whose gene pools develop over time in particular directions, some faculty interviewees suggested that intermixture between human populations had precluded the genetic isolation necessary for the development of distinct races, or that more recent interbreeding had erased racial distinctions that might have existed in the past.

Others explained that different human traits demonstrate different patterns of variation that do not necessarily overlap with each other, so that reliance on one trait to delineate race boundaries would lead to a completely different classification scheme than another trait would. In short, traits do not covary with each other in a way that results in stable, clear racial clusters. For example, a given population might develop one adaptive trait that distinguished it from its neighbors to the east but not those to the west, at the same time as it developed another trait that distinguished it from those to the west and not those to the east. As a physical anthropologist at City University explained:

> The line that I argue is that as defined broadly by biologists, I don't think the [race] concept fits the pattern of human variation very well. So I see race as defined in terms of subpopulations within a species that are characterized by a suite of distinctive traits . . . The thing I point out to students is that most of the characteristics that we look at, when we look at human variation, don't covary. So that you can't define a race on the basis of a suite of traits. Or more precisely, if you did try to do that, what you would have to do is carve the human race up into a very large number of races in order to find a set of people who share, really share a suite of attributes. And of course I argued that there's a number of reasons for that, that—for the lack of covariation, if you will—that the traits that we see are probably—that variation is probably adaptive, and it represents variation that's been favored by selection in relation to some environmental variable. Well in that case, if this trait, trait X is in response to environmental variable one, and trait Y is a response to

environmental variable two, unless those environmental variables covary, you don't expect the traits to covary. So what I argue to my students is that as someone who's interested in the adaptive outcomes of evolution, I'm much more interested in understanding the distributions of individual traits, because it's that that allows me to understand what they are adaptive responses to. So I argue in terms of more useful approaches, for example . . . maps of individual traits and ask how they covary with particular environmental variables. What is the goal of looking at human variation? Race used to be the way that we handled that concept, and race is a purely descriptive tool, it just allows you to name patterns or variations, but it's not only that, not only is it descriptive, not only is it limited in that regard, but it's not a good descriptive tool, because as I said these characters then covary. So I'm more or less arguing for chucking the concept as it applies to humans because it's unrealistic in terms of the pattern or variation, and because it doesn't let me do the intellectual work I want to do to understand the nature of these traits. Most students seem to buy that.

It is important to note that, as this quotation illustrates, the anti-essentialist faculty members who argued for "chucking the concept" of race did not deny or downplay the existence of biological variation among human beings; on the contrary, such variation was in most cases their intellectual topic of study. Instead, they felt that the race concept was a poor measure for capturing that diversity. Some suggested that geography would be a preferable and sufficient conceptual framework for studying human variation. "The only thing that's really relevant," a professor of physical anthropology argued, "is geographic variation and local adaptation to particular environments."

For these interviewees, the lack of clear racial boundaries among *Homo sapiens* meant that any dividing lines chosen were necessarily arbitrary. For example, a biologist at City University saw racial categorization as involving "false, overly stringent, or overly clear, unrealistically clear, distinctions between groups," and a physical anthropologist argued, "The boundaries are completely porous, completely moveable, depending on how—where you want to put them." Such arguments implicitly counter the essentialist belief that races are in some sense simply "out there," independent of human powers of perception or socially influenced classifications.

In these anti-essentialist statements, the critique of arbitrariness opens the door to human agency as a factor in categorizing races. However, it does not go so far as to explicitly identify social processes that spark and shape classification efforts. If anti-essentialists recognize scientists' decision making as a proximate influence on race identification, it is constructivists who place such decisions in a broader social context.

CONSTRUCTIONISM: RACE IS SOCIAL

In contrast to the scientists who defined race primarily in terms of its inaccuracy or fallacy as a biological tool, others sought to explain it as an idea that has emerged and been maintained in particular historical or cultural contexts and/or that serves particular interests. Constructionist arguments reject biological definitions of race by pointing to historical and contemporary social processes that shape the emergence, spread, and evolution of race thinking. As a faculty member in the State University biology department stated, "[F]or my definition, race is a social construct. It is defined culturally at the time, in the time period, and from a biologist's perspective it is not useful."

Although constructionist interviewees rejected the essentialist belief that biological difference dictates racial boundaries, they recognized that race is inherently an idea or claim about biology. One City University anthropologist summed up the difference by stating: "I think there are *ideas* of biological races, but I don't think that they exist." Winant (2001, 317) illuminates this "biologistic" element of the traditional race concept by noting that race "appeals to biologically based human characteristics (so-called phenotypes)"—even though "selection of these particular human features for purposes of racial signification is always and necessarily a social and historical process." In this view, biological (or other essential) difference is intrinsic to any idea of race, and it is precisely this notion of inherent, fixed qualities that makes race compelling and useful.

Moreover, unlike the anti-essentialist professors who criticized the biological race concept as being unscientific, the constructionists generally saw science itself as a social product and thus not antithetical to a culturally produced idea such as race. As a cultural anthropology professor at City University explained, "I have a really strong belief in sort of the way in which science is, sort of within culture, as opposed to be-tween, you know, here's science and it's factual and race is part of it and here is culture and it's invented." In a related vein, a few faculty mem-bers noted that the biological race concept derived much of its power from its appearance as scientific and thus unsullied by cultural value systems, but that it is nonetheless fundamentally a cultural product.

Constructionist respondents pointed out that even though race cate-gories are ostensibly grounded in human biology, they have always been interpreted as having important social and cultural implications. With that observation in mind, many interviewees cast race as one of several types of "construction of difference," such as nationality, ethnic-ity, religion, gender, and class. In this perspective, the deployment of racial classification is always part and parcel of larger processes of ine-quality and domination:

> And so that's where I think the point in teaching race is not to sort of say it's all cultural, it's not biological, but rather to say that constructions of difference, be they characterized as cultural or biological, you know, really operate in a sociopolitical framework that is about relations of inequality, or, to put it differently, unequal relations of wealth and power and social subordination.—*Cultural anthropologist, Ivy University*

Given its social repercussions, constructionist faculty members ada-mantly rejected the conclusion that race is not "real." As the cultural anthropologist quoted above contended, "Frankly, you know, race is in-finitely more real because it's social, than, you know, than anything that might make it meaningful at the biological composition." Another cul-tural anthropology professor elaborated:

> Well, the main message I think that I tried to convey was that race was a very real but social construct. It has real impact—and this was one thing that I really wanted to make sure that students, especially African-American students in my class, or students from different countries, that—the message that I wasn't saying it didn't exist, because I feel like sometimes that's what comes across from some of the anthropological discussions: "oh, it's just a social construct." You know, but if you're African American and male and you're looking for a cab in New York

City, it's going to be very real . . . but that's sort of real social effects from perceived biological differences.

In their comments about the "reality" of race, constructivist interviewees showed concern that the concept of race as social construct would make little headway outside the academy unless its holders could acknowledge and/or account for laypeople's observations of the social and physical world. In contrast to anti-essentialists' dismissal of the biological race concept as a fallacy that no biological scientist would accept, constructionists did not position it as antithetical to the scientific enterprise, but rather saw it as an unsurprising outgrowth of a socially embedded institution.

On the existence of biological races

After asking faculty interviewees the open-ended question of how they would define race, I also asked them to tell me whether they agreed or disagreed with the following statement, taken from Lieberman (1997): "There are biological races in the species *Homo sapiens*." The results are shown in Table 1.

AGREEMENT WITH THE LIEBERMAN STATEMENT

Nearly one quarter of the professors presented with the Lieberman statement agreed with it as is. When asked why, their answers included: "there are these genetic markers in terms of . . . frequencies and stuff like that have a biological basis" and "that aspect of biology is true, real, unambiguous, because we can trace it." The biologist from State University who had supported "the classical definition" of race offered:

> That's what we learned in college, and our observations over many
> years since we've left college seems to support the concept that we can,
> in a very general way, group people into three races, and it's I think
> the geography helps. So it's not like we have three races all intermixed
> all over the world and there are three types of people, like tall, me-
> dium, and short. It's that what we call the black race, Negroid, is
> found in Africa and places where Africans would have migrated. That

Caucasians are found in Europe and throughout the continent through Russia . . . and then you can associate Asians, focus on Japan and China, Vietnam, Thailand.

Determining what constituted "agreement" with Lieberman's statement was not always a straightforward task, however. In particular, almost a quarter of the interviewees took the position that they would agree with the statement if it were amended, usually by substituting other terms for the word *races*. Examples of the replacements or definitions for "(biological) races" that faculty suggested included "recognizable geographic variants," "species subgrouping," "different mitochondrial DNA haplotypes," and "human population group or breeding population." Although such comments could be considered as a mixed review of the Lieberman statement, I treat them as qualified or "contingent" agreements both because the interviewees themselves indicated a willingness to agree with the statement if their understandings of race were acknowledged, and because the substitutions they proposed retained the fundamental idea of naturally occurring, biologically distinguishable human subgroups. Consider, for example, the assistant professor of biology at State University who suggested replacing "race" because of its "negative social connotations," yet retained its basic premise of distinct groups:

I just think that the word *race*—because I've been brought up thinking that you can't use the word because it has all these negative social connotations and it's just completely inappropriate and not scientifically sound—but it's just hard for me to imagine having any adjective associated with race that would apply. I would certainly be willing to replace the word *race* with another word, like I would say there are "distinct genetic haplotype groups" within *Homo sapiens*, but I just can't imagine using the word *race* in any context.

It is noteworthy that this interviewee rejects the term *race* first for its "connotations" and being "inappropriate," and only later for not being "scientifically sound"; her reservations are not explicitly a critique of the underlying premise of racial difference.

Almost half of the faculty interviewees who were asked to comment on the Lieberman statement clearly disagreed with it. As with their open-ended definitions of race, professors drew on both biological and socio-logical arguments to refute the existence of biological races; however, in this case, they were even less likely to combine both types of argument.

Respondents who employed biological, anti-essentialist arguments against race again portrayed it as an unscientific notion, or more precisely, as an outdated notion no longer supported by modern science. As one biology professor at State University put it, "we have moved on" from such thinking: "modern genetics has dispelled the notion of race." These respondents found it hard to believe that their peers would argue for the existence of races. A biology professor at Ivy University called the Lieberman statement "nonsense," laughing, and continued: "My reaction is 'nonsense,' and I would imagine, so if it was given in the eighties, so this was after I went to—after I was undergraduate, I would be aston-ished, if either biologists or anthropologists said anything other than 'nonsense.'" In these anti-essentialist comments, support for the idea of biological race was cast as a matter of deficient intelligence, logic, or mod-ern scientific training.

The last comment also invokes another dimension of anti-essentialist argument that we saw previously: the claim that delineating human races is virtually impossible. "I don't think that the phenotypic characteristics are distributed in a way that allows the recognition of distinct races," a physical anthropology professor at City University said. A colleague in the same department stressed, "There are very, hardly any genetic dif-ference between breeding populations of *Homo sapiens*, very, very tiny amount of genetic material." And a biologist at State University explained, "Human history, human variation is much more complex than any rough categorization can approximate."

Faculty members who saw race as a social construct without biological underpinning expressed their rejection of the Lieberman statement in sev-eral ways. In one example that reflects constructivists' separation of social ideas of race from actual human biological variation, an anthropology professor at State argued, "There are not biological races in the species *Homo sapiens.* As I said before, I think that there are social groupings called races that have very real—that are very real, that have a very real social existence and that are based on perceived biological differences, but there are not biological races within the species *Homo sapiens,* as far as I know and as far as I've been able to read. I'm not an expert, but that's what I've determined from my reading and scholarship."

PATTERNS OF RACIAL CONCEPTUALIZATION

Differing views of race were not distributed randomly across the faculty sample; rather, certain perspectives were found more often in certain subgroups than in others. In this section, I identify a few factors as potentially relevant for subgroup variations. It is important to keep in mind, however, that with this small and unrepresentative sample, I cannot make statistical claims of association, let alone demonstrate causal relationships. The descriptive statistics I present are intended only to give readers an idea of how frequent certain views were among particular types of interviewees, and are not to be subjected to hypothesis testing. However, I use these data to consider whether existing hypotheses about scientists' racial conceptualization seem to be borne out—and to formulate an alternative model that takes into account the moral boundaries that my interviewees so frequently drew between their and others' ways of seeing race.

The role of institutional settings

ACADEMIC DISCIPLINE

In previous studies, the most common approach to explaining scientists' notions of race has involved making comparisons by academic discipline. However, my findings cast doubt on that strategy. To be sure, certain perspectives were more common among the anthropologists and others among the biologists I interviewed. In this faculty sample, the most frequent definition of race among biologists was one that treated race as a biological characteristic, whereas the mode among anthropologists was to portray race as a purely social construct (Table 1). Faculty opinions of the Lieberman statement ("There are biological races in the species *Homo sapiens*") showed a similar disciplinary pattern.

However, closer examination suggests that broad disciplinary boundaries are more porous than they may seem when it comes to racial conceptualization. First, taking subfield into account reveals that constructionist definitions of race were offered almost exclusively by the sociocultural specialists in anthropology departments; two-thirds of them took this approach, compared to only 14 percent of the physical anthropologists (and 23 percent of biologists). And whereas 57 percent of the physical anthropologists and 45 percent of the biologists defined race as a biological characteristic, only 17 percent of the sociocultural anthropologists did so. In short, the race concepts of physical anthropologists were closer to those of biologists than to sociocultural anthropologists.[5] (Biologists' views differed little by subfield, i.e., genetics or evolutionary biology). Moreover, it is important to note that in addition to such intradisciplinary variation in racial conceptualization, faculty notions of race varied considerably even within subfields. Three of the seven physical anthropologists opposed a biological reading of race, as did more than half of the biologists, while two of the twelve cultural anthropologists subscribed to a biological definition of race. In other words, even the practitioners within specialized subfields took varied positions regarding the nature of race.

UNIVERSITY SETTING

Two other measures of institutional exposure to race ideology—namely university eliteness and racial diversity—showed some evidence of a relationship to scientists' race conceptualization. Biological definitions of race as well as agreement with the Lieberman statement were less common among the professors interviewed at the relatively diverse State and Ivy campuses than they were in the faculty samples at the less diverse City and Pilot universities. Twenty-seven percent (or six out of twenty-two) of the faculty interviewees at State and Ivy subscribed to a biological definition of race, compared to 53 percent (or ten out of nineteen) of those at City and Pilot universities, and 39 percent at State and Ivy agreed with the Lieberman statement compared to 56 percent at the less-diverse schools. However, the share of faculty offering a specifically constructionist understanding of race varied little by campus racial diversity.

When it came to private versus public institutions, there was little difference in how often scientists defined race in biological terms, but a starker contrast in their adoption of a constructivist definition. Thirty-six percent of the professors interviewed at private universities (five out of fourteen) defined race as biological compared to 41 percent of those at public universities (eleven out of twenty-seven), but 36 percent of the former compared to 15 percent of the latter conceptualized it as a social construct. The same pattern held for the professors' opinions of the statement "There are biological races . . ." This finding contradicts the predictions of Lieberman, Littlefield, and their colleagues that faculty members at elite universities would be relatively likely to reject social constructionism. It may reflect, however, the greater presence of sociocultural anthropologists in the elite university anthropology departments and in the interview sample; whereas 55 percent of the anthropologists interviewed from the public State and City universities were in sociocultural fields, 75 percent of those interviewed at the private Pilot and Ivy universities were sociocultural anthropologists.

With all the academic variables, the possibility of self-selection into those settings requires drawing conservative conclusions about institutional context and racial conceptualization. As it turns out, however, anthropologists and biologists in my sample were very similar in terms of age, gender, nativity, religiosity, political orientation, and socioeconomic origins (even when examined by subfield), thus lessening somewhat the concern that any disciplinary divisions uncovered are mainly the product of socio-demographic heterogeneity. And faculty at public universities were fairly similar to their colleagues at private universities in terms of their definition of race as biological and their reaction to the Lieberman statement on the existence of race, regardless of any socio-demographic differences in their makeup. However, the difference in essentialism

between faculty at diverse and nondiverse campuses (27 percent support versus 53 percent) might be a reflection of higher proportions of
older and male faculty at the latter; as I will show, age and gender may
be related to racial conceptualization. To consider how such differences
in such socio-demographic characteristics might matter, I turn now to
results concerning some of the individual-level variables studied by
previous researchers.

Individual socio-demographic characteristics

A predominant hypothesis about racial conceptualization has been that
individual status predisposes individuals to embrace self- (or group-)
legitimizing understandings of racial difference. Unfortunately, the homogeneity of the faculty sample (and of the U.S. professoriate more
generally) along many status dimensions, not to mention its small size,
precludes a thorough assessment of that hypothesis here. Still, four characteristics emerged from this study as potentially playing a role in individuals' thinking about race—religious affiliation, socioeconomic background, age, and gender—and I discuss each briefly below. What is more
striking, however, is the finding that such personal characteristics seem
to help differentiate between the proponents of certain race concepts but
not others. In other words, the variables that previous researchers have
examined may only get us so far when trying to account for why people
conceptualize race the way they do.

RELIGION

A much greater share of faculty who described themselves as atheist or
nonreligious rejected the Lieberman statement on the existence of biological races (58 percent compared to 25 percent of the other interviewees),
and fewer offered a biological definition of race (46 versus 64 percent of
the other faculty interviewees). When the sect of respondents' religious
upbringing was taken into consideration, those from Jewish and Catholic
backgrounds rejected the Lieberman statement more frequently than Protestants (at rates of 86 and 57 percent respectively compared with 20 percent of Protestants). The same finding held for professors' open-ended

definitions of race: 78 percent of Jewish-origin and 71 percent of Catholic-origin interviewees eschewed a biological interpretation of race, compared to 50 percent of the Protestant-origin faculty. These results are consistent with Stark et al.'s (1979) contention that minority (religious) status lessens adherence to biological understandings of race.

SOCIOECONOMIC BACKGROUND (PARENTAL OCCUPATIONS)

To investigate a possible link between class and race concept, I used father's and mother's occupation to represent socioeconomic background. Interestingly, maternal occupation seemed to be more influential than paternal, but in both cases, faculty interviewees whose parents had held higher-status (i.e., professional or managerial) occupations espoused biological interpretations of racial difference less often than did other respondents. In fact, social constructionism was almost exclusively the province of the offspring of professional parents.

AGE

A clear age gradation emerged between the holders of different race concepts. The average age of the supporters of biological race was nearly fifty-three, whereas those who refuted race based on biological arguments were forty-eight on average, those who combined biological and constructionist arguments against race averaged forty-seven, and the proponents of a purely social constructionist were the youngest, at a mean forty-three years. The same relationship held when faculty opinions of the Lieberman statement were considered. Given the cross-sectional nature of these data, however, it cannot be determined here whether this scale reflects cohort experiences—for example, younger people today may have been exposed to constructionist discourse prevalent in the period of their youth—or alternatively, a life-course trend whereby young people in any time period are more likely than older people to reject essentialism.

GENDER

Gender is one of the variables to have received the most attention in previous study of scientists' racial conceptualization, and in this study it seemed to matter as well. Whereas 44 percent of male professors (twelve out of twenty-seven) defined race in biological terms, only 29 percent of female faculty (or four out of fourteen) did so. Moreover, almost twice as large a share of women described race as socially constructed: 50 percent compared to 26 percent of the male respondents. A similar pattern emerged in the levels of men and women's support for the Lieberman statement on biological race.

The pattern of gender differentiation in racial conceptualization, like those along the lines of discipline and university eliteness, has a striking feature. These variables all do a better job of distinguishing constructivists from other faculty than they do of accounting for differences between essentialists and anti-essentialists. For example, the biggest male-female gap in open-ended race definitions appeared in the proportions offering a constructionist perspective: the twenty-four-percentage-point difference between the shares of men and women who did so was larger than the gender divide for any other type of definition. Another way to look at this is to consider how similar essentialists and anti-essentialists were to each other—and how different from social constructionists—when they are compared in terms of the characteristics that have been emphasized in previous research. As the breakdown of open-ended race definitions in Table 2 shows, the essentialist ("Race Is Biological") and anti-essentialist ("Race Is Not Biological") camps were composed of equal shares of biologists (63 percent) and roughly equal shares of male faculty (75 and 73 percent respectively) and public university faculty (69 and 73 percent). In contrast, the composition of the constructionist ("Race Is Social") group was very different: only 11 percent of its members were biologists, 44 percent were men, and 44 percent taught at public universities.

It is not surprising that previous analyses identified factors that distinguished constructivists from others, because they operated within a dichotomous framework that divided race concepts into either essentialism or constructivism. My research, in contrast, points to a tripartite (constructivist/essentialist/anti-essentialist) breakdown of race concepts, and thus raises the additional question of which characteristics distinguish essentialists and anti-essentialists from each other.

How can we account for the ways in which faculty members who share a common biology-based approach to the race question divide

Table 2.   Faculty Characteristics by Definition of Race and by Opinion of Lieberman Statement

Of the interviewees who held the following views . . .		*. . . what percentage were:*		
Race Definitions		*Biologists?*	*Male?*	*At a Public University?*
	(N)			
Race is biological	(16)	63	75	69
Race is not biological	(11)	63	73	73
Race is social and not biological	(5)	80	60	80
Race is social	(9)	11	44	44
Total	(41)	54	66	66
Opinions of Lieberman Statement on Biological Races		*Biologists?*	*Male?*	*At a Public University?*
	(N)			
Agree	(8)	63	88	75
Contingent agreement	(8)	75	50	63
Neutral / Don't know	(2)	100	0	0
Disagree (biological argument only)	(7)	57	100	86
Disagree (biological and social arguments)	(2)	100	50	50
Disagree (social argument only)	(7)	29	43	71
Total	(34)	62	65	68

themselves into either the essentialist or anti-essentialist camps? Not only did my essentialist and anti-essentialist interviewees resemble each other empirically in their individual and institutional characteristics, but they share a great deal in common as scientific thinkers. They have largely the same understanding of the nature of human biological variation, its evolutionary roots, and the contemporary contours of human diversity, as well as reliance on the same tools and analytical methods for describing these phenomena. Their debate about race is nothing like the conflict between creationism and evolutionary theory, where opponents draw on different types of evidence, authoritative knowledge, and reasoning. When both supporters and opponents of the biological race concept agree that such groupings are "fuzzy" and not sharply delineated, what makes some scientists content to use racial labels to describe human variation and others unwilling to do so? As Stark, Reynolds, and Lieberman (1979, 90) put it, "We have, among authorities in the same discipline who employ similar techniques to analyze similar bodies of facts, different patterns of discovery and interpretation." What factors contribute to their diverse conceptualizations of race, or more precisely, to their varied acceptance of the proposition that racial groupings can be reliably distinguished in our species?

Drawing boundaries: Disciplines, real science, political correctness, and racism

One potential explanation may have to do with the way that people attribute particular qualities or meanings to various concepts of race. For example, they may associate a certain perspective with respected practitioners (Gieryn 1999), or feel that some ideas "fit" their intellectual self-image (N. Gross 2002). As I will show, interviewees clearly assigned very different values to different positions on race so that they seemed not so much to opt between empirical interpretations or analytical conclusions as they did to identify themselves with larger complexes of meanings that they associated with particular views. What essentialism meant or symbolized differed depending on whether the commentator identified him- or herself with an essentialist position. These findings suggest then that in order to fully account for individuals' concepts of race, we must understand why they come to associate certain standpoints with appealing or distasteful properties.

In his influential book *Cultural Boundaries of Science: Credibility on the Line* (1999), Thomas Gieryn argued that scientific controversies often involve "credibility contests" where "bearers of discrepant truths" not only joust over the accuracy or validity of their claims, but deploy discourse that links their views to values such as "objectivity, efficacy, precision, reliability, authenticity, predictability, sincerity, desirability, tradition" (1). Gieryn likened this process to mapmaking, where participants employ strategic rhetorical maneuvers to draw boundaries between their own ostensibly "scientific" position and the "less authoritative residual non-science" of their opponents (1999, 5).

As it turns out, such rhetorical "boundary work" (Lamont and Molnár 2002) was plentiful in my faculty interviewees' comments. Nowhere was this more evident than in the professors' comparisons of their understandings of race to those of others. To draw these out, I asked each interviewee to guess how three groups would respond on average to the Lieberman statement, "There are biological races in the species *Homo sapiens*": (1) members of their own discipline, (2) members of the "other" broad disciplinary division (i.e., social scientists for biologists, or biological scientists for anthropologists), and (3) the American public. These comparisons made it clear that interviewees' positions on the nature of race are not simply the product of abstract calculations or assessments of empirical data; they also carry with them values or associations—sometimes explicit, at other times less so—that play an important motivational and emotional role in the debate on race. In particular, two bases for evaluating racial concepts dominated the interviews: first, the question of which view was "scientific," and second, the issue of which was racist.

SCIENTIFIC VERSUS NON-SCIENTIFIC CONCEPTS OF RACE

Interviewees often presented certain ideas as being more "scientific" than others, and both essentialist and anti-essentialist views could be perceived as scientific. Faculty who believed that biological races exist, for example, depicted like-minded people as scientifically knowledgeable and experienced. One biologist in this essentialist group said, "I think that a lot of us see where biologists, particularly evolutionary biologists, see geographic variation within a species and we see it in *Homo sapiens* too. It's all sort of part of the same sets of processes." Another speculated about her colleagues, "I think people who work on model systems . . . like yeast or worms or flies . . . might agree" with the Lieberman statement on biological race. Such essentialists felt that people who rejected a biological interpretation of race did so out of either a lack of knowledge or a more basic rejection of scientific practices and attitudes. One biologist suggested that most of the public would disagree with the statement on the existence of races because they would be "afraid of the implications" rather than remain "detached like biologists."[6] Social scientists were also suspected of "try[ing] to deny the genetic truth," as one biologist put it, either because of lack of knowledge (they "wouldn't understand race as an example of species polytypism," according to one interviewee) or because they "reject the idea of a data-driven reality." Yet another biologist attributed what he believed to be social scientists' rejection of the race concept to an extra- (or non)scientific agenda, namely their "need" for race because "they are professionally invested in race and racism."

Although essentialists demarcated science from nonscience, particularly when asked to compare their views to others, it was the anti-essentialist respondents who were most likely to invoke science in all facets of their discussion of racial conceptualization, whether open-ended definitions or focused comparisons between disciplines. Comments in this vein included: race is "scientifically untenable," "a useless concept," or a "non-concept"; it "doesn't make sense," "has no biological basis," or "doesn't have scientific validity in a biological sense"; "there's no biology attached to it," "Biologists don't find those categories to be very useful," and, "To a geneticist, there's only one race." For these interviewees, the falsity of the biological race concept was underscored by emphasizing its distance from current scientific knowledge, locating it outside the realm of modern science. As a biology professor at Ivy University maintained: "Nobody who knows any current biology would agree with that statement, whatever their professional status is." These respondents found it hard to believe that their peers would argue for the existence of races:

> I don't think there's any biological evidence to support the fact that there are things such as biological races. I would hope that when you were asking other people this that they would be smart enough to recognize

that this is true. That if they took a logical—you know, like I said before, for there to be biological races two things had to happen. You needed to start different and maintain differences.—*Biologist, State University*

Anti-essentialists' perception of their view as that of "smart" people acquainted with "modern" science meant that belief in biological race indicated ignorance. In the following comment, that ignorance verges on religious credulity, evoking the public debates about creationism that many faculty interviewees felt they faced all too often in the classroom:

Unfortunately, there's probably some still uneducated people in certain areas of the country, and they might tend to agree with this [Lieberman statement]. I don't know what the problems—what the frequency would be, hopefully not that high, 10, 15, 20 percent maybe, but I'm sure there are a number of individuals out there that still believe this, [like] that men have one less rib than women.—*Anthropologist, City University*

In anti-essentialist attempts to position the boundaries of science to exclude a biological notion of race, references to the public often served to signal ignorance of contemporary science.

Despite the disparity in their conceptualizations of racial difference, both essentialists' and anti-essentialists' attempts to claim "scientific" status share an idealized vision of contemporary science as blameless when it comes to race.[7] Essentialists criticize anti-essentialists' for not being "scientific" enough, whereas anti-essentialists accuse essentialists of not keeping abreast of current science and instead cleaving to old, outdated principles. Either way, modern science appears to be free of any problematic views about human difference, because any such troubling perspectives are associated with the past. And biologists' recurring criticism of social scientists as being attuned to nonscientific, political concerns suggests that "real" science is conducted in a space free of such contaminating biases.

Constructionist interviewees, in contrast, expended much less effort on distinguishing scientific from unscientific ideas. They generally saw science itself as a social product that did not automatically confer superhuman prestige and which is always intertwined with political concerns.

In this view, a human enterprise such as science is not intrinsically anti-thetical to a culturally produced idea such as race. A few faculty inter-viewees noted that the biological race concept derived much of its power from its appearance as scientific and thus unsullied by cultural value systems, but that it is nonetheless fundamentally a cultural product.

RACIST VERSUS NONRACIST CONCEPTS OF RACE

As important as it was to lay claim to scientificity, this was not the only symbolic boundary that my interviewees struggled over. Scientists sought simultaneously to distance themselves from any association with "rac-ism." Indeed, the claim to be antiracist is in some sense the antidote to the charge of political correctness (or "unscientificness"). Both racism and political correctness are devastating ethical accusations—the antitheses of antiracism and scientificity—and like trump cards, they seem to neu-tralize each other. If political correctness is the charge commonly leveled at scientists who reject essentialist ideas about race, racism is the label slapped on those who accept them. Political correctness and racism are the touchstone moral errors that underlie the debate on the nature of race.

The most common rhetorical move in this realm was to equate belief in biological race with racism, as in the following comment:

> If you took a random survey across the United States, probably most people would agree with that [Lieberman] statement. Because many people in the United States are racist, so they want to believe something like that, something that fits with what they already think.—*Biologist, State University*

Another biologist predicted that the public would support the state-ment on races because "they don't want diversity." Academics who op-pose the equation of race with biology see themselves as modern scien-tists who have rejected the racist, erroneous thinking of the past. In their view, humans all too easily translate diversity into hierarchy; thus the resemblances between race, gender, nation, religion, and other schema are highly pertinent. Without disavowing human biological diversity, these academics are deeply skeptical of both the motivation for and ulti-mate impact of classifying by race.

Yet there is no simple mapping of racism and antiracism to diverse concepts of race today. Many proponents of the biological race model also see themselves as antiracist: they are objective scientists untainted by social influence who are searching for knowledge that would benefit people who have been disadvantaged by racism (e.g., Risch et al. 2002). Consider again Professor A.'s comments:

> So you say, for example, that blacks have higher rates of hypertension and males have much higher rates of prostate cancer. Why? And then you get the . . . "there is no such thing as race." People's . . . origins and so forth and background mean nothing in terms of medicine. And we'd say, "Wow." I was wondering, if I were black and had prostate cancer, I'd want the medical association, you know, to have paid a little more attention to the diversity. You know. And they have to call me black, even though my—one of my great-great-grandmothers was white. I think I'd still want that to happen.

It is no accident that the realm of medicine has become a key site for heated debate about the nature of race. In this field devoted to human well-being, those who see race as a useful biological tool can sidestep the implied link between essentialist race and racism by casting their support of racial categorization as part of a humanitarian and antiracist health agenda. In this vein, it is worth noting that the Association of Black Cardiologists supported the introduction of the race-specific pharmaceutical drug BiDil; it is difficult to claim that this association's promotion of a medicine that may have reinforced essentialist thinking about racial difference was motivated by racism.

The other way in which essentialists can fend off accusations of racism is to counter that anti-essentialism is nothing more than a superficial brand of "political correctness," one that is not motivated by any genuinely antiracist concern and which can lead to the denial of basic and important truths about the human body. One biologist at City University maintained that social scientists "would try more to be politically correct or some perception that this is politically incorrect, which I can imagine that people would think that way, but I don't see there's any real reason to try to deny it. It's a function of the genes that you get." Another biologist reasoned:

So some people might actually have prejudices, but they know that that's wrong, so they might say, "Oh, I don't believe in races," but they're saying that because they have these beliefs and they just don't want their colleagues to know that or whatever.

Whether essentialism or anti-essentialism is racist or nonracist, then, was far from a settled matter among the biologists and anthropologists I interviewed.

In the contemporary debate about the nature of race, scientists have to engage in moral boundary-marking (Lamont 2000) on two fronts simultaneously. On one hand, they have to assert their position within the highly authoritative enterprise of science and demonstrate their fidelity to such ostensibly scientific norms as honesty, openness, and impartiality (Gieryn 1999). On the other, they must also show they are free of racist assumptions and objectives. To date, neither essentialists nor their opponents have been able to decisively lay claim to both the mantles of science and antiracism. Perhaps this is why scientific opinion on the true nature of race remains so unsettled. Until the outcomes of these distinct but related boundary-marking struggles are determined—that is, until a consensus forms about which racial concept is ultimately most scientific *and* least racist—everyday academics lack clear guideposts to signal where their support should lie.

The vehemence with which interviewees dismissed notions of race that conflicted with their own, and the ways in which they did so, offers a new direction for research on the determinants of scientists' racial conceptualization. As we saw, once we turn attention to the majority of the faculty who grounded their race definitions in accounts of human evolutionary history—that is, the essentialists and the anti-essentialists—we find many socio-demographic similarities between those who accept the idea of biological race and those who reject it. Moreover, all these faculty invoke the same body of research on genetics and evolution to make their diverse cases, which may simply be "half full, half empty" judgments about how much physical differentiation is necessary to delimit a race (Morning 2005). Given their shared analytical framework for approaching the question of race, what may most distinguish the two camps are not the logical conclusions they draw, but rather the value characteristics they attribute to different concepts of race. What remains to be explained then is not why some scientists embrace biological race and others reject it, but rather at a deeper level, why one person's "science" is another's "racism."

CONCLUSION

Key findings

My interviews with university anthropologists and biologists strongly refute the frequent claim that scientists have arrived at a consensus about the nature of race, let alone a constructivist one. It is worth keeping in mind, moreover, that the popularity of racial essentialism among scientists has probably been underestimated by this research. For one thing, given a non-white interviewer of predominantly white faculty members, some degree of "socially desirable" conversation may have lessened the frequency with which interviewees reported thinking of race as a matter of fixed biological difference. For another, my sample is one in which anthropologists are highly overrepresented (compared to their share of the total professoriate in the United States), which may mean it is one where racial constructivism was more widely embraced than it would be in a random sample of social and biological scientists.

Why then have so many observers—especially social scientists—asserted that scientists are in agreement when it comes to the race concept? This research offers a potential explanation. When I asked anthropologists and biologists whether they thought the members of other disciplines would share their views on biological races, I discovered a striking asymmetry. Cultural anthropologists—the strongest supporters of the constructivist model of race—were extremely confident that biologists shared their perspective: 78 percent made that prediction. In contrast, none of the physical anthropologists made this prediction, and when I asked biologists whether social scientists saw race as they did, only a minority—less than one-fifth—thought so. In other words, only the racial constructivists in my sample were quite certain that their perspective had been adopted throughout academic science.

This asymmetry is likely fed by the imbalance in prestige accorded the social versus the natural sciences. In today's academy, social scientists have more to gain from claiming alliances with natural scientists than the other way round. It is not surprising then that when I asked my interviewees whether their views of race were largely shared by the public, anthropologists guessed their ideas were closer to those of biological scientists than they were to those held by laypeople, but biologists suspected their own views were closer to those of the American public than they are to those of social scientists. In yet another example of boundary-marking in the debate on race, the social scientists I interviewed were more likely than the biologists to convey the sense that they were partners in an interdisciplinary and expert conversation about race that was far from mass discourse.

In addition to the centrality of boundary-marking to contemporary scientific race conceptualization, my research findings also point to a new way of mapping the race debate. Instead of the usual dichotomous depiction of essentialists versus constructivists, a tripartite scheme including anti-essentialists better fits the empirical data. One reason is that anti-essentialism emerged as a distinct rhetoric in interviews, one that not only draws on its own line of reasoning but which is usually not combined with constructivism when individuals explain their reasoning about race, despite the two concepts' commonalities. Another reason to distinguish anti-essentialism from constructivism is that their frequent separation in discourse may help explain why they have made fewer inroads in the academy than some presume. In other words, their rhetorical combination might make for a more effective weapon against racial essentialism. For example, if social scientists rely solely on constructivist arguments about historically malleable categories, they may not be equipped to answer the biological questions that laypeople raise: Don't different races have different diseases? Why do doctors take note of their patients' race? As one cultural anthropologist confessed about her lectures on race, "I always worry that I'll get trapped by people asking a question about biology that I cannot answer." A purely history- or sociology-based constructivism runs the risk of seeming unpersuasive, incomplete, or downright Pollyannaish. A physical anthropologist touched on this danger in describing her teaching on race:

And what I say is that, well, the social concept as it's enhanced with all of these stereotypes and us-thems and da da da da da, has no usefulness at all, but the biological concept of geographic variation, I'm sorry geographic variation exists. It's not pre-determinate. It's not all those things. And so I actually—I—while I'm sympathetic with what the people who say race doesn't exist are trying to do socially, I kind of think they're being irresponsible because it's like saying to a kid that boys and girls don't differ.

In her view, it is not enough to simply assert that race is a "social concept" that "doesn't exist" biologically. To give students a full and convincing account of race, their teachers have to join the history of "stereotypes and us-thems" to biological knowledge of human geographic variation.

From academic conceptualization to academic instruction

What scientists teach students about race can be enormously influential. In the next chapter, I describe numerous interviews where undergraduate students draw on their college coursework when reflecting on the nature of race. As a prelude, I will close this chapter with the comments that professors made about how race figures in their classrooms.

To learn how scientists' thinking about race actually translated into their teaching, I asked my faculty interviewees whether and how they thought the topic came up in the courses offered by their departments. I found that while most anthropologists saw a place for race in their discipline's instruction, most biologists saw it as only tangentially related to their primary areas of interest.

Virtually all of the professors of anthropology reported either mentioning race in their own teaching or expecting that the topic had a place in the teaching of their colleagues. More specifically, they linked the mention of race to classroom discussion of human physiognomy and its adaptation to the environment, skeletal biology and forensics, disease, the history of the anthropological discipline itself, social hierarchy, race relations, linguistics, and the cultural construction of race. They also saw the discussion of race as being interwoven with classroom lectures on ethnicity, identity, gender, class, and nationalism. "When I teach cultural anthropology," a professor at City University reported, "we talk about race in a number of lectures specifically, but then questions of ethnicity, identity politics, questions of hierarchy, gender hierarchy, class, all of those things blur with considerations of race." For a professor at Ivy University, race was an analytical element in her study of colonialism: "when you talk about colonial history, what is it that links—what is the framework in which you understand colonialism? It has to be some kind of racialized understanding of the world." In other words, anthropologists saw race as both a topic worthy of dissection in its own right and an example of a broader class of social differences that could shed light more generally on what one professor called "the play of difference."

When asked what messages they attempt to convey to students regarding race, anthropology professors emphasized both the social nature of racial categorization and its failure to accurately capture biological patterns of human variation. Some faculty expressed this by distinguishing the "social concept of race" from "the biological concept of race." Another described his efforts to "break down essentialist thinking" by confronting students "with the fact that race, racism and racial classification change through time." Several professors mentioned the importance of teaching that "race was a very real but social construct," and "that that exists in the world, that there have been these systems of domination, they have been racialized." One anthropologist turned around the usual depiction of race as malleable to open up the possibility of change for the better: "we therefore have to have radically open-ended political imaginations about the possibility of the future that we create in the present, and understand our implicatedness in the production of—or conceivably the deconstruction and demolition of—certain kinds of ways that racialized distinctions organize social life."

In contrast to the anthropologists' consensus that race had a place in their disciplinary instruction, biologists were evenly divided over the question of whether they expected race to come up in their departments' course offerings. In discussing their own teaching, many professors reported not referring to race, either for lack of time or relevance or because they felt the notion was fundamentally flawed. One professor stated that race "has no scientific basis"; another described it as "an emotionally and a psychologically and socially burdened term that doesn't have a clear biological meaning." A department chair thought the sparse coverage of race in his department might be due to the interests of his colleagues: "Most of our faculty are not well-versed in population genetics or diversity, they're more molecular geneticists, and they always put the population genetics at the last lecture in the syllabus." Interestingly, however, one member of the department who did discuss race in the classroom thought the chair did not approve: "I expect my chair now doesn't even like it. 'What does that have to do with genetics?' But it has a lot to do with genetics." Echoing the chair's comments, another faculty member said, "I teach diagnostics, molecular genetics, molecular physiology, so that [race] doesn't come into any of the teaching I do." Finally, a professor of evolutionary biology in another department saw race as out of his realm because it dealt with human beings: "I'm a biologist; I don't even have to worry about people," he said.

Race may appear more frequently in biology courses than their instructors realize, however. One professor who said "It'd be even hard to imagine how one could bring it [race] up" nonetheless went on to describe a class exercise where students genotyped their own DNA and then compared their findings to various racial groups' allelic frequency rates as reported in a class-distributed research article. Moreover, biologists had little trouble listing topics to which race could potentially be connected in biology lessons. Most of these related to differential rates of phenotypic expressions of genetic traits across racial groups: sickle cell anemia, cystic fibrosis, skin color, ear wax quantity, enzyme production, and "syndromes related to the Jewish community." Other areas in which interviewees thought race might figure in biology instruction were: population genetics more broadly; metabolism, in biochemistry classes; differential rates of heart disease by race or different average body temperatures; evolutionary debate on the African-origin versus multiregional hypotheses; the Human Genome Project; and the abuse of genetic methods or logic (e.g., with respect to intelligence). Generally, however, biologists' expectations concerning the place of race in their discipline were so minor as to be easily overlooked; for most of these interviewees, race might appear briefly as an illustrative example in broader discussions of genetics, biochemistry, or human evolution, but was largely implausible as a subject to which a biology professor would devote focused attention.

Anthropologists' greater efforts to convey their concepts of race to students are likely mitigated by their relatively small numbers. Biology is a much more frequently selected course of study than anthropology, by a ratio of more than six to one (National Center for Education Statistics 2002, table 258). As a result, biologists' notions of race, even if less frequently and explicitly presented in the classroom, are likely to reach a much wider audience than anthropologists' concepts of human difference. And since biologists are relatively unlikely to depict race as socially constructed, we might expect this understanding of race to have made few inroads among students. How American college students think and talk about race is the topic of the next chapter.

FIVE

Learning Race

STUDENTS ON HUMAN DIFFERENCE

> I just think about how much my—like how I think about
> race has changed and how—to me, I think of it as almost
> being a construction, like a social construction. Whereas
> before I thought of it as being very much based on biology.
> And while I think it fundamentally is, it's being used in a
> way which is not biological. And I think the type of educa-
> tion we're getting here, everyone is exposed to that.
>
> —Biology major, Ivy University

The twenty-one-year-old student from Madison, Wisconsin, quoted above describes an experience that many proponents of a constructivist approach to race would like to see more widely shared. In her account, coming to college meant exposure to a new way of thinking about race that changed her previous views considerably. Having originally thought of race as "very much based on biology," she now believes it to be "a social construction." Moreover, she feels that through her college's coursework, "everyone is exposed" to that perspective. In many ways, this student's college career exemplifies the role that many constructivists believe formal education can and should play in reshaping Americans' conceptualizations of race.

But how common among today's college students is the transformative experience described by the biology major from Madison? In later comments, she herself guessed that not all universities convey the constructionist message, and that people without university training would have a "very different" outlook. Similarly, many supporters of such an educational agenda are pessimistic (e.g., Graves 2001). Nicholas (2001, 142) suspects "there may be significant differences between what anthropologists themselves think of race and what their students are learning or at least being given to read." Shanklin (1999, 672) concludes that students "probably have little occasion to assume that anthropology has anything useful to say about race or racism." Yet the sentiment that education is an important potential ally in the effort to transform traditional American views of race endures (e.g., Obach 1999). As cultural anthropologists Mukhopadhyay and Moses (1997, 525) outline the challenge to their colleagues, "We must understand and be able to explain to students and the public the weaknesses of typological/classificatory approaches to human diversity and be able to demonstrate alternative clinal approaches." And Lieberman et al. (1992, 303) feel that college professors in particular have a special responsibility in this area because "high school students learn very little about race from biology textbooks and teachers in high schools."

As in the previous discussions of high-school textbooks and college professors, this chapter takes up again the thread of how scientists' race concepts are conveyed to the public through formal education. It does so, however, from the perspective of college students who describe the messages about race they hear in the classroom. In the following pages, I address the question of how students receive or react to scientists' messages about race by exploring the understandings of racial difference they take away from the classroom. College students constitute perhaps the largest public audience for academic knowledge, and an especially important one since future policy makers are most likely to emerge from their ranks. Moreover, undergraduates have an unusual degree of access and exposure to research scientists, thus offering a special window onto laypeople's reception of the racial beliefs that are promulgated by "experts." In interviewing young people who often draw on their university coursework to make sense of race, I aim to learn, as Swidler and Arditi (1994, 321) put it, "how ordinary people actually take up and use (or reject) the knowledge" generated by elites.

After a brief description of the students I interviewed, the chapter presents three main sets of empirical findings. First, I describe the ways that undergraduates depicted race when asked to define the concept. Second, I report the extent to which they agreed with the claim that our species is divided into biological races. And third, I analyze the ways in which they actually used race as a conceptual tool when I asked them to explain real-life race differentials in outcomes as diverse as health and professional sports participation. This last set of findings is of crucial importance because it shows that the students' reasoning about race in the abstract—for example, when they are asked to define the term—is not the same as the way they think about race when they have to account for racial disparities. Notably, difference in "culture" was the most popular way to define the nature of race among my student interviewees, yet references to concrete cultural differences (in practices, beliefs, norms, or values) were relatively rare when respondents were asked to explain why racial groups had different outcomes in health or sports. Their comments also pointed to another fundamental finding about Americans' racial conceptualization: we do not have a consistent, uniform metric of racial difference whereby all races differ from each other in the same ways and by the same degree. In my young interviewees' views, deep-rooted biological difference separates blacks from all other races, who in turn are distinguished from each other by cultural differences in practices and norms. In short, these students' racial conceptualization is heavily colored by what might be called "black biological exceptionalism."

The final sections of this chapter are devoted to the question of which factors, either individual or institutional, seem to help account for variation in college students' conceptualization of race. As I find that sociodemographic characteristics such as gender or region of origin seem to matter little, I focus instead on the role that academic training plays. Here the discipline of anthropology emerges as playing a pivotal role in transmitting the idea of race as socially constructed. Moreover, the views of the professors I interviewed are clearly mirrored by their students: the share of undergraduate majors in a department who define race as socially constructed reflects the proportion of professors in the same department who do as well. However, the undergraduate academic experience is not limited to the classroom; my results suggest that aspects of college life such as institutional eliteness and racial diversity are also related to the ways that students think about what race is.

HOW DO COLLEGE STUDENTS CONCEPTUALIZE RACE?

Student sample and interview strategy

The demographic backgrounds of the students I interviewed varied considerably from campus to campus (Table 3). On the whole, the student sample also differed notably from my faculty interviewees, and not just in terms of age.[1] The proportion of women in the student sample was nearly twice that in the faculty sample, and the proportion of nonwhites was greater. A larger share of students than faculty identified with centrist or right-leaning politics, and nearly twice as many reported some religious affiliation compared to their professors.

As with professors, I tried to gauge students' racial conceptualization by asking first for their open-ended definitions of race, then whether they agreed or disagreed with the Lieberman survey statement on the existence of biological races (see the student interview questionnaire in Appendix D). In addition, however, I went on to ask students how they would account for two types of real-life race differential (to be described below). My aim was to find out whether different kinds of question seemed to elicit different conceptions of racial difference. And as I show next, the ways that students thought about race did indeed seem to vary depending on what kind of question I put to them.

Defining race

When I asked undergraduates how they would define the word *race* or explain what it was, they often gave multiple answers, drawing on more than one theme to try to convey a sense of what race is. This was

Table 3.   Student Characteristics by University

Percentage of Students in Sample	City U. (n = 14)	State U. (n = 13)	Ivy U. (n = 17)	Pilot U. (n = 8)	All (n = 52)
Major in natural sciences	38	58	29	63	44
Female	71	31	82	63	63
White	78	69	71	75	73
Politically left of center	57	54	88	75	69
No religious affiliation	36	31	47	38	38
From Northeast U.S.	86	69	29	50	58
Foreign-born	0	23	12	13	12
Father in professional occupation*	57	54	71	100	67
Mother in professional occupation*	38	38	71	75	55

*Parental occupations classified according to 1990 U.S. Census occupational codes for both professional and managerial categories.

something that faculty interviewees did not do much, but which recalls Apostle et al.'s (1983) finding that people frequently use more than one "explanatory mode" to account for race differences.

RACE AS CULTURE

In a major departure from faculty definitions of race, students had a pronounced tendency to equate race with culture. Over two-thirds of the students (thirty-six out of fifty-two) relied on some aspect of culture to help explain the nature of race. In many cases, they explicitly referred to culture, for example when defining race as "the different cultures people are from" or "about the culture, the tradition, the beliefs that a particular group has." In other instances, students referred to elements that are associated with culture, such as beliefs, values, and practices. A female psychology major at City University summed up race as follows:

> I think it kind of has a lot to do with like what culture you're coming from and like you're different, I mean everything from like how you eat,

what you eat, to what you wear to like, I mean, the language, everything. So it's like this entire package of pretty much who you are.

Other definitions included:

So it definitely has to do with your family background, both parents
combined, their parents, whatever the mix is. Like people say I'm half
Italian. It's just your family background, where they're from, what their
culture is. I guess. What their beliefs are.—*Accounting major, State
University*
   I think there's a little bit of your culture, your background, kind of
those values that your parents teach you. It's not different from other
races, but the kind of traditions that you have.—*Biology major, Pilot
University*

By combining culture with ancestry ("family background"), the student interviewees effectively cast race as ethnicity: a group identity that
depends on a sense of common origins or history, coupled with shared
values and behaviors (Weber 1978/1956). In so doing, students desensi-
tized the notion of group difference, shifting it from the problematic realm
of racial difference to the less charged discussion of ethnic identity.

This shift to ethnicity defuses the topic of race in several ways. First,
the emphasis on culture circumvents the linkage of race to biology that
is emblematic of the "old" racism that respondents might wish to avoid.
Second, it evades engagement with the history of oppression that has
been part and parcel of racial stratification. Instead, ethnicity discourse
emphasizes markers—such as "what you eat," "what you wear," or "values that your parents teach you"—that are unlikely to entail the same
discriminatory consequences, particularly for this largely white sample
of respondents. In this way, it avoids questions of power, inequality, and
contemporary racism (Bonilla-Silva 2003; Frankenberg 1993). Third, students' equation of race with ethnicity treats group identities as voluntary to some extent, the product of freely made individual choices to
engage in particular behaviors. It depends on whether you have "maintained old values" or on which place "you most identify with" as some
students put it, and as Waters (1990) has shown, among white Americans
the choice of peoples and places with which to identify—as well as to

what extent to do so—is largely optional. One student at Ivy University made this connection explicitly when asked to define race:

> I think more and more it's something that has to do with completely, you know, self-definition, what group you kind of identify with. And, I mean, in that way I think "ethnicity" might be a better term in a lot of ways for that.

By suggesting that racial classifications are a matter of volition, students circumvent discussion of the coercive nature of external racial categorization.

Students' conflation of race and ethnicity had clear limits, however. The boundary emerged when students were asked whether groupings such as the Irish, Polish, or Vietnamese—the kinds of groups that students often referred to when seeking to illustrate the differences in cultural practice that animated their definitions of race—should in fact be considered "races." When asked directly which groups they considered to be races, students usually listed the same groups as those on the U.S. census (i.e., white, black, Asian, etc.).[2] Thus a disjuncture appeared between their invoking ethnic differences when asked to define race and their implicit acknowledgment that ethnic groups were in fact not really racial groups when asked to catalogue the latter. For example, a student who had defined race as "the different cultures people are from," based on "the country that their relatives came over from, however long ago it might have been," described the following groups as races when asked for a list:

> Like, you know, like the Asians, which lots of people—that kind of get offended because I know my friends that are Asian, because you know, people call them Chinese and they're Korean, and stuff. Or else like African Americans or like white Americans and stuff like that. Indians.—*Anthropology major, City University*

As it turns out, the traditional racial groups this student names (e.g., "Asians") do not in fact correspond to the two basic elements of her race definition. The list does not specify particular "countr[ies] that their relatives came over from," and the groups are too broad to reflect specific "cultures people are from." As with many of my interviewees, when it came to demarcating racial groups, this student did not actually apply the ethno-cultural criteria that had featured so prominently in her more abstract definition of race.

The transformation of race into ethnicity may be no more than a discursive strategy that sidesteps uncomfortable discussions of externally imposed identities and racial discrimination. However, it may also genuinely reflect the students' perceptions of racial groups as being marked by noticeable and significant cultural practices. Students were quite attentive to the differences in speech, dress, music preferences, etc. that they observed among the roommates and classmates they associated with distinct races. In this vein, culture also helped them explain their numerous observations of people who "were" one race but "acted" like another. Moreover, the role of cultural practice in distinguishing groups may have been particularly salient for this largely white sample, whose own ethnic identities as Italian, Slovak, or other were likely sustained over generations by such references. Finally, this generation's exposure to the discourse of "multiculturalism," which is all too often a euphemism for racial and not cultural diversity, likely contributes to the equation of race with culture.

The elision of race and ethnicity is a two-way street. Just as students' definitions of race took on the volitional and inconsequential aspects of "optional" ethnicity, their understandings of (ethnic) cultural difference acquired something of the permanence, breadth, and depth that usually characterizes portrayals of racial difference. Behind their accounts is a presupposition that large, meaningful, and fixed cultural differences exist between races, even when they have little evidence or experience to support the hunch. As one psychology major at City University contended:

> There's a lot of African Americans that have never lived in Africa, you know. So a lot of them grew up here and act a lot like most white people act, you know, but there are still different things like—I don't know, I'm not, like I've never lived in an African-American family or anything like that. But I'm sure there are some different things that they value that we don't. Like I mean I know that women are much more assertive, and much more, I don't want to say aggressive, but, you know, I mean, if you

look at the factor of eating disorders, I mean eating disorders are like predominantly white, middle-class American things.

It is striking that this student is persuaded there are significant cultural differences between African Americans and whites ("I'm sure there are some different things that they value that we don't"), even though she provides limited evidence of such differences and observes that "a lot of [African Americans] grew up here and act a lot like most white people act." The conviction that different races—and in particular, blacks and whites—inhabit very different cultural worlds, despite common nationality, residence, language, religious foundations, and political and economic values (Hochschild 1995), is firmly rooted among the undergraduate students interviewed here. Recalling Balibar's (1991, 23) description of cultural "racism without races," the students emphasize what he termed "the insurmountability of cultural differences" and "the incompatibility of life-styles and traditions."

RACE AS BIOLOGY

For all the discussion of race as stemming from cultural difference, student interviewees were almost equally likely to define race with reference to physical characteristics: thirty-four out of fifty-two (or 65 percent) sounded this theme. This stable coexistence of cultural and biological understandings of race suggests that the notion of cultural difference has not so much replaced biological accounts of race as been seen as an extension—or a more socially acceptable rendering—of them.

Perhaps the most common way of invoking physical difference as the basis for race was through students' references to skin color and other phenotypical features:

> Yeah, so I guess race in a sentence is, people—the way people perceive one another on the basis of their appearance, specifically their skin color, hair texture, you know, maybe facial features, and, you know, national origin in some cases.—*History major, Ivy University*

> I'd say I understand it [race] just by the person's skin color.—*Biology major, City University*

Some students defined races as the product of more extensive biological difference, alluding either to genetic difference, other non-phenotypical differences, or—like their professors—to evolutionary processes that resulted in racial differences:

> Like I personally think it's just a matter of, you know, physiological differences that occur simply because of environment.—*Biology major, State University*

> I guess it relates to the human origin. Where people are from, what skin color they have. Just like what background.—*Biology major, Pilot University*

Students who touched on physical difference in their definitions of race were divided on whether it also entailed behavioral or cultural differences. Many suggested that races should be defined as stemming from both cultural and biological differences:

> Like I think race has to do with like the—like what skin color you are and if you like identify with like a particular sort of—if there's something about like people who wear that skin color that you particularly identify with. Like if something else goes along with that skin color, like culture. I'd say like skin color plus culture is maybe race, or something like that.—*Anthropology major, State University*

> I think that the way that people usually define race has to do with like the way people look, but I think that the way people understand race when you think about it more has to do with the way people act.—*Anthropology major, Ivy University*

In contrast to this "skin color plus culture is maybe race" approach, however, other students were adamant that race had to do only with biological (phenotypical) difference, but nothing more. If the former group's approach could be labeled "race is more than biology" (or as one student put it, "I think race is a lot more than just different colors"), the latter group's message was, "race is nothing more than biology."

> It's the color of your skin. But it's really—that's all it should be. Like it shouldn't be anything more than that. That's it. And I think some people take it as more than that. You know, they make it cultural I think. But as

Americans, what makes our country so great is that it doesn't matter—it doesn't matter what color of skin you are. You're an American. So in my opinion I don't think race should be an issue ever—for anything, anymore, but unfortunately there are some people who think that—that think it should be. So I don't think—on the outside it's the color of your skin, but other than that, that should be it.—*Meteorology major, State University*

So the genes make them different, but, because they look different—we look different—the environment is going to play a role. People have darker skin; they might be less prone to skin cancer because they have that protective layering. But it doesn't make them different people, so . . . I don't think people act—if you just take the U.S. and different races here, and if they were born here, and they're different races, I don't think that makes them act differently, makes them any different.—*Biology major, Ivy University*

This student's stressing the idea that different genes or skin colors "doesn't make them different people" is reminiscent of another argument that appeared in student definitions of race: the claim that "we're all the same." As an Ivy University anthropology major put it, "I think everyone is basically the same. We all have the same physical functions regardless, you know, what your culture is or what your race is. So I don't see the biological differences."

RACE AS SOCIAL CONSTRUCT

A minority of student interviewees (nine, or 17 percent) took a constructivist approach to race. When asked how she would define race, an anthropology major at Ivy University answered, "I guess I would say that I agree that it's socially constructed and that it is a way that over time people have been organized into groups." The idea of racial categories as dependent on time and place also came across in a State University anthropology major's response to the same question:

Well, I would just basically describe that there's no biological differences amongst, you know, the races and that the only difference is in how we, I guess, view, you know, the phenotypes. Like you know, somebody who has a different color skin is seen as a different race and that it—how it all has like a historical, you know, value to it, and political

and, you know, social politics as well, and just try to explain that, that
there's no actual biological difference. I think that's, you know, the key
there.

Another anthropology major at State University, who stated "I definitely agree with the anthropological idea that it's socially constructed,"
continued:

> I'd say that it's—the idea of race is the idea that race—that the concept of
> race is the idea that there are differences between groups of people
> based on biology essentially, but that in reality those—the ideas that
> are—the attributes or stereotypes that are associated to people based on
> biology, which isn't even really that accurate to begin with, is culturally
> formed or historically formed.

Moreover, many of the students who adopted a constructivist definition of race went on to portray it as a concept that is not only historically
or geographically anchored, but which also arises to serve social and
political ends. This view was articulated particularly forcefully by anthropology majors at Ivy University; here are three examples:

> *Example 1.* I define race as a system of classification that uses outside
> markings, usually the color of people's skin, but it also could be facial
> configuration, to place people in different categories of sort of belonging
> or otherness.

> *Example 2.* I would say like social categories, or race is a, you know, social
> category that's based on appearance and that is used to distinguish
> people from one another. But that actually there is no difference. There is
> no biological basis for the difference, but there is—but at the same time
> like it doesn't mean those categories aren't important to people or aren't
> important categories to think about or work with. You know, not just like,
> oh, race doesn't matter. But that—I mean, because how you identify in
> terms of your race can be really important I think. But it derives more
> from social systems of hierarchy and power than it does from any sort of
> difference in your genes or like something like that.

> *Example 3.* So for me race is a concept that has been used to do more
> harm than good to other people. It's a very politically charged word that
> doesn't reflect any reality but reflects our reality. Race is a way of

classifying other people and attributing them certain characteristics that make them in one way or the other; usually if you're classifying like you're not giving the person the chance to classify himself or herself. So you're already doing something there that is about power. I mean, you're saying something about some person and the person is being quiet. And then I feel like race is—I just can't detach it from the concept of racism because racism is not only saying you're of that one race but it's also a violent concept when it's put into practice.

Although the constructivist definition of race was only a minority viewpoint among students compared to the more widespread cultural and biological conceptualizations of racial difference, it was clearly a very compelling one for its small group of undergraduate supporters.

On the existence of biological races

As with the faculty interviewees, students were next asked to comment on the statement taken from Lieberman's survey (1997): "There are biological races within the species *Homo sapiens*."[3] Nearly twice as many students as faculty members agreed with the statement as is: 47 percent of the former did so compared to 24 percent of the latter. If "contingent" agreements are included as well (i.e., responses in which interviewees agreed to a modified statement), then 57 percent of students can be considered to have agreed with the Lieberman statement versus 48 percent of the professors.

Student arguments about the existence of biological races, pro or con, revolved around their judgments of biological similarity or dissimilarity between racial groups. As evidence they pointed to human physiognomy, genetic makeup, evolutionary history, or disease susceptibility. Examples of their agreement that biological races exist include:

I think there really are because like there are different genes that can lead to different expressions, or can lead to different, like how, behaviors in people. And I think that will define a race.—*Anthropology major, City University*

Well, I mean it's a fact that humans, like we're not all the same. I mean, we all have the same or similar genes but there are differences between people that—we've all evolved in a somewhat similar way but I think that different groups of people are different.—*Biology major, Pilot University*

Among the 43 percent of students who disagreed, arguing that biological races do not exist, the following perspectives emerged:

I disagree because I know some small facts about this type of thing . . . and, although I don't remember numbers specifically, I recall hearing somewhere that races, quote, unquote, make up something like 2 percent, or .1 percent, of the genomic makeup of a person, whereas similarities between cultures are 99 percent. Genetically. Biologically. Whereas, separate—I mean, the differences are only like 1 percent or something ridiculous like that. So, I mean, and even—I mean, there's pigmentation. You know. That's basically—that's what I see as the difference between races. Difference between cultures is a different thing. Difference between identities is a different thing. But biologically I don't see any difference.—*Economics major, Ivy University*

Like *Homo sapiens* is referring to human beings, like we're all human, and I think it just comes down to that. You know, I think there are like cultural differences within the species *Homo sapiens*, but there's not that much; we all have the same number of genes. There's, you know, the variation in the genes, you know, is just random. Like what Darwin says or whatever. Yeah. That's how I feel.—*Anthropology major, State University*

On both sides of the fence, however, students often wove notions of behavior and especially culture into the discussion, sometimes as a counterpoint to biologically grounded race, but sometimes in harmony with it.

As did the faculty interviewees, students often hesitated in formulating their opinion of the statement on biological race. Some vacillated, starting with "agree" but ending with "disagree," or vice versa. (In tallying the counts of each, I took into account only students' final answers.) Students were not as likely as professors to resolve their concerns by proposing an alteration to the statement; whereas 24 percent of the faculty took this route, only 10 percent of the students used this "contingent agreement" approach. Instead, a more common way for students to express their reservations about the statement was to voice ethical concerns about its motivation or likely impact. It is noteworthy, moreover, that students on both sides of the biological race divide (i.e., those who agreed with the statement and those who did not) expressed reservations about the idea of biological race. They did so by noting both their emotional discomfort with it (e.g., "honestly, it does make me uneasy") and their moral disapproval (e.g., "it's a very shifty statement").

Several students found the statement troubling because they felt it reinforced divisions among human beings:

> I think it emphasizes the differences between us. Rather than the same. I mean, there's a lot more things in common than are different . . . But. And I think a lot of, like, you know, race—like, I mean, I guess like—I know one black kid that acts totally just like me. Like he's no different than me.—*Biology major, State University*

> Well, I just think, just divisions, always. I don't understand why there have to be divisions, why we have to categorize all the time. You are who you are, and that's just who you are, you shouldn't be limited to a certain category or identification. It should be limitless, you know, your race. So here, I mean like I said, it should just be that species are *Homo sapiens*, and you know, that's all you need, so that's why I'd say that.—*Political science major, Ivy University*

Closely related to this concern about encouraging racial divisions was the fear that the idea of biological race—whether or not the student deemed it accurate—could be misinterpreted or manipulated to promote negative actions or beliefs:

> So the funny thing is that when I read it on paper like that it makes me angry . . . not like angry, angry—like I wanted to kill someone—but I feel like the person who's like saying it is going to follow this sentence, like, "therefore, let's do something bad to other people." . . . And, yeah, like seeing it written down makes me unhappy.—*Anthropology major, Ivy University*

> Because I think that it gets to be a pretty dangerous thing to say that there are different—that there are like fundamentally, like, different races on the basis of—on the basis of like biology or I don't know what. Genes or something. Kind of absurd because—it's not absurd; maybe it's true and I don't know—but because I feel like it can be manipulated in

many ways to perpetuate things like fascism and Nazism that really strongly upheld this sort of statement. And so I'd venture to say that it's not true.—*History major, Ivy University*

As we have seen, faculty interviewees were also very sensitive to the moral implications of arguments about the nature of race. Students, however, tended to express their reservations in more emotional terms. And the last quotation above exemplifies a kind of reasoning that most professors would likely denounce: the idea that because racial essentialism might be dangerous, it therefore cannot be true. This logic represents the kind of "political correctness" that many of my faculty respondents suspected was afoot in the academy, but to which none them admitted. As I will show later in this chapter, however, students had a visceral sense of inhabiting a social world that condoned some beliefs while condemning others—and of being participants in the maintenance of those norms.

Explanations for observed race differentials

After asking students for their open-ended definitions of race and opinions of the statement on biological race, I also asked how they would explain two real-life situations in which differences between races have emerged.[4] Rather than rely entirely on their responses to abstract questions or statements, I used these factual scenarios to learn something of how their concepts of race worked "in action" by exploring the ways in which their understandings of difference would actually help explain a given outcome. This approach turned out to be extremely rewarding because it demonstrated that the abstract statements that students made in earlier parts of the interview did not necessarily correspond to their applied uses of race, or to the concepts of racial difference that truly helped them make sense of the world.

RACE DIFFERENCES IN INFANT BIRTH WEIGHTS

For the first "real-life" question, I purposely chose an outcome with which I did not expect students to be familiar: the observation that infants associated with different races have different median birth weights.[5] The question was:

> Researchers have discovered that at birth, babies of different racial groups tend to have different weights. For example, white babies have among the highest median weight, black babies among the lowest, and Asian babies' weights tend to be in the middle. In your opinion, what are some possible explanations for this finding?

I expected that providing students with statistics for white, Asian, and black babies would make the question less sensitive than if it required a strictly black/white comparison. Moreover, I asked interviewees for more than one potential explanation in order to gauge the range of causes that seemed plausible to them, rather than force them to stand by one choice only. In this way I hoped to obtain a more accurate reflection of how they thought race might matter, even in areas where they might not feel knowledgeable enough to offer a definitive answer. In retrospect, I think this item also offers insight into how people make sense of biomedical research findings, which today are frequently reported in the mainstream press (not to mention in the original scientific literature) in terms of differential outcomes between races.

Three general characteristics emerged sharply from students' speculation about the causes of racial differentials in infant birth weight. First, the "culture" concept that they had drawn on so heavily when defining race became much less prominent. Second, the concepts of race that students described differed depending on which racial groups they were discussing. And third, the phenomenon of racial discrimination was virtually nonexistent for students as a potential cause of racial disparities.

Students' grappling with observed racial differentials evoked very different approaches to race than the ones they espoused in their open-ended definitions. This disjuncture was best illustrated by their references to cultural difference. Recall that when asked earlier to define race, most students emphasized culture (e.g., "everything from like how you eat, what you eat, to what you wear"). When confronted with race differentials in infant birth weight, however, "culture" was the least frequently mentioned among the four major explanations I recorded, which also included (1) genetics, (2) socioeconomic inequality, and (3) maternal diet and health. Only 27 percent of the students explicitly drew a picture of culturally specific values, beliefs, or practices contributing to birth weight differentials. In these instances, students portrayed culture as influencing choice of foods ("if you're Chinese or Japanese, you eat a lot of non-fattening foods like sushi or something like that") or the quantity of food pregnant women eat ("maybe white people think it's good to eat more or to indulge in a pregnant woman's need to have different kinds of food"; "it might be something like having a large child is not as important to other cultures, like in the United States it is to like a white culture").

In contrast to students' limited use of culture, they were most likely to offer genetic explanations for birth weight differentials: 70 percent suggested this possibility. Two arguments predominated: either that infant birth weights reflected disparities in adult sizes, which varied by race, or that birth weight was a function of evolutionary adaptation. Examples of the former included "Asians are shorter than most people" and "if [the parents] tended to be taller then they might have babies with higher birth weights." The evolutionary approach inspired explanations such as:

> Maybe like low birth weight may be—the races that have low birth weights are races that were—like way back when they were very nomadic, did a lot of moving. Maybe it was beneficial to have a child that was—that weighed less.—*Anthropology major, Ivy University*

> Maybe, in terms of evolution maybe it's better for the white people to have bigger babies than the other countries, I don't know.—*Biology major, State University*

As these responses suggest, particular racial groups evoked particular concepts of racial difference.[6] For example, the possibility of birth weights simply reflecting adult size was invoked almost uniquely to account for white/Asian infant weight differentials, even though students were told that the greatest variation in median birth weights was between whites and blacks. Such asymmetries were even more apparent, however, in students' speculations about the roles played by maternal diet and health (mentioned by 51 percent) and by socioeconomic inequality (brought up by 57 percent). When students mentioned diet specifically, it was usually to distinguish white from Asian eating patterns, often citing the latter more favorably than the former. When discussion turned to maternal health independent of nutrition, however, students illustrated this potential factor with unfavorable images of blacks. In particular, drug abuse came up only when students considered African American birth weights:

> It might just generally be that Asian babies are smaller. Maybe American babies are bigger. I don't know how that ties with the black babies. I know, you know, if the mom uses drugs or anything like that, the babies can have a lower birth weight. But I don't think that's a particular one, like black mothers versus white mothers or Asian mothers. —*Biology major, City University*

As with other students who raised the issue of drug abuse, this student avoided explicitly naming blacks—at least at first—and she qualified her comment by suggesting it does not apply to "a particular one, like black mothers versus white mothers or Asian mothers." Instead, the blacks/drugs link was at first only implied, through her mention of drugs as soon as she mentioned black babies. Yet a minute later, she recounted, "Just according to one of the articles that I've read recently, the black babies because of drug use among the mothers." This kind of furtive linking of blacks to drugs was echoed in other students' explanations.

Socioeconomic inequality was another potential factor that came up only when students compared black to white birth weights. Specifically, interviewees commonly speculated on the role that African Americans' relatively low incomes, limited access to health care, insufficient food, and poor education might play. However, discrimination rarely figured in the discussion as a possible cause. Consider the following comments by a meteorology major at State University:

> I guess for blacks, they're typically always found like in lower-income housing, lower socioeconomic status, so they may not have been educated and have like the resources. They may have been, you know, pregnant in a bad situation, so maybe they don't know the proper prenatal care. They may not have access to the proper prenatal care. And so as a result they may be like drinking or doing these drugs or smoking or something. That could be a reason for low birth weight. That could be a reason. I mean, obviously, whites, I guess, typically still have better access to, you know, more education in terms of taking care of the baby, like going to Lamaze class, you know, things like that, knowing what not to do while you're pregnant.

In his account, blacks' low birth weights are largely attributed to their engagement in illicit behaviors: "drinking or doing these drugs or smoking," or getting pregnant "in a bad situation." When group inequalities are mentioned, they are normal outcomes, simply given, and unconnected to any mention of discrimination, whether in residential location, wages, or health service delivery. Notice this interviewee's use of the passive voice: blacks are "typically always *found* like in lower-income housing, lower socioeconomic status" (emphasis added); they "may not have access to the proper prenatal care"—but discrimination does not enter the picture. In fact, the handful of students to mention discrimination in their explanations for birth weight differences dismissed it as having operated only in the past:

> African Americans might be more stressed. I mean, now they have all these minority programs, but when these mothers or something were growing up like twenty years ago, maybe they worried about finding jobs, whereas white people are already settled here, they don't have to worry, or something.—*Biology major, Ivy University*

> That most—like because of the inequalities that existed prior to—well, black people weren't given the opportunity to prosper and therefore couldn't get good jobs and therefore couldn't make money . . . —*Biology major, Pilot University*

When faced with race differences in a biomedical outcome, then, students largely identified genetic factors and freely made choices as key determinants. In this perspective, discrimination hardly exists, and pervasive social stratification is simply part of the backdrop. In a world without racism, individuals too are absolved of the suspicion of racism that so often hangs over discussion of the nature of race.

RACE DIFFERENCES IN PROFESSIONAL SPORTS REPRESENTATION

The other "real-life" question I put to students read as follows:

> The second scenario I'll describe has to do with sports, and the overrepresentation or underrepresentation of certain racial groups in certain sports, compared to their share of the total population of the country. To give you an example from football: in the NFL, blacks make up 67 percent of the players and white athletes are in the minority. But

in the total population of the United States as a whole, whites make up the majority and blacks count for only 12 percent of the population.[7] In your opinion, what could be some plausible explanations for why the racial composition of the National Football League is so different from the racial makeup of the country as a whole?

Like the previous birth weight question, this sports outcome was chosen to permit a wide range of potential explanations (e.g., biological, environmental, cultural, etc.). However, in selecting the numerical overrepresentation of blacks and underrepresentation of whites in football as the second case, l deliberately targeted an outcome that I expected to be (1) familiar to students, both in terms of their exposure to televised sports and more particularly to the occasional debates that flare up in the media about the role of race in professional sports; and (2) a more sensitive topic, both because it narrowed down to a black/white contrast and because in so doing it focused on blacks—my own racial group— thus potentially exacerbating any interviewer effects.

Despite the controversial tone that discussions of race in sports have often taken on, students were again most likely to turn to biological accounts (74 percent), followed by socioeconomic explanations (50 percent). In contrast to their hypothesized solutions to the birth weight dilemma, however, culture figured more prominently in the football scenario, evoked by 48 percent of the students. Finally, discrimination also came into play in some sense: one-fifth of the students thought that sports recruiters might favor black athletes. In other words, "reverse discrimination" that put whites at a disadvantage seemed the most plausible way in which prejudice might have something to do with the racial makeup of professional football.

Discrimination against blacks again played the largely invisible or taken-for-granted role it had in students' discussions of infant birth weights. Although half of the interviewees mentioned racial differentials in income, access to good schools, career prospects, and safe housing— as well as minorities' exposure to role models in particular occupations and to diverse sports—they did not necessarily describe these as unfair inequalities resulting from racism. Students were most likely to perceive discrimination at work in the area of education. Even in this realm, however, unequal opportunities were described as matter-of-fact realities unconnected to either individual or institutional racism. As a State University student put it, "there's more opportunity for white people to be more educated so that certain groups, like black people, maybe develop more of their social aspects in sports," and lean toward sports "rather than an intellectual career." Another noted that whites have "more educational opportunities" and that "if you start higher, then you have a potential to go higher." The acknowledgment that "whites have more opportunities" simply leaves open the question of how racism might play a role. The invisibility of racism was even more evident when conversation turned away from the quality of education available to minorities to their disproportionate exposure to poverty and unsafe neighborhoods. Racial discrimination hardly registered in the following account from a State University student, even though it touches on poverty, violence, residential segregation, and incarceration:

> Another reason may be—blacks—I read a lot of articles in *Sports Illustrated* about athletes, and they always grew up in like poor settings, so they found sports is their only outlet to like get away from the drugs and the violence and whatever was associated with their lives. That was the only thing they could do, so they got really good at it. And then they would be recruited by colleges and then they would—you know, they got really good and then they eventually become the pros. Whereas, whites typically don't grow up in those kind of settings, where they don't need sports as an outlet to rescue them from, you know, dangers and stuff like that, from the streets. So that's why, you know, whites grow up to do like other non-sports-related activities, I think. I mean, I read so many articles in *Sports Illustrated* about an athlete who was black, who grew up where his father was in prison or he was raised by his aunt, he was always around drugs and stuff like that. And sports was their only outlet. So that could be a reason why you have so many more, I guess, blacks in the NFL.

Again, note the passive acceptance of race differentials in poverty and segregation as neutral phenomena unrelated to discrimination: blacks "always grew up in poor settings," "whites typically don't grow up in those kind of settings." At most, anti-black racial discrimination figured as a phenomenon of the past only. As an Ivy University biology major reasoned, "they weren't allowed to get really great education until the 1950s or around then, so it might be that they would spend their time practicing sports." And a student who thought "it's a lot easier to get onto a football team as an African American, than to get onto the executive board of a company" chalked it up to blacks' business advancement being slowed by the lingering presence of people "who were fighting for segregation in, you know, in those sixties and seventies."

A more frequent mention of contemporary discrimination was raised in students' speculations that the recruitment process into professional sports might be biased in favor of black athletes. An anthropology major at State University suspected that blacks have an edge in draft picks due to "the general underlying idea that blacks are better at athletics than whites in general." A psychology major at City University thought it was the image of blacks as "aggressive and violent" that would put them in good stead; if a coach "had a choice between like a white player and a black player, they would probably go for the black player." But the students left ambiguous the extent to which they thought of such prejudices as unsubstantiated biases. The avid reader of *Sports Illustrated* quoted above believed both that blacks appeared more "intimidating" than whites and that they were naturally superior athletes who coaches would naturally seek to recruit. In other words, coaches' hypothesized preference for black players falls in the category of "statistical discrimination": a kind of bias that is grounded in past experiences with different kinds of people. As such, it is not clear whether most students would consider it a prejudice so much as a sound judgment based on coaches' past observation of blacks' superior physical abilities.

Indeed, nearly three-quarters of the student interviewees suggested the possibility—and in most cases seemed quite persuaded—that differences in sports representation were due to blacks' natural physical superiority vis-à-vis whites. As a City University anthropology major explained, "black people are physically superior to white people. They can run faster, jump higher." Similarly, a State University biology major thought that "black people have like a difference in their cardio-vascular system that enables, you know, their muscle structure to develop differently." Students were for the most part quite matter-of-fact about such racial differences; they presented them as patently obvious, as did this Urban Studies major at Ivy University:

> You see like the Williams sisters come on and start just killing everyone. It makes you think like, what happens if more black people are given the ability to play tennis? . . . Does it ever end? I feel like it just goes on forever.

Blacks' physical prowess was largely attributed to musculature; students spoke of muscle length, muscle tone, muscle mass, extra leg muscles, "slow twitch" versus "fast twitch" muscles, "more defined" or "cut" muscles, "lean" muscle, and the ability to build muscle. In some cases, these were differences that students had previously discussed with friends, family members, and authority figures such as teachers or coaches; in others, students reported having personally observed such differences, particularly among their peers. A varsity swimmer commented, "Just from what I've noticed, like in people that I know that are black, they just seem to have such like awesome muscle tone. Like really—you know, I don't know, how or why it is, but they seem to have just like more muscle mass than white people."

As in the case of infant birth weights, students' discussion of sports quickly revealed that their concepts of race—in particular, of what kinds of differences distinguish races, and how those differences develop— depended a great deal on which races they had in mind. In general, interviewees drew on ideas about human evolutionary history to explain why blacks and whites were disproportionately employed by the NFL. However, their evolutionary accounts displayed two striking racial asymmetries. First, their notions of how evolutionary forces acted to create race-specific traits differed when they reflected on blacks, whites, or Asians. Second, they seemed to suggest that while the black race was distinct from all others due to biological differences, other races differed from each other along cultural lines.

In students' understandings, evolutionary pressures had exercised a decidedly distinct effect on Africans and their descendants. While blacks' natural selection had led them to develop certain physical capacities, Europeans and others had bolstered their intellectual faculties over time. When interviewees sought to explain the racial composition of the NFL, they largely presumed that blacks had a natural physical superiority compared to other racial groups, and they came up with two evolutionary narratives to account for it. One explanation was that slavery in the United States had exercised a selection effect on the African American population, either because the harsh conditions had weeded out all but the strongest or because slave owners had purposely bred slaves for strength:

> I think part of that might have to with slavery because they would take the best fit man and the best fit woman and they would, you know, they would have children and those children would be—so they were sort of like bred to be fit and muscular, like work horses. So just coming from that, like they've been bred for that. And I hate that about whatever, that past, people's history, but I think that might be part of it.—*Biology major, City University*

> If Africans were slaves, there might have been some mutations in their DNA that might have allowed their bodies to keep up with this, and then eventually it gets passed down, and then football players can cope with all the stress.—*Biology major, Ivy University*

The second explanation that students gave for blacks' physical superiority stretched further back in history to African ancestors and their adaptation to the exigencies of their environment.

> Well, obviously—I mean, not obviously—I think the easiest explanation is that there's some—that there's some biological reason that because African Americans [*sic*] had to run and catch their game in Africa, that made them fast and fleet-footed and able to nimbly tackle the prey or something.—*Biology major, Pilot University*

> [I]f they were different way back when, you could probably associate it to circumstances as to why someone needed to be bigger and stronger, if they were like a hunter as opposed to like a—probably hunters everywhere though. But maybe they're hunting smaller animals or bigger animals, or there's like a certain heat, there was a certain cold, there were different reasons for why.—*History major, Ivy University*

If evolutionary processes had forced Africans to develop physical ability, however, other races' survival had required them to adapt in different, more cerebral ways.

[Blacks] tend to be more athletic, maybe because where they were living, they had to be—it required them to be more athletic to get food or something. When I think of Caucasians, where they originated, the first thing I think of is medieval times where they're all kind of domesticated, they're wearing clothes and they're just not being, not really running around, and riding horses or something.—*Biology major, Pilot University*

It could also be just that we came to depend in Europe, because of climatic situations and everything that we had to concentrate on, not consciously, but you know, our adaptation was less in terms of physical adaptation as technological. So, in order to survive in a harsher climate like rough winters, we came to depend more on technology than just on physical superiority.—*Anthropology major, City University*

I have images of Africa, of like walking around, . . . buckets of water, pails of water, and like Europeans I just see them as like judges, I don't know why, I'm just getting a big judge . . . I don't know why, and people with black skin have a lot more—are more cut, have a lot more defined muscles, as I see a lot less fat with black males than I do . . . white people, the more I see are more defined, more built than whites. —*Undeclared major, City University*

Similarly, I asked a State University biology major who was born in India whether her reasoning—she had guessed that "their ancestors in Africa, they had to always run"—would explain Asian Americans' relative underrepresentation in professional sports. She responded:

Yes, maybe they're more education-oriented so that they spend all their time reading books or something; that was more conducive to their environment, and they were farmers or something, so that generally it's not necessarily like brute physical strength to go hunt something, it's more tending to their fields. It is also physical development, but a lot of them had labor forces, in their terms of different castes and everything, so the upper class would sit there reading books or something, so they're not going to be developing their physical abilities as much.

As this comment illustrates, students' grasp of the evolutionary processes of natural selection was shaky at times, even when it came to biology majors. It is not clear, for example, why the characteristics of the upper class suffice to color the traits of an entire race, or how an activity such as reading books would ultimately impact the physical abilities of later generations.[8]

To make sense of sports, students consistently grounded contemporary race differentials in long evolutionary pasts of marked biological difference. Their hypotheses—namely, that present differences must have developed in response to previous generations' exigencies—are clear examples of the ways in which assumptions about the present (such as that Asians "spend all their time reading books") are simply transported to the past. As Gifford-Gonzalez (1995) points out, these stories are a kind of science fiction that projects our contemporary social configurations onto the past rather than the future. When thinking about the human past, students imagine early Africans (and in fact contemporary Africans, who they see as living the same life as previous generations) as having been at the mercy of their environment (particularly animals) for their everyday survival. Europeans, on the other hand, have mastered the environment: they domesticate animals, not flee them; they insulate themselves from the dangers of their surroundings by wearing clothes and building cities; they develop technology that spares them having to carry water or farm land; and they embody authority, as in the figure of the judge. Where Africans brought only brute force to bear, like the animals with which they were locked in struggle, early Europeans were able to bring superior intelligence, the hallmark that separates man from beast.

The result of these distinctive evolutionary pathways, according to students, was that blacks in particular were uniquely identifiable by physical difference; the distinctions between other races were not measured along a metric of biological difference. Instead, whites and others were recognizable for their cultural characteristics. This asymmetry emerged when I asked interviewees why, if blacks were such superior athletes, there were so few in some sports, such as professional hockey. I expected the same kind of evolution-framed answers I had gotten in response to the question about professional football: something along the lines of whites being naturally physically adapted for hockey. But this was not the case. Instead, students felt that for the most part, cultural traditions explain white predominance in hockey, as well as the presence of other groups in various sports such as Caribbean baseball players, Hispanics in boxing, or Brazilians in soccer. Reasons that Canadians and eastern Europeans dominate ice hockey included: "it's just what they've learned, . . . like how they grew up"; "that sport is more expressed, is more important there in those cultures that train more"; "that I think might be a cultural thing . . . It's always been associated with hockey, cold climates, cold European climates . . . Just like more white kids will probably be introduced to it when they're younger"; "maybe certain groups are just not interested culturally in anything to do with ice hockey." In other words, I learned that only *blacks'* presence in a sport could be explained by biological characteristics, and even their *absence* from certain sports could be attributed to their physical capacities (e.g., lack of body fat to swim). When whites or other groups were at issue, however, culture replaced biology entirely as the most plausible explanation for the racial makeup of professional sports leagues. In contrast, fewer than half of the students thought cultural traditions could explain blacks' football participation.

In a further bifurcation of racial conceptualization, it became apparent that the term *culture* took on different meanings depending on whether students spoke about blacks or nonblacks. For example, to explain why hockey was a predominantly white sport, the students invoked culture in the sense of traditional custom or habitual practice. When discussing black predominance in football, however, students used "culture" to describe a broader, more diffuse value system that prized physical activity in general over intellectual occupations.

> I mean, it could be a social or cultural thing, where different races, you know, or the cultures, stress physical, you know, participation in physical sports, you know, more than others.—*Biology major, State University*

In promoting a physical versus mental dichotomy, students' cultural explanations for race differentials in sports representation closely mirrored their biological accounts. As one student put it, blacks had come to value "body knowledge" versus whites' prizing "book knowledge," and he elaborated:

For a racial explanation, you could say you know if you want to look at it socioeconomically, there's more of a stress on, you know, blacks—I guess more as a culture then—to perform well athletically as a means of bettering themselves, versus whites being you know—there's a big emphasis on education and studying. Staying in the library as you're growing up and reading books. Not as much on being outside and running around.—*Biology major, Pilot University*

The same contrast was developed by a City University anthropology major as she sought to explain why "in general, black people are physically superior to white people":

It's just, you know, they're definitely, I don't know if that's cultural, but it does seem that they seem to inherently have a better—it kind of also has something to do with we have a—maybe Europeans have a longer tradition of mind/body dualism. If that hasn't been as ingrained into African culture and African American culture, they might just be more in tune in with their bodies and know how to use them better.

Again, culture in this account does not designate specific practices but rather a broad value system privileging physical over mental activity. So even though students' "cultural" explanations present differential sports representation as a matter of choice or preferences, they arrive at the same scenario as the evolutionary biology accounts that suggest that differential tendencies toward these activities are hardwired. When it comes to blacks in the United States, culture functions like biology (Balibar 1991).

In discussing how individuals' race concepts vary according to which particular group(s) they have in mind, I have so far emphasized the phenomenon of black biological exceptionalism. In this way of thinking, racial difference between blacks and whites is interpreted as physical in nature, whereas different outcomes between whites and other races are attributed not to biology, but to cultural preferences. In my college interviews, blacks figured as an anomaly, uniquely designated by students as physically a group apart—a perception that is quite striking given African Americans' mixed ancestry as well as the common African origins of our entire species. However, the "real-life" scenarios also pointed to three other kinds of group difference that had an impact on interviewees' conceptualization of race. First, gender mattered: the image of the superhuman strengths of black male athletes was a sharp contrast to students' association of black mothers with disease and drug abuse in the discussion of infant birth weights. To be sure, part of the difference lies in the nature of the scenarios themselves, one of which associates African Americans with athletic success and the other with poor health, but it also has a gendered dimension, pitting debilitated women against men of superior strength. Second, students' discussions of infant birth weights revealed a marked tendency to equate Asianness with foreignness, for example, by contrasting "Asian babies" with "American babies," or casting the comparison as an international one ("maybe it's better for the white people to have bigger babies than the other countries"). Accordingly, the students' portrayal of Asians as foreigners paved the way for a cultural concept of racial difference, one that emphasized diversity in cultural practices and values. Finally, it must be noted that race difference was always interpreted by interviewees as a matter of comparison between whites and nonwhites: for example, between whites and blacks, or whites and Asians, but never between blacks and Asians. This means that the individuals' concepts of race were systematically informed by their understandings of the characteristics of the white race, characteristics for which other races represented the opposite reflection. In short, ideas about race are always ideas about whiteness.

Comparing different measures of racial conceptualization

In comparing my interviewees' open-ended definitions of race to their reactions to the Lieberman statement on biological race and to their explanations for race differentials in birth weights and sports, it is clear that students' concepts of racial difference varied considerably depending on the context and manner in which they were asked to think about it. For example, race was linked to cultural differences in 69 percent of the student definitions of race, but only 48 percent of their accounts for sports representation and 27 percent of those for birth weight. Similarly, race was equated with biological differences in 65 percent of students' open-ended definitions and in over 70 percent of their explanations for sports and health differentials, but only 47 percent were willing to agree when asked point-blank whether the Lieberman statement on the existence of biological races was true (although an additional 10 percent offered their conditional agreement).

These fluctuations in the prominence student gave to biology and culture when they thought about race were likely due both to their judgments about the sensitivity of certain questions and to the mental associations evoked by differences in question content, language, and format. It seems that the bald Lieberman statement was interpreted by students as a sensitive one, whereas the birth weight and sports questions were not. The relative obscurity of debates about the causes of low infant birth weight may have rendered the subject less delicate, while the sports question's apparent depiction of black superiority vis-à-vis whites might have similarly rendered it less sensitive. A different sports question in which blacks seemed to be at a disadvantage—for example, on their relative underrepresentation as quarterbacks or coaches in the NFL—might have left students less willing to offer biological explanations.

Similarly, students' varying references to races as cultural groups may also be due to differences in the perceived sensitivity of the questions posed. The fact that mentions of culture reached its highest point in students' open-ended definitions of race (but subsequently appeared much less often in explanatory accounts of racial differentials in sports and birth weight) suggests that cultural differences are not in fact central to the way students think about the nature of race; culture did not seem to offer students much of a tool for working out actual cases of real-life race differentials. Instead, the language of (multi)culturalism may simply be perceived as a diplomatic or neutral way of discussing race. Culture came up most frequently in the sports and health scenarios as a descriptor of unproblematic differences between nonblack races, one that carries the connotation (in the United States at least) of an inoffensive reference to racial difference.

Regardless of the explanation for why an individual might conceive of race differently when it is placed in different contexts, this research demonstrates that the measures we apply to racial conceptualization matter enormously. Perhaps no single indicator of racial conceptualization is sufficient in itself; instead there are likely to be several dimensions of such thinking that can be captured only through the use of multiple measures. Exploring those dimensions and developing methods to analyze them will be a fundamental task for future research in this area.

EXPLAINING VARIATION IN STUDENT RACIAL CONCEPTUALIZATION

As we have seen, undergraduate students—like their professors—show considerable diversity in the ways they conceptualize race. One way to understand that diversity is to explore, as I did with faculty interviewees, whether individuals' socioeconomic characteristics seem to be related to their thinking about racial difference. Interestingly enough, however, the kinds of characteristics that previous researchers have investigated seemed to have even less to do with students' race concepts than they did with those of the professors. In my sample, region of origin, gender, religious affiliation (e.g., Jewish, Catholic), and parental occupation showed virtually no association with student racial conceptualization. The two exceptions were religiosity and political orientation. Students who declared they had no religious affiliation—about two-fifths of the sample—were substantially more likely than others to depict race as socially constructed and to deny that biological races exist. So were interviewees who located themselves left of center in political terms. Indeed, it was left-leaning students alone who proposed constructionist definitions of race; no student identified with the political center or right did so. Instead, the relatively conservative students defined race in terms of either biological or cultural difference. Overall, it is worth noting that the socioeconomic characteristics that did not prove to be associated with student concepts of race—such as gender or region—were all variables that represent statuses (e.g., female, Midwestern) that individuals acquired prior to developing their views of race, and so could have been considered potential determinants of students' racial conceptualization. Instead, the two variables that did show some relationship to race conceptualization— political orientation and religiosity—were ones that reflect ideological leanings that could well have been acquired later in life, and thus be either causes or effects of particular racial understandings.

The finding that young people's racial conceptualization is more closely linked to their ideological views and exposure than to the circumstances of birth suggests that the academic settings in which they find themselves are likely to play an important role in their thinking about race. Again, the causal mechanism is not clear-cut: colleges may well shape undergraduates' concepts of race, but it may be equally likely that students with particular, preexisting notions of race are more likely to choose certain kinds of campuses and not others. What I explore below, then, is how particular kinds of educational institutions seem to house specific ways of approaching the question of defining race. In particular, I look at how my student interviewees' views of race varied by university eliteness, campus diversity, field of major, and concepts of race held by the faculty teaching in their major. In the process, I pay special attention to how the message that race is socially constructed fares among college students.

University setting

Undergraduates' understandings of race varied notably across college settings. Ivy University students in particular stood out as both especially familiar with and supportive of the notion of race as construct (see Table 4). They were the most likely to define race as socially constructed and the least likely to believe biological races exist, whereas City University students were least likely to define race as a construct and most likely to agree that biological races exist. These two campuses are at opposite ends of my sample in terms of the two college characteristics I measure: eliteness (or selectivity) and racial diversity. Ivy is both elite and relatively racially diverse, whereas City is not an elite school and is the least racially diverse in my sample.

The relevance of both eliteness and diversity for students' race thinking is borne out when we simply order the campuses along different measures

Table 4.   Student Race Concepts by University

	City U.		State U.		Ivy U.		Pilot U.		All	
Race Concepts	N	%	N	%	N	%	N	%	N	%
Defined race as:										
Biology	11	79	9	69	8	47	6	75	34	65
Culture	12	86	9	69	8	47	7	88	36	69
Construct	1	7	2	15	5	29	1	13	9	17
(Total sample n)[a]	(14)		(13)		(17)		(8)		(52)	
Agreed with Lieberman statement[b]	11	79	7	64	6	38	4	50	28	57
(Total sample n)[c]	(14)		(11)		(16)		(8)		(49)	

NOTES:

[a] Percentages of students offering various race definitions do not sum to 100 because interviewees frequently offered more than one type of definition.

[b] "Agreement" includes contingent agreement.

[c] The Lieberman question was omitted from three student interviews due to time pressure, resulting in a sample size of forty-nine for this item.

of racial conceptualization. If we rank the four universities from those with the greatest share of student interviewees to define race as biological to those with the smallest share, they follow in order of their racial heterogeneity (Table 4). The same is true when we rank the schools in terms of their proportions of student interviewees defining race as socially constructed. However, if the universities are ranked in terms of their student interviewees' agreement with the Lieberman statement on biological races, school eliteness seems to matter more. Much larger shares of students at the public universities City and State than at private universities Pilot and Ivy agreed that biological races exist.

These results imply that both college eliteness and diversity matter for student concepts of race, but that each of these two campus characteristics is related to different aspects of thinking about race. It is on relatively diverse campuses that racial constructionism may be more widely taught, or more readily accepted by students, according to their open-ended definitions of race. In contrast, the eliteness of a college may have an impact on what kinds of statements about race are considered socially acceptable, as reactions to the "biological races" statement suggest. In the next subsection (on academic training), I will delve further into professors' transmission of the constructivist perspective; first however, I explore the climate of intellectual tolerance at elite universities.

Concern about social acceptability is a constant theme when analyzing how people talk about race, as my interviews with both college faculty and students illustrated. One indicator is the comments that respondents explicitly made about feeling uncomfortable or vulnerable to critique when expressing certain ideas. Another measure of the role of social desirability in race discussion comes from comparing what interviewees were willing to say in different contexts—or more precisely, in response to different questions. Across the board, the question on the existence of biological races was the measure where students were least likely to voice essentialist beliefs about racial difference, in contrast to what they said in their open-ended race definitions and in their discussion of real-life differentials in sports and health. In other words, the point-blank question "Do you agree there are biological races in our species?" seemed to be an especially sensitive one that provoked a certain amount of anxiety on the part of interviewees. More than any other item, it was a barometer of self-consciousness, self-censoring, socially desirable reporting, or simply "political correctness."

Comments by students at Ivy and Pilot universities suggest that elite colleges foster especially strong cultures of political correctness; it was in these settings that interviewees spoke most vividly about normative regimes for the discussion of race. Consider their responses when I asked them to speculate on whether other college students in general would agree or disagree with the Lieberman statement on the existence of biological races:

> Like I guess we're kind of—at least here at school we're hit over the head with, you know, social Darwinism. Like, "oh, gosh, that ugly thing that happened." You know. And so that almost produces like this gut

reaction, like, "oh, we stay away from all of that." So I think they would almost—a lot of them would disagree. Yeah.—*Biology major, Ivy University*

I think you'd cause a lot of internal dilemma for a lot of people. I think that also largely because this campus is perceived as being a liberal campus, people are reluctant to have conservative views . . . So taking that into account, I think you might get more "disagrees," but I don't—I don't know. You'd get a lot of "disagrees" and "I don't knows" than you'd get students, "well, like I agree." You know. What are you going to do about it? And I think a lot of that has to do with the atmosphere and the fear of agreeing . . . I think more people would agree than they would care to admit necessarily—[if] it wouldn't be an act or something that they perceive as going on the record.—*Anthropology major, Ivy University*

I think there's a large, large conservative element in their beliefs on the campus and that they don't—I mean, that they're—to my mind, they're kind of racist. I mean, that's kind of the feeling that I've encountered. But—and I just think—but on the surface, they don't feel like they could ever kind of allow that to show in a general way, that they don't. I mean, it just seems like there's a lot of pressure today at [Pilot University], or anywhere, to go with the kind of politically correct view. And that to say that there are biological races would be to kind of admit that you're racist, in a way. I mean, just to say that. And I just can't see a lot of people saying that.—*Biology major, Pilot University*

In describing the tone on elite college campuses, students conjured up a judgmental and unforgiving atmosphere where the social penalties for taking an unpopular view are immediate and considerable: students are "hit over the head" with warnings about "social Darwinism," there is the "fear of agreeing," and as one Ivy anthropology major put it, someone who did affirm the existence of biological races would not get "any sort of positive response." This sense of an oppressive intellectual milieu came across particularly strongly in the interview with the Pilot University biology major quoted above. When asked where he thought the "pressure" he had described came from, the student elaborated:

I feel that, well, number one, the press. But, I mean, you come to high school and— or even middle school and there are always these diversity weeks, which I'm not saying are bad. But, I mean, they definitely give a feeling that you have to be very—very, very careful about what you say and, you know, guidance counselors say things. And I mean, it's pretty much, you know, the whole Antonio Gramsci—it's feeling a cultural—he called it "cultural hegemony"—but like you're influenced by everything around you and like whether it's the press, whether it's your teachers, whether it's you get to [Pilot University] and you have RAs and you have all these talks during freshman week about, you know, diversity and so you get this feeling that you have to be very—and even today, I mean, look at, you know, if a senator makes one wrong statement and expresses some—maybe it's a racial statement, which I'm not agreeing with, but if he expresses a personal view, everyone jumps on top of him immediately. And it's that kind of feeling that if you say one wrong thing in a study break, everyone jumps on top of you immediately because you're not supposed to say anything that might be controversial.

Like his peers, this student depicts an elite social sphere in which accusations of racism or political incorrectness can suddenly spring to life on the basis of innocuous comments—and where "cultural hegemony" dictates the range of ideas we permit ourselves to entertain and express. Thus, a particular code of social acceptability may leave students at the most selective colleges least likely to openly agree that races are biological in nature.

Academic training

At the heart of this book is the contention that academic training has the potential to play a major role in how Americans come to think about race. If this is true, university settings matter not just because of their eliteness or racial diversity but because of the intellectual orientation they provide. To explore this possibility, I examine how students' choice of disciplinary major in general is related to their concept of race, and then consider the specifics of their academic experience on each of the four campuses studied here. In particular, I look at what students report is taught in the classroom, the concepts of race that faculty hold in different anthropology and biology departments, and the role that coursework in other disciplines—such as English or sociology—may play in shaping students' understandings of race.

DISCIPLINARY MAJOR

Regardless of university, anthropology majors overall approached the question of race differently than did biology or other majors. Almost 40 percent of the anthropology majors I interviewed defined race as a social construct, whereas no biology major on any campus adopted this definition (see Table 5). Conversely, over 80 percent of the biology majors defined race as a physical phenomenon, compared to less than 40 percent of the anthropology students. When it came to the linkage of culture to racial difference, however, the students did not vary as much by major. In other words, their training seemed to influence their thinking about the roles of biology and/or social construction when it comes to race—which is not surprising since these are the terms in which their professors frame the race debate—but did not leave as much of a mark on their ideas about the role of cultural difference.

The discipline of anthropology appears to play a unique role in transmitting racial constructionism. Not only did anthropology coursework emerge as a necessary (if not sufficient) condition for constructivist student conceptualization, but its closest neighbor in the social sciences—namely, sociology—made no such contribution, at least not in this small sample. Regardless of the major students ultimately chose, those who took at least one course in anthropology were the most likely to define race as a social construct; in contrast, taking at least one course in sociology had no such effect.

That anthropology majors embraced a constructivist view of race more often than other students comes as little surprise if we take into account the definitions of race that their professors hold. As I reported in Chapter 4, anthropology professors defined race as socially constructed twice as often as biologists: 47 percent of the former did so compared to 23 percent of the latter.

For professors' concepts of race to have an impact on students, however, they have to be communicated in some way. Here lies the other key to anthropologists' role in transmitting the idea of racial constructionism to students: they discuss race in the classroom much more often than biology professors do. In our interviews, professors of anthropology claimed to mention race frequently in their course lectures while biology

Table 5. Student Race Concepts by Academic Major

Race Concepts	Anthropology		Biology		Other		All	
	N	%	N	%	N	%	N	%
Defined race as:								
Biology	7	39	15	83	12	75	34	65
Culture	11	61	14	78	11	69	36	69
Construct	7	39	0	0	2	13	9	17
(Total sample n)	(18)		(18)		(16)		(52)	
Agreed with Lieberman statement	8	44	12	71	8	57	28	57
(Total sample n)	(18)		(17)		(14)		(49)	

instructors felt race had little place in their teaching. Undergraduate students largely corroborated this depiction when asked whether race had come up as a topic in their classes. Their comments also shed light on why anthropology coursework in particular—as opposed to other social sciences or humanities—seems to have a particularly strong influence on students' race notions. According to my student interviewees, anthropology professors seemed much more likely to address the question of defining race, and in response the social construction of race.

> [T]he [anthropology] professors that I've had here have always been very adamant about discussing why race doesn't exist. So it always seems to come up in that context. I don't know if that's across the board in this anthro department or if that's just the professors I've had, but it always comes up. You know, dispelling the myth of race.—*Anthropology major, Ivy University*

> Anthropology, I guess, they really try to enforce the whole idea that, you know, race is culturally constructed and there's no such thing as race. So and that's just like reinforced and like, you know, they repeat it like eight times in the lecture when they discuss race.—*Anthropology major, State University*

CAMPUS DIFFERENCES AMONG ANTHROPOLOGY MAJORS

Despite the apparent link between anthropological teaching and student belief in racial constructionism, however, a closer look at the interviews reveals that not all anthropology departments promoted such thinking. As Figure 8 shows, it was particularly at the racially diverse Ivy and State campuses that anthropologists emphasized the social construction of race in their open-ended definitions. Accordingly, the anthropology majors at Ivy and State were the most likely—indeed the only students interviewed—to cast race as a social construct. Not only do these results suggest a close connection between specific departmental faculties and their students' race concepts, but they even hint that something of a critical mass is necessary for professors to convey an effective message about race to students. In this sample, the only majors to define race as socially constructed were those in departments where at least half the faculty interviewed also approached race in constructivist terms.

Why didn't any of the anthropology majors at City University draw on the notion of social construction to define the concept of race? The "critical mass" explanation would be that not enough of their professors subscribed to that view to transmit it effectively; perhaps City students received less exposure to it. From City anthropology majors' accounts, however, another factor emerged: their professors seemed to talk about race in a different way. Specifically, City University students tended to describe the race-related content of their anthropology coursework as grounded in the examination of diverse groups and their cultures. When asked why she had stated that race figured in anthropology teaching, a City University anthropology major responded:

> Well, I guess it would have to come down to specific people that we're studying, perhaps. There are areas that were like focused in. Like on a certain day we would cover like a certain tribe of people, to get like that exotic, I guess . . .

This student's account suggests that City University anthropologists were more likely than their counterparts at State or Ivy to adopt a "multiculturalist" approach to race, similar to the equation of race and

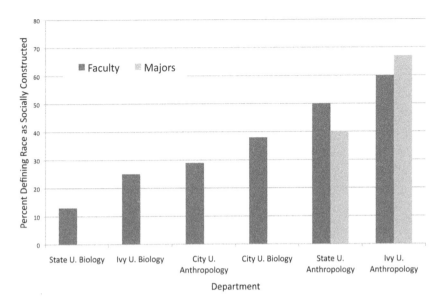

Figure 8.   Percentage of Department Faculty and Majors Defining Race as Socially Constructed

N O T E :   Pilot University interviewees are not included in the comparison due to their small numbers.

culture that appeared in the geography textbooks I described in Chapter 3. However, her words also raise the possibility that City students were less likely to fully comprehend the anthropological message that "race is constructed."

Such misunderstanding is hardly limited to the City campus. Interviews with students at all the universities made clear that exposure to teaching racial constructionism did not necessarily result in students' comprehension of the idea. At times they interpreted the idea of race as "cultural construct" to imply that racial categories mirrored cultural boundaries; that is, race should be understood as "cultural" not because it is an ideology that has evolved in particular cultural contexts, but because it is a mapping of culturally distinct groups. For example, an anthropology major at City University argued that one could use "a cultural construct" to identify racial groups, taking into account "differences like what they eat, and how they eat." An Ivy University student who had learned in an anthropology class that "race does not exist, it's just a completely artificial construct," said of his professor:

> He was very adamant about it. I think when he was saying that and how I understood it was that it's all about culture, about individual cultures. And people throw around the word race in a different context, and it's almost inherently racist, the way they use it. You kind of, you kind of assume that black people are fundamentally different or Latino people are fundamentally different, when really each person is part of a distinct culture, whether it's country or—actually the way I see it, it's not just country, it gets down to the village level.—*Urban Studies major, Ivy University*

Clearly, the classroom message that race is a "cultural construct" has led some students to conclude that races are fundamentally cultural groups, without internalizing the argument that the production of a racialized worldview is a culture-bound process. And perhaps at an institution such as City University, where a smaller share of the anthropology faculty subscribed to the constructivist perspective on race, such miscomprehension is more common.

Although anthropology majors at both Ivy and State often defined race as socially constructed—in sharp contrast to their peers at City University—their professors' intellectual orientation and teaching approaches also produced differences in the ways students on the two campuses spoke about race. Interestingly enough, the Ivy University anthropology majors who had so clearly articulated constructivist definitions of race were not as confident in referencing biological arguments that support this perspective—in other words, "anti-essentialist" arguments. This first became evident when they were asked to evaluate the Lieberman statement on the existence of biological races; although they uniformly rejected it, they could not support their positions with the same degree of elaboration they had used to depict the sociohistorical construction of racial classifications. One responded:

> I think partly I feel like—I feel a little bit that I don't know. Since I don't know as much about physical anthropology, it's hard to say what I think or sort of come from a completely informed point of view. But I guess

just, again, like I don't see it as a biological category, so that's why I disagree.

Another, when asked what claims or evidence faculty had presented to argue that race was socially constructed, responded:

It's genetic evidence that—I don't know, man . . . I don't remember . . . But I know that there's like scientific hardcore DNA things that sort of—I don't know.

In some way, the Ivy University anthropology students' familiarity with the social origins of race seemed to have precluded fuller consideration of just how human biological variation fit into the picture. Their responses reminded me of what an anthropology professor at Pilot University had told me about his graduate students' grasp of racial constructionism:

You see, that's become so deeply embedded as a political point that people have lost sight, I think, of how it is we know this to be true. And I guarantee you there are two things, if you go and interview our graduate students—I love them; I'm saying this for the record: they're intelligent, fine folks—there are two things you will not be able to get them to do: You will not be able to get them to give you the evidence upon which one can base the assertion that race correlates with nothing, and you will not be able to get them to give you an effective anti-creationist argument. They can't do it, one of the predominant reasons being they believe these things to be so and they don't learn what it is you would need to know in order to handle them. But, trust me, they will get into an intro course some day with a student who's a creationist, and boy will they not be able to respond. They won't likely get into a conversation with somebody who's a racist, but ask them to write a review of *The Bell Curve*[9] and I guarantee you they cannot make the argument effectively. What they will be doing is saying it's obvious. And I know it and we all know it. But, wait a minute, no you don't.

State University anthropology majors, in contrast, drew more often than others on their knowledge of human biological variation when explaining why race is socially constructed. That is, they often made anti-essentialist claims. For example, one major based his argument on the lesson from his "Introduction to Biological Anthropology" course that "there really is no true genetic difference between humans." After making the same claim, another State University anthropology major explained, "the only difference is in how we I guess view, you know, the phenotypes."

The difference in Ivy and State students' grounding of racial constructionism likely reflects the intellectual orientation of the universities' anthropology departments. Both Ivy and Pilot University's anthropology departments are heavily weighted toward cultural anthropology, whereas physical anthropology has a much higher profile at City and State University. As the professor quoted above went on to explain, the demise of four-field anthropology prevents many current anthropology students from gaining exposure to both cultural and physical anthropology, and thus from developing a familiarity with the biological, anti-essentialist arguments underlying claims that race is socially constructed. This may well explain the emphasis of the Ivy University undergraduate anthropology majors on social constructivism without taking into consideration human evolution or patterns of biological variation to the same extent as their peers elsewhere.

ROLE OF NON-ANTHROPOLOGY COURSES

The exceptional reach of constructionism among Ivy University students also points to a final aspect of undergraduate intellectual training that may shape young people's racial thinking: the role that non-anthropology courses can play in reinforcing the constructionist perspective. At Ivy, courses in other social sciences, the humanities, and even occasionally the biological sciences also incorporated the idea of race as a social construct. For example, one student described an English class on Shakespeare that entailed "talking about how race was constructed or perceived in Renaissance England." A student in a course on Asian Americans recounted:

> It's a history course. And in that sense you know race is going to be a topic. You know the constructions of, you know, Asian identity are going to be brought up, and you're going to really kind of break down ideas of race and you're going to talk about, you know, even in like some

sense you're going to talk, again, about *Orientalism*. You know, and drop
Edward Said's name. Yeah, I think that also often it's—in my experience,
it has been about constructions of identity. That's really been the focus,
rather than any kind of—as a history major—histories of discrimination
or histories of racial experiences. You know. It's more contemporary or
even past construction.—*Political science major, Ivy University*

Ivy students also frequently described their university's core humanities program, required of all students, as conveying a constructionist
message about race:

And we did a lot of kind of questioning the origin of the concept of race
and how that has been used to justify things. That was really eye-
opening for me. I had no idea how contemporary the idea of race is. I
mean, it's a pretty recent development, at least as we think of it now.
—*Biology major, Ivy University*

This dissemination of constructionism across the disciplinary spectrum may explain why Ivy University students appeared distinct from
others along the measures of racial conceptualization described previously, even when compared to students at the similarly diverse State
University or the similarly elite Pilot University. At Ivy University, student exposure to a constructivist perspective did not depend on the
teaching of the anthropology department alone, but rather was broadened and reinforced by the active role of other departments on this front.

As in the case of academic scientists, college students' notions of race
seem less strongly tied to their socio-demographic characteristics than
previous researchers have assumed. In both cases, training in anthropology plays a crucial role in fostering a constructivist perspective on
race. The relatively small size of this discipline, however, in terms of the
numbers of students who pursue it and the number of practitioners who
teach it, does not bode well for the future transmission of this outlook,
at least through the mechanism of higher education. Given its limited
reach in the contemporary academy, it is not surprising that only a minority of students defined race as a social construct, and even fewer
found the notion of social construction useful when thinking about the
real-life racial differentials that characterize our social world.

CONCLUSION

With this chapter, I conclude the book's empirical study of the race concepts that scientists hold and convey to the lay public via formal education. I end with college students because they make up an extremely important group to examine, for two reasons. Although they are hardly "typical" of the U.S. population at large, they come to campus with beliefs about racial difference that are common in their home communities, including their families, neighborhoods, and schools. In other words, the university undergraduates I interviewed offer a window into the kind of race thinking that circulates widely in our country. However, they are also in the unusual position of having extensive contact with academic scientists. In attending class lectures, reading scientific textbooks and articles, or meeting with professors during office hours, they are exposed to scientists' views in an extraordinarily direct manner. This is the second reason then that college students make up an important community to study in terms of lay receptions to scientific concepts of race. Having encountered social and biological scientists' notions of race, what do these young people make of them?

Undergraduate students' position at the crossroads of the lay public and the academy, while ideal in some ways for studying the interaction of scientists' and nonscientists' ideas, also poses a challenge. How can we discern which of their comments reflect their upbringing in society at large, and which testify to the influence of their college professors? Two assumptions have guided my analysis. First, I note that some student discourse is unique to them, and did not appear in my interviews with faculty. Examples include their frequent equation of race with culture, or their depiction of blacks as a race exceptionally distinguished by physical difference. I consider such discourse to reflect students' socialization prior to college, and thus ideas that circulate widely in the American public. Second, I presume that other kinds of discourse are largely academic in origin: namely, racial constructivism and anti-essentialism. Both are grounded in arguments that have been developed by academics: for example, the historical observation that American racial categories have changed considerably over time, or the genetic discoveries of the similarities in DNA across racial groupings. Consequently, I treat student references to such claims as evidence of the influence of social and biological science on their racial conceptualization. What these two bodies of "lay" and "scientific" discourse leave out is the considerable mass of essentialist commentary, found in both student and faculty interviews, that locates racial difference in human bodies. In other words, I view racial essentialism as a shared discourse that is mutually reinforced by laypeople and academic scientists.

With these working assumptions in mind, to what extent are undergraduate students' race concepts influenced by the scientists with whom they come into contact? To answer, it is worth distinguishing two kinds of "influence." If we are looking for "modification," the response seems to be that exposure to scientists' race conceptualization has done little to change students' ways of seeing it. For one thing, the depiction of races as cultural groups that was so popular among students did not seem to come from professors—it was a portrayal that was foreign to the academics I interviewed. For another, the idea of race as a social construct, which was fairly widespread among anthropology professors, had not made many inroads among the students I interviewed, and certainly not among non-anthropology students. On these two counts, then, academics seemed to have exercised only limited influence on their students.

If "influence" includes "reinforcement" of students' preexisting notions of race, however, then university scientists may play a bigger role in young people's racial conceptualization than is immediately apparent. For example, students' emphasis on biological difference when defining *race* may have its roots in thinking they developed before college, but their references to gene expression or evolutionary history may be elaborations that they have adopted from their undergraduate coursework. In other words, college instruction may provide some with new tools with which to make old arguments.

When considering the impact of the academy on young people's race concepts, we must take into account the likelihood that the college setting beyond the classroom matters as well. University eliteness and racial composition may play an indirect role; what came across more directly in interviews though was the extent to which students, particularly at the most selective institutions, felt a diffuse pressure to conform to certain ways of thinking about race and not others. Such communal norms are not surprising given the extent to which interviewees (both student and faculty) perceived the question of the nature of race as having ethical implications. In varied students' words, the suggestion that races are biological entities "evokes a feeling" of "stuff that you're taught is bad," it provokes a "gut reaction," and it is likely to "cause an internal dilemma for a lot of people."

The students' anxieties about political correctness—shared in some measure, as we have seen, by their professors—speak to the difficulty of establishing a clear boundary between what is racist and what is not. The distinction between the two is experienced as an externally dictated convention; rather than formulating for themselves what constitutes prejudice and what does not, students were fearful of falling unwittingly on the wrong side of the divide and being convicted in the court of public opinion. The wide-ranging specter of political correctness instills fear of being judged racist more than it imparts any sense of what racism is. As a result, students voiced a wide range of notions of racial difference, but consistently sought to present their opinions as nonracist. Again, this is reminiscent of the faculty interviewees, who presented both their constructionist and essentialist viewpoints as being antiracist. Where professors protected themselves from the potential charge of racism by invoking their authority as scientists and their humanitarian motives, students portrayed themselves as enlightened: educated, at home in a multicultural world, and thus free of the prejudices that cripple other people. A common strategy in this Northeastern university sample was to portray less-educated people and those from the South or the Midwest as those most likely to be racist. Clearly, boundary-marking was an important tactic for disassociating oneself from racism.

My student interviewees vividly conveyed the imperative of avoiding racism yet being unsure of what exactly counts as racist—especially when racism is not supposed to exist in one's own social world, but only in geographically distant places. Hence the attentiveness to political correctness: it is not just an instrument of punishment, but a guide to public behavior. Yet in reality, political correctness offers little insight into what constitutes racism, but rather holds out only an injunction against the mention of race (as Frankenberg (1993) found). Paradoxically, this proved a boon in several interviews. As a result of their dire expectations about the consequences of talking about race, some students were pleasantly surprised and relieved by the end of our interview that nothing had gone wrong, and thanked me for providing a safe opportunity to reflect on the nature of race.

SIX Race Concepts beyond the Classroom

NEW YORK, Feb. 7/PRNewswire/—GenSpec Labs, LLC.
has announced that it has formulated the world's first
genetically specific nutraceutical product line which effectively addresses the unique metabolic needs of African-
Americans, Hispanics, and Caucasians . . . In the near future,
GenSpec should be found at local retailers nationwide such as
Walgreen's, USA Drug, Duane Reade, and Kmart.

—GenSpec LLC (2006) press release

Schools are not the only places where scientists' concepts of race make
their way to a lay audience. Instead, formal education is just one of many
institutions that reflect and convey scientific notions of racial difference
to the public. Through their statements, practices, policies, and products,
a wide range of public- and private-sector organizations play important
roles in this dissemination process. In other words, textbooks and course
lectures are not the only vehicles for spreading scientists' concepts of
race; laws, regulations, news reports, bureaucratic practices, and commercial goods and services also embody and communicate notions of racial
difference. For example, a race-targeted vitamin such as the GenSpec
product advertised above sends as much of a message about the nature
of race as any textbook lesson. It tells potential consumers that different
races have distinct, indeed "unique" needs, and that these diverse needs

are rooted in our biological—here, metabolic—differences. This product line also provides customers with a particular racial taxonomy, where "Hispanics" figure alongside "African-Americans" and "Caucasians." Finally, its makers' prediction of placement on the shelves of such national chains as Duane Reade and Kmart—a hope that has yet to be realized (Kerr 2006)—suggest that the equation of race with biology is a widely accepted truth.

In this chapter, I situate formal education in a broader context of institutions that interpret, act upon, and transmit to the public scientists' concepts of race. Specifically, I examine a series of institutions that claim to discern or identify individuals' race based on scientific knowledge and/or techniques: census enumeration, the legal system, criminal forensic profiling, and recreational ancestry testing. In these cases, as well as in the field of medicine, I show that both institutional discourse and activities convey particular understandings of race to the public.

A central motive for canvassing these institutions is of course to gain an empirical overview of how contemporary science overall—not just in its educational outreach—may influence lay concepts of race. However, by comparing the messages about race disseminated through formal schooling to those conveyed by other institutions, I also consider to what extent educational interpretations of scientists' race concepts are aligned with those emanating from other kinds of organizations. Ultimately, this chapter argues that the essentialist interpretation of race that has found solid footing in the academy is also promoted in the noneducational realms I study. In other words, when it comes to racial conceptualization, high-school and college education is largely in sync with other important social institutions.

This inquiry into "race concepts beyond the classroom" also has a theoretical objective: to further develop the idea of racial conceptualization that was introduced in the first two chapters of this book. Previously, race conceptualization has been presented as an individual-level phenomenon; indeed, I defined it in the Introduction as "the web of beliefs that an individual may hold about what race is." In this chapter, however, I expand that definition to argue that race concepts are not only individual as they can be institutional as well. Ideas about racial difference often animate, inhabit, structure—and are expressed by—institutions. The role of institutions in disseminating racial concepts, moreover, cannot be overlooked. It is not enough to consider how science affects race in an abstract, unspecified manner, but rather, scholars must grapple with the intermediary organizations and practices that are concrete conduits for scientists' race thinking.

This chapter also aims to expand our theoretical perspective on racial conceptualization by broadening the range of institutions (and institutional characteristics) that we understand as channeling scientific thinking about race. Scholarship on science popularization usually focuses on organizations and texts with explicitly communicative or educative functions, such as textbooks, schools, "popular science" magazines, or mass media science reporting (see for example Bucchi 1998; Jacobi 1986; Shinn and Whitley 1985). As I show below, however, other institutions also send messages to the public about the nature of race, but they generally do so in a way that is much less direct than journalism or formal instruction. For one thing, explaining the meaning of race may be a very minor aspect of such organizations' activities: the U.S. Census Bureau, for example, presents a definition of race on its website, but explaining the nature of race is hardly its central mission. For another, such entities may not broadcast any explicit verbal statement about race, but instead engage in activities that reflect and convey certain understandings of racial difference. When we visit a doctor who records our race, check off race categories on a school form, or buy vitamins advertised for our race group, we encounter subtle ideas about racial difference that are not accompanied by any overt definition of the concept. In short, race concepts can be embodied in and communicated through practices and objects, not just language. Therefore if we limit consideration to only those organizations that expressly aim to communicate a particular vision of race, we exclude a wide range of influential institutions that transmit, amplify, and recast scientists' ideas of human difference—and which may also reach a large number of people as they go about their daily lives.

Exactly which institutions convey concepts of race to the public? Arguably, a large number. The entertainment industry, for example, is no doubt enormously influential in shaping Americans' thinking about racial differences. My scope, however, is limited to institutions that draw on—and thus in some sense project—science-based concepts of race. Educational and (science-reporting) media organizations are examples of this class, which also includes public, private, and nonprofit organizations whose activities rely to some degree on operating definitions of race that are informed by scientists' input. Among these, however, I will focus specifically on institutions that meet three conditions: (1) they are situated outside the academy, (2) they aim to discern or assign individuals' race, and (3) they do so through some scientific method or process of scholarly deliberation. The first criterion serves to identify institutions that do not fall under the rubric of higher education, and thus whose messages about race are not likely to be transmitted directly through the kinds of formal instruction I have already investigated. The second criterion—namely the claim to "measure" race directly—denotes organizations whose messages about race, I argue, carry a special power. They purport to have special knowledge about the nature of race and to have expertise in "seeing" individuals' race. This implies in turn that race can be directly observed or apprehended. Third, in keeping with this book's overall theme of the transmission of scientists' views of race to the public, I focus on institutions whose strategies for identifying individuals' racial membership are in some way grounded in current scientific knowledge or methods. That scientific input may come from university-based research scientists or from scientists employed in the private or public sectors (for example, in corporate laboratories or government health institutes). The important thing is the institutional utilization of ideas and practices drawn from the scientific establishment, which is not confined to universities.

Which institutions meet these three criteria? Foremost among them I place the Census Bureau, the legal system, the criminal justice system, and the recreational genealogy industry. I will also examine the medical establishment because its practices have come to play an important role in debates about the nature of race even if doctors do not usually meet my second criterion—that is, the claim to measure race directly. (Instead, they tend to rely on patients' or research subjects' racial self-identification.) All these institutions transmit ideas about human difference through their activities or products, regardless of whether they explicitly communicate their working models of race to the public.

The list of institutions I investigate can be organized into three groups. First come the two public institutions that have perhaps the longest history of classifying Americans by race: our census and our legal system. Next I explore two of the newest sectors to make determinations about racial membership, both of which emerge from genetic science: criminal justice forensics and private sector genealogy testing. The final group is made up of medical actors—specifically physicians and pharmaceutical companies—who do not claim to measure race directly, yet suggest to differing degrees that racial classification is necessary or beneficial for their practice. All of these groups are worthy of much more thorough study than I provide, but my aim here is simply to highlight the concepts of race that their activities reflect and convey, explicitly or implicitly, intentionally or not.

The U.S. census and racial classification

Often when I tell people I do research on racial classification, they ask me about the U.S. Census Bureau's race categories. More specifically, they want to know how the Census Bureau would categorize particular types of people. "If my mother is Belgian and my father is Tunisian, what box should I check?" "I'm Indian and my husband is white; what should I put down for our kids?" The presumption is usually that there is a single correct answer, and that the Census Bureau is the ultimate arbiter of such decisions, thanks to its expert knowledge of race.

Certainly, the decennial census is the most high-profile instance of official racial classification in the United States. Although it actually follows, rather than sets, the federal government's racial categories—these are in fact established by the U.S. Office of Management and Budget (OMB) and enshrined in OMB Statistical Directive 15—and although all federal agencies must follow Directive 15's standards, it is the Census Bureau's use of these categories in particular that draws the greatest public attention. When Directive 15 was revised in 1997, affecting the entire federal government, the change was largely interpreted in the press as a matter of new census categories (e.g., Winslow 2001).

Given its highly visible practice of identifying U.S. inhabitants by race, what message does the Census Bureau convey about the nature of racial difference? I will examine two significant dimensions of that message, one that explicitly defines race and another that does so implicitly.

First, on its 2010 Census "Frequently Asked Questions" website, the Census Bureau provides the following "Meaning of race" (which is very similar to the definition it published for the 2000 census):

QUESTION: What does the Census Bureau mean by race?

ANSWER: The Census Bureau collects race data in accordance with guidelines provided by the U.S. Office of Management and Budget and these data are based on self-identification. The racial categories included in the census questionnaire generally reflect a social definition of race recognized in this country, and not an attempt to define race biologically, anthropologically, or genetically. In addition, it is recognized that the categories of the race item include racial and national origin or socio-cultural groups. People may choose to report more than one race to indicate their racial mixture, such as "American Indian and White." People who identify their origin as Hispanic, Latino, or Spanish may be of any race.

This brief statement links race to many phenomena—"social definition"; biological, anthropological, and genetic difference; national origin; cultural groups; and Hispanic origin—yet does not clarify the nature of those connections. Although the census categories do not reflect "an attempt to define race biologically, anthropologically, or genetically," we do not know whether such attempts are impossible—that is, because races do not in fact correspond to biological or anthropological groupings—or whether such an exercise would be perfectly feasible, but is simply one the

Census Bureau and OMB have decided to forgo. Furthermore, the observation that "racial and national origin and socio-cultural groups" make up the list of census race categories raises the question of what (if anything) distinguishes races from national and cultural groups. By noting them separately, the Census Bureau seems to suggest that races are somehow different from cultural and national groups, but then why do the latter appear as part of a question about race? Just as it is left unclear what the census race categories have to do with biological or anthropological classifications, it is equally confusing how they relate to culture and national origins. To be fair, the "social definition of race" to which the Census Bureau alludes probably contains all these contradictions and more. But even this formulation is ultimately a vague one: is the Census Bureau trying to say that race is socially constructed and that by its very nature does not correspond to biological populations or cultural communities? In the final analysis, this explicit definition of race manages to invoke all the competing concepts of race that my interviewees voiced—the biological/ essentialist, culturalist, and constructivist/anti-essentialist perspectives— without coming down firmly in any one camp.

Census race categories are dictated by the OMB's racial classification framework, which contains much of the same ambiguity and indeed introduces its own. The current *Standards for Maintaining, Collecting, and Presenting Federal Data on Race and Ethnicity* (Office of Management and Budget 1997) maintain that "The categories in this classification are social-political constructs and should not be interpreted as being scientific or anthropological in nature." This language hints at a constructivist orientation, but the caveat that the categories are neither "scientific" nor "anthropological" might come as a surprise to those who are aware that scientists have historically contributed to their construction. Moreover, it raises the same question as that posed by the Census Bureau definition: does the claim that these are not "scientific" categories mean that race cannot be classified "scientifically," or just that the OMB has chosen not to do so? The confusion about what race fundamentally has to do with biology, anthropology, or anything else is compounded in the standards' "Supplementary Information" preface. "The racial and ethnic categories set forth in the standards," it maintains, "should not be interpreted as being primarily biological or genetic in reference. Race and ethnicity may be thought of in terms of social and cultural characteristics as well as ancestry." Here the OMB categories are not "primarily" biological— does that mean they are "somewhat" biological, or not at all? And what does it mean that race "may be thought of in terms of social and cultural characteristics"? As with the census definition, the OMB's model connects several phenomena to race without making clear exactly what kind of criteria delineate racial membership. Indeed, in the standards' section on "OMB's Decisions," the OMB notes that these decisions do *neither* of the following:

— establish criteria or qualifications (such as blood quantum levels) that are to be used in determining a particular individual's racial or ethnic classification

— tell an individual who he or she is, or specify how an individual should classify himself or herself.

Yet Directive 15 goes on to explicitly define the membership of each racial category. Its instructions read:

— **American Indian or Alaska Native.** A person having origins in any of the original peoples of North and South America (including Central America), and who maintains tribal affiliation or community attachment.

— **Asian.** A person having origins in any of the original peoples of the Far East, Southeast Asia, or the Indian subcontinent including, for example, Cambodia, China, India, Japan, Korea, Malaysia, Pakistan, the Philippine Islands, Thailand, and Vietnam.

— **Black or African American.** A person having origins in any of the black racial groups of Africa. Terms such as "Haitian" or "Negro" can be used in addition to "Black or African American."

— **Hispanic or Latino.** A person of Cuban, Mexican, Puerto Rican, Cuban, South or Central American, or other Spanish culture or origin, regardless of race. The term, "Spanish origin," can be used in addition to "Hispanic or Latino."

— **Native Hawaiian or Other Pacific Islander.** A person having origins in any of the original peoples of Hawaii, Guam, Samoa, or other Pacific Islands.

— **White.** A person having origins in any of the original peoples of Europe, the Middle East, or North Africa.

These category definitions emphasize biological descent from the "original peoples" of particular geographic areas. In doing so, they add another ingredient—geography—to the list of factors previously associated with race: biology, anthropology, nation, and culture. And they leave open the question of why these geographic labels in particular are equated with races. What is the logic that identifies a small group such as Native Hawaiians and Other Pacific Islanders as a race just like the enormous category of "Asians," billions of people strong? That is, what is the underlying concept of racial characteristics and difference that identifies both Pacific Islanders and Asians as races?

In sum, there is no single and straightforward explicit definition of race among the public communications of the Census Bureau and the OMB regarding the nation's official racial categories. Proponents of just about any concept of race can find something to like in these public statements— while a person who is simply searching for a clear-cut explanation of what race is will likely come away disappointed.

These organizations also communicate ideas about racial difference to the public implicitly in the very way their question formats are structured. A powerful example comes to us through the federal government's distinction of "race" from "ethnicity." In a study of census race and ethnicity items from around the world (Morning 2008a), I found that this feature distinguished the U.S. census from the 137 other nations I examined. Only in the United States do we use separate questions to elicit an individual's "race" as opposed to his or her "ethnicity," and moreover, only the United States fields an "ethnicity" question that measures membership in only one nonindigenous group: Hispanics or Latinos. (The closest parallel elsewhere would be questions on indigenous status, but even those questions usually include a range of indigenous groups from which to select.) There are historical reasons our nation does not count Hispanics as a racial group (Morning and Sabbagh 2005). But more importantly for this discussion, what does the federal bureaucratic distinction between race and ethnicity, embodied in the practice of providing separate questions for each, convey to laypeople about the nature of race?

In its explanation of who is counted as Hispanic (reproduced above), the OMB includes people "of Cuban, Mexican, Puerto Rican, Cuban, South or Central American, or other Spanish culture or origin, regardless of race." What stands out here from the other categories, all of which are premised on "origins," is the unique reference to culture. In other words, Hispanics constitute a group, an ethnic group, which is delineated by a shared culture. What then does this imply about race? That races are demarcated by some other kind of difference. This view is reinforced by the statement that being Hispanic or not depends on culture, "regardless of race." In contrast to my undergraduate interviewees' frequent equation of race with culture, in the OMB perspective race has nothing to do with culture. So what other criteria are left as potential bases for determining a person's racial membership? Judging from my interviews, the two other contenders are the essentialist conviction that patterns of human biological variation dictate racial boundaries, and the constructivist claim that racial groups are artificial inventions that need not be anchored in any characteristics of individuals themselves. Given the weak transmission of academic constructivist thinking to the public, however, the OMB and Census Bureau's apparent elimination of culture as the basis for race effectively opens up the field for Americans to interpret race as a matter of biological difference. Although this is not what the two government agencies say explicitly, it is a message that is embodied in their applied practice of drawing a sharp distinction between race and ethnicity.

Census-taking then—in the United States and elsewhere—is an institution that broadcasts ideas about the nature of race through both its explicit official discourse and its routine practices. This holds true even though public education is not the Census Bureau's mission. And despite the disclaimer that census race categories are not "scientific," they are shaped by the input of demographers and other social scientists in addition to bureaucrats who use anthropological and biological research as reference points. Perhaps most importantly, these categories are *perceived* as the product of specialist expertise. Thus, the conceptualization of race they embody is likely to be an authoritative one for many Americans.

Law and racial determination

Today the idea of a court of law determining someone's racial identity would probably offend many Americans. The official imposition of a racial label comes squarely into conflict with the notion that individuals have a right to identify themselves as they wish. This contemporary belief in a right to self-identification was particularly evident in the multiracial movement of the late 1990s, which successfully pressed the OMB to revise Directive 15 to permit the recognition of mixed-race identity (Skerry 2000). The perception that individuals' self-identification should trump legal or administrative classifications was also apparent in the 1983 case that Susie Phipps brought against the State of Louisiana. Phipps claimed she had always understood herself to be white and should be officially recognized as such, even though the state maintained that she was "three thirty-seconds black" and therefore "legally black" (F. Davis 1991, 9–10). The multiracial movement and the Phipps case attracted national media attention in part because they struck a chord with the contemporary sentiment that government imposition of racial labels was anachronistic at best, and a serious abrogation of civil rights at worst.

Prior to the second half of the twentieth century, however, Americans lived with laws and regulations that were much more active in assigning individuals' racial status. Beginning in the colonial era, race was a key determinant of political, social, and economic rights, and a relatively extensive legal apparatus developed to establish just who could enjoy which rights (Smedley 2007). Over the course of our history, courts determined individuals' race in order to rule on who could do what, where, and with whom. Which people could enter together into intimate relationships of sex, marriage, or adoption (Kennedy 2003), who could become a naturalized citizen (Haney López 1996), and who could have access to public spaces or facilities (F. Davis 1991)—these are just a few examples of the domains in which individuals' "correct" racial identification was central to deciding the rights and privileges they might legally enjoy. Moreover, judges were guided in those decisions by a body of state laws that explicitly dictated formulas for racial classification. For example, in 1785 Virginia passed a law defining as black any person with a black parent or grandparent, and in 1910 changed this "one fourth"-ancestry rule to a "one sixteenth" one. Other states implemented a "one eighth" law, but as F. James Davis (1991) has shown, over time state legislatures generally adopted stricter provisions that defined as black anyone with "one drop" of "Negro blood."

Historically then, the U.S. legal system has been a major institution to grapple with and disseminate concepts of race. It has functioned as an authoritative arbiter of racial membership. Referring to laws that provided rules, algorithms, or procedures for discerning individuals' race, and examining the evidence they deemed pertinent, courts determined people's racial identity. All these activities imply working concepts of what race is: which races exist in the world, how each is distinguished from the other, and what characteristics or actions reveal a person's true racial status. To take an example from late nineteenth-century census regulations for the correct classification of people of American Indian and white ancestry, enumerators were told to take into consideration the communities in which the people lived and "their habits of life and methods of industry . . . In a word, in the equilibrium produced by the equal division of blood, the habits, tastes, and associations of the half-breed are allowed to determine his gravitation to the one class or the other" (U.S. Census Office 1872, xiii). Like these administrative instructions, courts admitted a wide range of evidence—corporeal and contextual—when deciding an individual's racial status (Kennedy 2003; Lewis and Ardizzone 2001; Pascoe 1996).

Today the U.S. legal system is much less involved in making determinations of individuals' race. Since the mid-twentieth century civil rights movement largely eliminated the traditional legal framework that had made race a key factor in determining the rights that Americans could enjoy—for example, in limiting nonwhites' access to educational institutions or workplaces—the judiciary no longer has to assign bodies to racial categories for purposes of deducing their rights and privileges. Moreover, the administrative practice of racial self-identification—as opposed to the imposition of one's racial classification by government fiat—became more widespread in the same period. Notably, in the 1960s and 1970s the U.S. Census Bureau moved from a system of external enumeration—that is, one where designated officials visited people's homes and filled out the census schedule on their behalf—to a mail-back system where people receive the census questionnaire at home and fill it out themselves as they see fit. This places the responsibility for choosing a racial identity squarely with the person completing the form.

Nonetheless, there are still instances in the United States when race is determined through legal deliberation. This is because racial membership still matters in certain legal situations. Affirmative-action measures, for one, hinge on differential treatment by race. In one case, *Malone v. Haley* (1989),[1] the Supreme Judicial Court of Massachusetts was called on to decide whether two brothers, Paul and Philip Malone, should be considered black by their employer, the Boston Fire Department (Ford 1994). When they first took the Department entrance exam in 1975, identifying themselves as white, their scores were too low to be accepted. In 1977 they took the text again, this time claiming to be black, and their new scores were high enough to be placed on the separate minority candidate list that the Fire Department was required to maintain under a court-ordered affirmative-action program. After being hired, they served for ten years, but when they sought promotion to lieutenant, Department officials noticed they had identified themselves as black in 1977, and determined the brothers had falsified their racial identity. The Malones were fired, thus motivating their legal appeal to uphold their black status. The Massachusetts judge, however, rejected the brothers' claim because he deemed they failed to meet three criteria that would ostensibly have indicated their blackness: (1) physical appearance as black—they had fair coloring and "Caucasian" features, (2) documentary evidence: at least three generations of Malones were consistently recorded as white on their birth certificates, and (3) consistent self-identification as black. According to the judge, "there was no evidence that the Malones identified themselves personally or socially as Blacks." To make a determination of the brothers' race, the court considered their physical traits, bureaucratic records, and social behavior as relevant types of evidence.

These heterogeneous standards also figure in contemporary legal determinations of American Indian status. On one hand, recognition as American Indian depends largely on enrollment with a recognized tribe; this makes it more of a political and bureaucratic identifier than a racial one. On the other, both tribes and federal case law often equate being Indian with possessing a particular ancestral heritage, frequently measured in terms of "blood" fractions or quanta. In this sense, designation as American Indian is "based on a totality of circumstances, including genealogy, group identification, and life style."[2]

Thus, although called upon less frequently to make individual determinations of racial status, the law must nonetheless be included among the major social institutions that develop and disseminate concepts of race in the United States. As Ford (1994, 1231) notes, our legal system still undertakes the twin tasks of "defin[ing] the nature and boundaries of the groups to whom remedial preferences are addressed" and then " 'accurately' sort[ing] individuals into these groups." Both are part and parcel of racial conceptualization: forming notions about the nature of races and the characteristic markers that signal membership in them.

What may be less obvious, however, is why I locate the law among institutions that convey *scientific* understandings of race. I do so for two reasons. One is simply that courts have often turned to scientists' writings and testimony when forming their conclusions. In early twentieth-century naturalization cases, for example, when petitioners from around the world sought court recognition as white in order to be eligible for U.S. citizenship, judges often made reference to the arguments of anthropologists (Haney López 1996). In this way courts, in the same way as the Census Bureau, have circulated scientific ideas about race (no doubt albeit via a process of translation and transformation as well). The second, more fundamental motive for treating legal institutions as conveying scientific ideas about race to the public is that they generate notions of human difference through a process of learned deliberation that— although we do not usually label it "science"—shares some basic features of knowledge building with what we normally recognize as science, the "decided and deliberate . . . path to knowing" (Duster 1984, 2). Legal decisions involve rules (methodology) for the collection and analysis of evidence (data) for coming to conclusions; in short, they entail a knowledge-gathering process—a science—of their own. This in turn means that the legal system presents itself—and is taken to be—an authoritative arbiter of what race is. It claims to dispose of a certain expertise that permits it to directly discern or ascertain individuals' race, an expert status that is shared with few other institutions.

Discerning race in DNA: Criminal forensics and recreational ancestry testing

In this section I bring together the practices from two realms that are very different in their goals and organizational framework: forensic science and ancestry testing. Forensic science—and more specifically, the discovery of an individual's characteristics or identity from specimens of physical evidence such as blood or saliva—is a crucial activity of the criminal justice system. It supports investigation into the identities of criminals, victims, or both. It is also employed by public authorities to identify disaster victims. Genetic ancestry testing, however, is largely a service that is sold by private firms to consumers for recreational purposes. Its objective is to provide customers with genealogical information about the racial or ethnic makeup of their family tree, based usually on saliva samples that clients furnish. In other words, criminal forensics and genetic ancestry testing could not be further apart in terms of their missions and institutional bases: the former is an arm of the public-sector criminal justice system, employed to adjudicate cases of life and death, whereas the latter is a leisure pursuit that private-sector firms market for corporate profit.

However, these activities have at least three important features in common. First, they both claim to discern or measure individuals' race directly, using scientific theories and methods. Second, they both base their determination of racial identity on biological evidence alone; they purport to "read" a person's race from his or her physical constitution, whether from skin color, skeletal dimensions, DNA, or other features. And third, their identification techniques have a great deal in common. In short, specialists in criminal forensics and genetic genealogy all make determinations (or estimates) of individuals' race using similar reasoning about the nature of racial difference and similar methods.

How important are these institutions in terms of conveying their science-based notions of race to the public? Most Americans will probably never have any direct experience with either field (although television crime shows such as *CSI: Crime Scene Investigation* and *Cold Case* have been so popular that the term "CSI effect" has been coined to describe the public's now-exaggerated expectations of forensic investigators). I contend nonetheless that criminal forensics and genetic genealogy are key professions in terms of engaging in activities that reflect and express a particular conception of racial difference. Outside academic research laboratories, these two technical fields are those that are most closely positioned to the direct biological measurement of race. As such, they powerfully convey the message that race is something to be read from a person's body, and that such a method of identification bears the imprimatur of science.

As we saw previously, the other primary institutions that wield the authority to establish racial categories or assign individuals to them—the legal system on one hand and the decennial census on the other—look to a wide range of factors in determining racial membership, such as cultural practice, documentary evidence, and social relations. They also turn to biological evidence, taking into account surface phenotype (skin color, facial traits, hair texture, etc.) or information about ancestors' identities—but not to the exclusion of other forms of proof.

In contrast, criminal forensics and DNA ancestry testing require only the body—or parts of it. In particular, they scrutinize two sets of physical characteristics that courts and census-takers do not take into consideration for racial assignment: anatomical structure and genetic profile. Forensic anthropology in the United States has traditionally focused on determining age, sex, height, and race from skeletal attributes such as skull measurements and dental characteristics (Duster 2003b, 2; Sauer 1992). In these efforts, the dimensions of a given specimen are compared to those recorded among archived samples of skeletons—some dating from the early nineteenth century—that have been labeled as "white," "black," "American Indian," etc. (Brues 1992). In other words, previous generations of researchers determined which kinds of bodies belonged to which race—and which races existed in the first place—and then established physical averages or ranges for each race that resulted.

This is the fundamental reasoning that underlies the biological measurement of race in general. Scientists start with beliefs or assumptions about what "the races of mankind" are—that is, they do not ascertain empirically which races naturally occur or exist (or if they do at all). Instead, they gather human biological data and sort them into preconceived racial groups, then deduce these groups' typical characteristics, whether in terms of skin color, skull width, or genetic variants. To illustrate, if we were followers of Prof. Leonard Jeffries' theory that humanity can be divided into "sun people" and "ice people" (Morrow 2001), we would collect physical specimens from individuals we believed to belong to these groups, sort them accordingly, and then record the biological measurements typical of each. Armed with those data, we could then attempt to estimate any given individual's race (i.e., sun or ice) based on our tables of the average measurements for each group.

Although it uses data, measurements, and analytical techniques that are probably less transparent to most people than the traditional methods of measuring femur length or tooth shape, the new genetic approach to identifying race relies on the same underlying logic. In other words, it involves (1) settling on a taxonomy of races; (2) gathering physical data—in this case, DNA—on these preselected races; (3) selecting and then measuring what are considered to be the representative (genetic) characteristics of those race groupings; and (4) applying these aggregate sample statistics to an individual case to estimate in some fashion the group(s) to which he or she is most likely to belong. To be sure, there are differences in the type of genetic data that have been utilized to identify a person's race (Ossorio 2006). In criminal justice work, "ethnic" DNA profiling began in the United Kingdom in the 1990s with analyses of short-tandem repeats (STRs) (Lowe et al. 2001; Ossorio and Duster 2005), "stretches of DNA where the DNA replicating mechanism appears to 'stutter,' resulting in different numbers of copies of repeated sequences" (Greely et al. 2006, 249). Such racial identification procedures are in keeping with the STR analyses that police authorities rely on for matching crime-scene specimens to specific individuals. In the ancestry testing industry, however, biotech companies work largely with some combination of mitochondrial DNA (passed on from mother to child), Y chromosomes (passed from father to son), or "ancestry informative markers," genes whose alleles or variants are thought to reflect ancestral origins (Bolnick et al. 2007; Obasogie 2009). Yet these data sources and the analytical approaches applied to them are not strictly segregated by profession. At least one genetic genealogy company, DNAPrint Genomics, successfully sold its services (under the brand name of DNAWitness) to police departments for purposes of identifying the likely race of criminals for whom investigators have only biological samples (e.g., blood or saliva). According to Ossorio (2006, 282–83), "To assess a sample source's ancestry, forensic scientists use the same genetic tests, the same methods and markers, as biomedical researchers and commercial testing services."

In the cases of forensic and recreational DNA ancestry profiling, we find public- and private-sector organizations that convey two very powerful messages about race. One is that race is an objective feature of human bodies that can be directly observed or discerned. The second is that the categories with which we are familiar from daily life—groupings such as "black" or "Caucasian"—are an accurate representation of biologically distinct human groups that appear "in nature." The assumptions that have gone into producing ancestry estimates—assumptions about which racial groups exist in the first place and who their representative members are—are obscured by the claim to deliver an accurate, "scientific" product. Indeed, the grounding of such government and commercial activities in scientific theory, data, and techniques lends considerable authority to their activities and conclusions. This is an authority they share with the medical establishment, which I discuss next. But the legitimacy of their pronouncements comes from another aspect of their positioning, which I argue they share with the legal system (and to some extent the Census Bureau): forensic and recreational genetics are located on the frontline of what we imagine to be the direct observation and measurement of race. We ascribe to them the ultimate expertise in "seeing" or detecting race. And the very belief that experts can confidently discern race from human bodies is of course a deeply essentialist one.

Medicine: Locating race in the body

In contrast to the institutional actors described above, medical practitioners and researchers are not for the most part in the business of scientifically discerning or measuring individuals' race. Instead, they largely solicit and accept the racial self-identification of their patients and clinical trial subjects. This means that the medical establishment signals less clearly the conceptualization of race that underlies its activities: it does not purport to measure race, so it does not indicate where the source of racial difference is presumed to lie. Nonetheless, I touch on the broad field of medicine here because not only do its practices suggest that racial information is necessary for care of the body, but it brings the authoritative imprimatur of "science" to that message. Furthermore, medicine has played a prominent role in scientific and public debates about the nature of race (Graves and Rose 2006; Holden 2003; Phimister 2003; Stolberg 2001). Physicians and other medical actors also constitute an important conduit for science-based views of race because they are widely familiar to the public, so their conceptual approaches to race can be conveyed to laypeople in millions of everyday encounters.

The intersection of race thinking and medicine has received a considerable amount of scholarly attention in recent years. Prominent examples include Steven Epstein's (2007) *Inclusion: The Politics of Difference in Medical Research*, Wailoo and Pemberton's (2006) *The Troubled Dream of Genetic Medicine*, and "The Meanings of 'Race' in the New Genomics: Implications for Health Disparities Research" (S. S. J. Lee, Mountain, and Koenig 2001). However, my intention here is not to describe or summarize the wide range of literature on this topic, but to identify and connect several distinct medical practices that each reinforce the notion that race is a biological marker. In particular, I look at the role race plays in physicians' diagnoses, organ transplantation, and pharmaceutical development. In each area, routine practices and not necessarily overt statements send strong signals to laypeople about scientific understandings of race.

DIAGNOSIS AND PRESCRIPTION

Sally Satel's (2002) *New York Times Magazine* essay, "I Am a Racially Pro-filing Doctor," brought to public attention a debate that had already be-gun in professional publications such as the *Journal of the American Medical Association* (Osborne and Feit 1992), *Annals of Internal Medicine* (Witzig 1996), and *New England Journal of Medicine* (Schwartz 2001; Wood 2001). Her provocatively titled article raised the question of whether physi-cians should take race into account when diagnosing their patients' medical conditions and prescribing remedies.

It is unclear how many of Satel's peers are also "racially profiling doc-tors." However, she is unlikely to be alone. Published evaluations of the merit of race-based diagnosis and prescription suggest that it is not an insignificant dimension of medical practice (Braun et al. 2007; Burchard et al. 2003; Ellison et al. 2007; Garcia 2004). So do the numerous studies that show patients receive different treatment regimens depending on their race (see for example Todd et al. 2000 on pain relief). The existence of laboratory tests that require patients' racial identification for their analyses—such as the prenatal tests for congenital disorders I have described—further indicate that race is a fairly well-established ingredi-ent in medical diagnosis in at least some realms. A more direct measure of the place of race in medical practice comes, however, from the focus-group research that Vence Bonham and colleagues conducted with ninety black and white physicians. They found that most of the doctors believed that a patient's race has "important clinical implications" (Bonham et al. 2009, 284), and their respondents reported using a variety of methods for identifying their patients' race. However, the doctors they spoke with were far from any consensus about why or how race mattered in medi-cine, and they expressed considerable skepticism about race being a proxy for individual-level genetic variation. These results suggest that race is often likely to figure in physicians' diagnosis of their patients' symptoms, but the treatment they prescribe varies "depending on their physicians' views of what 'race' means or represents" (284).

Consequently, doctors' use of race in daily practice is unlikely to send any one message to their patients about the nature of race. For some physicians, race is a meaningful guide to cultural practices that directly bear on health: diet, physical activities, willingness to seek medical care, etc. Other doctors interpret race as relaying relevant information about patients' social status: economic position, educational attainment, or likely exposure to discrimination. For still other practitioners, race is first and foremost a proxy for genetic makeup, suggesting inherited tendencies toward particular medical conditions. In short, no simple consensus about the nature of race exists among physicians. Yet their frequent recourse to the practice of racial classification is likely to send some message about race to their patients, even if it is not one that is consistent across the profession.

ORGAN TRANSPLANTS

The transfer of human organs (or other materials such as blood or bone marrow) constitutes a specific case in the overt use of race to guide medical treatment. In this realm, race is commonly and explicitly portrayed as a biological characteristic for which donors and recipients should be matched. As explained by the United Network for Organ Sharing (2009), the nonprofit organization that administers the U.S. Organ Procurement and Transplantation Network:

> Successful transplantation often is enhanced by the matching of organs between members of the same ethnic and racial group. For example, any patient is less likely to reject a kidney if it is donated by an individual who is genetically similar. Generally, people are genetically more similar to people of their own ethnicity or race than to people of other races.

As it turns out, some research disputes the claim that racial matching is associated with better transplant outcomes. For example, one study of bone marrow donation concluded that "race mismatch between recipient and donor did not affect outcome" (Kollman, Howe, and Anasetti 2001, 2043; on cord blood, see also Wofford et al. 2007). What is more important here than judging between different claims about race and transplantation is simply that race is so frequently and openly linked to professional and public discussion of this set of medical procedures. The research literature on transplants is replete with studies of the effect of racial matching (or mismatching) on patient outcomes (Lepage-Monette 2008; Mahle, Kanter, and Vincent 2005), the distribution of particular genetic characteristics (particularly human leukocyte antigen alleles) among different racial groups (Beatty et al. 2000; Cao et al. 2001; Rizzuto et al. 2003), and the impact of different procedural protocols for taking race into account when matching donors to recipients (King et al. 1996; J. Roberts et al. 2004; Segev et al. 2005).

This concern with the role of race in matching organ donors to recipients has in turn made its way to media coverage of the procedure. For example, a newspaper report on a California case (Barbassa 2009) began with this dramatic opening:

> If Nick Glasgow were white, he would have a nearly 90 percent chance of finding a matching bone marrow donor who could cure his leukemia. But because the 28-year-old bodybuilder is one-quarter Japanese, his doctor warned him the outlook was grim. Glasgow's background would make it almost impossible to find a match, which usually comes from a patient's own ethnic group.

Publications such as these, whether in professional journals or the mass media, not only reinforce the essentialist idea that race (and indeed "ethnicity") correspond to biologically marked human groups, but bolster the symbolic belief that distinct races are in some fundamental way incompatible. "White" organs do not fit "black" bodies, or even three-quarter white and "one-quarter Japanese" bodies. In other words, human organ transplantation as currently practiced and conceptualized reifies visceral notions of human difference.

PHARMACEUTICALS

A much newer development at the intersection of medicine and race appeared in 2005, when for the first time, the U.S. Food and Drug Administration (FDA) approved a pharmaceutical drug intended to be marketed to one racial group in particular. As described by the drug's maker Nitromed (2007), BiDil was "approved for use in addition to routine heart medicines to treat heart failure in black patients, to extend life, improve heart failure symptoms, and help patients stay out of the hospital longer."

(Elsewhere Nitromed specified "African Americans" as the target market, leaving it unclear whether the drug might also be useful for black people outside the United States, such as Nigerians or Jamaicans.)

Although race-targeted drugs are a new commercial product, the idea that pharmaceuticals (or other medical interventions) may have different effects on patients of different races is not. This reasoning underlay the National Institutes of Health Revitalization Act of 1993, which required that NIH-funded clinical trials enroll members of minority groups as research subjects (S. S. J. Lee, Mountain, and Koenig 2001). This new legal requirement is emblematic of what Epstein (2007, 5) calls "the inclusion-and-difference paradigm," embodied in the "series of federal laws, policies, and guidelines issued between 1986 and the present that require or encourage research inclusiveness and the measurement of difference." This perspective presumes meaningful biomedical differences between races and prescribes group-specific analysis as the appropriate strategy for an equitable system of health care.

As in the case of organ transplantation, however—and perhaps even more so—the actual role of race in pharmaceutical efficacy is debated. Critics of race-targeted pharmacology have pointed out that the clinical study that led to the FDA's approval of BiDil—the African American Heart Failure Trial (A-HeFT)—included only self-identified blacks, thus precluding direct comparison with any other racial group that would make it possible to assess whether the drug worked differently for members of different races (Ellison et al. 2008a; Obasogie 2009). Moreover, A-HeFT did not analyze its human subjects' genetic markers, ruling out any demonstration of whether genetic differences between racial groups help explain differential reactions to pharmaceutical drugs (Kahn 2007). Instead, commercial patent protection laws provided a substantial incentive to develop a race-specific drug (Kahn 2006). It is telling that the FDA panel that approved BiDil was agnostic as to what causal mechanism might explain the A-HeFT outcomes; its members acknowledged "[n]ot understanding the reasons for the difference in treatment effect by race" (Temple and Stockbridge 2007, 58).

Despite such uncertainties, other race-targeted pharmaceutical products are in the works. In 2004, biologists Sarah Tate and David Goldstein published a review in *Nature Genetics* listing twenty-nine medicines that "have been claimed, in peer-reviewed scientific or medical journals, to have differences in either safety, or, more commonly, efficacy among racial or ethnic groups"—even though the authors found those claims to be "universally controversial." Despite the absence of any "consensus on how important race or ethnicity is in determining drug response," the authors found that 8 percent of the pharmaceutical products introduced from 1995 to 1998 indicated some race- or ethnicity-specific effectiveness (Tate and Goldstein 2004, S34). Obasogie (2009) details several cases where pharmaceutical companies have pursued or are pursuing the possibility of targeting their products to a specific racial demographic (see also Kahn 2007).

Although the question of whether "a pill should be color-blind" (Stolberg 2001) is far from settled, the fact that a race-targeted medicine has entered American pharmacopoeia and others are in the pipeline sends a powerful signal to the public about the nature of racial difference. First, it suggests that race is a meaningful factor in medical outcomes—even though just what role it plays (if any) is highly debated. Second, it is often interpreted as evidence of intrinsic, genetic differences between races. A *New England Journal of Medicine* article title neatly summed up this view: "Racial Differences in the Response to Drugs—Pointers to Genetic Differences" (Wood 2001). In this connection, it is worth noting that while the FDA panel that approved BiDil acknowledged that no causal pathway for the drug's outcomes had been decisively established, its members did not hesitate to assert that race or ethnicity "can be a useful proxy" for "the genomic and other physiological characteristics that cause people to differ" (Temple and Stockbridge 2007, 58). In short, the use of race to guide the prescription of pharmaceutical drugs reinforces the essentialist belief that racial categories are anchored in natural and self-evident biological patterns of variation (Ellison et al. 2008a; Kahn 2007; Winickoff and Obasogie 2008).

What does color-blindness convey?

Above I have examined a series of institutions that overtly incorporate racial classification in their practices, often making explicit statements about the nature of race—for example, about the indicators that identify one's racial membership, or the characteristics that distinguish one racial group from another. In so doing, I have emphasized the impact of direct messages about race. This raises the question, however, of whether institutions that do not systematically incorporate racial distinctions in their practice also broadcast notions of race—perhaps anti-essentialist ones. For example, are clothing stores—which do not segregate their wares by race, but by size and gender—implicitly suggesting that race is not a bodily characteristic? Are publishers, who do not market books with specific font types for specific races, quietly telling us that eyesight does not vary by race? In other words, to truly consider the ideas of race that institutions convey to the public, is it necessary to also take into account the gamut of organizational practices that do not distinguish by race?

This is a real possibility. But the absence of explicit mention or use of race—that is, "color-blind" practice—is not easily interpreted. It might reflect and reinforce a constructionist or anti-essentialist orientation, it might mask essentialist presumptions that practitioners prefer not to elucidate, or it might simply mean that such actors have not thought about whether or how race is relevant to their field. As Frankenberg (1993) showed, color-blind—or "color-evasive" discourse—is not necessarily incompatible with racial essentialism. Consequently, it is difficult to predict what analysis of a wider sample of institutions would reveal in terms of what color-blind organizations can be said to broadcast about race. Perhaps the variety of racial concepts that are projected to the public by institutions that explicitly grapple with race—from the constructivism of certain quarters of the academy to the bare-boned essentialism of forensic genetic testing—is mirrored by a similar eclecticism among those actors whose engagement with race is much more subtle.

Another way to think about what the broader panorama of institutions signals to the public about race might be to take into consideration the failure of certain firms that are grounded in essentialist assumptions about human difference. As it turns out, DNAPrint Genomics, which offered DNA ancestry tests, went out of business in 2009; Nitromed, the company that produced the race-targeted heart medicine BiDil, has suspended its promotion of the drug due to lackluster sales (Stewart 2008);

and the CEO of GenSpec, the vitamin company described at the start of this chapter, was sentenced in 2010 to more than seven years in federal prison after being convicted of mail fraud and money laundering (Voyles 2010). Although the performance of these companies doubtless depends on multiple factors, it is possible that some of their troubles stemmed from weak demand for products and services that incorporate a biological model of racial difference. However, it must be kept in mind that other companies offering the same products have survived. As I reported earlier, numerous pharmaceutical firms claim that their drugs have special utility for specific racial groups (Tate and Goldstein 2004), and Obasogie (2009) lists over twenty companies as offering DNA ancestry tests. In other words, the difficulties faced by a handful of firms do not yet spell trouble for industries that are based on marketing race-specific biomedical goods and services. Still, it is worth keeping in mind the global overview of race-grounded and science-based organizations when considering what notions of racial difference they convey to the public.

CONCLUSION

The fact that very different kinds of organizations collect and use data on race—from marketing firms to police departments—implies that we are exposed to a variety of signals about what race is, what kind of information it contains, and how and why it matters (Nelson 2008). Schools, as I have shown, are not the only places where we learn about the nature of race. For example, a hospital's racial classification of an inpatient might imply that race reflects her genetic predisposition to disease. But that is not why colleges collect race data from their applicants. Encounters with different institutions lend themselves to varied conclusions about what race represents: our genetic code, outward appearance, socioeconomic background—or all of these and more. They also expose us to different kinds of messages about race: overt statements in press releases or online FAQs, or subtle notions suggested by organizational practices, procedures, and structures. From our vantage points as patients, consumers, or citizens, what are we to make of the panorama of signals about the nature of race?

The institutions highlighted in this chapter, along with the education case I investigated earlier, certainly convey a diverse range of racial concepts that are grounded in scientific thinking. Where genetic genealogy tests imply that racial membership is encoded in our DNA, court decisions have promoted the idea that racial identity can be inferred through social behaviors (at least in part). Moreover, as the legal system further demonstrates, even a single institution can broadcast or act upon multiple concepts of race. In law, social behavior, physical appearance, and kinship documentation have all provided clues for determining an individual's race; similarly, a patient may take away from her doctor's visit the notion that race affects health through—and is rooted in—genes, behaviors, or experiences.

Yet there is one concept of race that all the institutions I have featured have in common to some extent: the essentialist understanding of race as a property or marker of our bodies. In previous chapters I have shown how this perspective informs the textbook lessons that are a fundamental channel for the transmission of scientific race concepts in formal education. In this chapter I find that even in institutions that diffuse multiple interpretations of race, such as census enumeration and the legal system, essentialism is one of the elements they showcase, even if inadvertently. The other institutions that are more unified around a single interpretation of race—such as criminal forensic profiling—have simply converged on a biological model of race. Unlike constructivism—which is disseminated at times through education, census-taking, and legal precedents—or culturalism, which may come through in the census, law, or medicine, essentialism is the one concept of race that is promulgated to some degree by all the institutions I have investigated.

The predominance of essentialism in institutional concepts of race suggests it is the stream of scientific thinking about race that is most widely diffused to the public. Moreover, the presence of multiple institutions that transmit a biological vision of race may well compound the power of any single institution's message in this vein. The essentialist beliefs about racial difference that I observed in formal education, then, are much more likely than its constructivist teachings to be amplified by similar messages from other domains. Consider, for example, how a high-school biology textbook may point to forensic practices of racial identification, or present statistics on medical disorders that are classified by race. Simply put, the concept of race as a biologically rooted human characteristic likely receives more institutional reinforcement than any of its competitors.

These similarities across institutions raise questions about the role played by our broader social context in nurturing some understandings of race and not others. What does the wide reach of biological essentialism among institutions that utilize and communicate scientific race thinking say about its purchase in the wider society? In the next and final chapter, I take up the question of how contemporary social and political developments in the United States have preserved essentialist beliefs about race.

SEVEN

Conclusion

THE REDEMPTION OF ESSENTIALISM

The second time I was pregnant, I had the good fortune to be living in Italy thanks to a Fulbright research fellowship. This time my encounters with the medical establishment were quite different from those I had experienced as a first-time mother in New York. As I went through various rounds of doctors' appointments and laboratory tests in Milan, no one ever asked me what my race (or ethnicity) was. I never had to fill out a form describing myself as "black" or "white," yet it seemed that doctors and technicians were perfectly able to care for me and interpret my test results without that element of information that had seemed indispensable back in the United States.

Perhaps my Italian physicians were simply not up to speed on the latest techniques. Judging from their use of technology such as ultrasound imaging, however, I doubt that. Maybe they did not collect race or ethnicity data because Italy is a homogeneously European country, with little variation to keep track of. Except it's not: not only does Italy receive larger net numbers of immigrants annually than any other country in the European Union save Spain, but its foreign-born population is extremely heterogeneous, counting Romanians, Moroccans, Chinese, and Indians among its largest immigrant communities (Blangiardo 2009, 39; Eurostat 2010). If race were an important characteristic of our physical constitution, then why wouldn't Italian doctors take it into account as assiduously as their counterparts in the United States?

The simple answer is that although our bodies do not differ greatly between New York and Milan, our ideas about our bodies do. Either race is a characteristic of our biological makeup on both sides of the Atlantic, or it is on neither. The real difference between us lies in the ways we link race to biology—and to culture, and to social organization. Those links, moreover, are not only conceptual: they are institutional. As an American my experience in Italy was striking not just because of what people thought or did not think; it was also notable because of the kinds of encounters I had—or did not have—when I interacted with institutions such as the medical establishment, universities, and government offices. Unlike in the United States, where such institutions routinely require individuals to identify themselves in terms of racial categories, no one in Italy ever asked me to fill out my "razza" on a form. Clearly, ideas about racial difference and its significance depend a great deal on national context.

In this concluding chapter, I take up the question of what social and political characteristics of the United States might help account for the concepts of race that I have described in this book. To address it, I consider what the findings reported in previous chapters imply about underlying trends in how we see and think about racial variation. These empirical observations point to two contemporary dynamics in particular: the post–civil rights era appeal of individual (rather than societal) explanations for racial inequality, and the implications of our nation's changing demographics for the conceptualization of race. Both offer potential explanations for why essentialism remains such a dominant stream in American racial conceptualization. Although some might consider simple inertia to be a sufficient answer, I argue that scientific and popular race beliefs have undergone significant transformation over time, reflecting a process of continual "reconstruction" (Morning 2008b) that suggests anything but dependence on vestigial notions of difference. Instead, the race concepts I have documented resonate with the social landscape of today.

RACIAL CONCEPTUALIZATION IN FORMAL EDUCATION AND BEYOND: A SUMMARY

Over the course of this book, I have traced a cycle of knowledge dissemination by asking how scientists understand the concept of race, what kinds of scientific interpretations are actually conveyed through schooling, and how laypeople react to those ideas. I draw several conclusions from this empirical research. First and foremost, I find that social and biological scientists hold a wide range of beliefs about the nature of racial difference; contrary to some scholars' expectations, they are far from any consensus, either within or between disciplines. In particular, constructivism and anti-essentialism have hardly conquered the academy (despite repeated claims to that effect), even in my highly particular sample where anthropologists make up half the interviewees. In contrast, the essentialist proposition that races are biologically grounded entities remains a compelling view for many contemporary scientists. To be sure, my interview sample is small and far from generalizable to the U.S. professoriate as a whole, so it cannot be used to estimate the proportions of all faculty who might subscribe to one school of thought or another. However, the variety of opinion it shows, with respondents being almost evenly split on the question of whether race is biological in nature, suggests that a larger and more representative sample would be unlikely to reveal a broad consensus.

In moving from what scientists think to what is represented to the public as scientific thought, the message that race is a social construct seems to get lost in transmission. In high-school biology textbooks, the constructionist message is all but absent; instead racial essentialism is reinforced in several ways, both direct and indirect. Even social science texts largely fail to make a strong constructivist case. And although I do not collect data directly on class lectures, the university students I interviewed clearly identified racial constructionism with anthropology teaching, but not nearly as much with teaching in any other discipline. In short, scientific instruction that challenges biological notions of race, though compelling or at least intriguing to the students it reaches, does not appear to be a widespread feature of formal education in the United States today.

Nor does constructivist or anti-essentialist teaching necessarily leave a deep mark on undergraduates. Even in a sample where one-third of the students interviewed were anthropology majors, and thus among those most likely to be exposed to the academic idea of race as socially constructed, less than one-fifth of the respondents defined race that way. Only students who had taken a course in anthropology (regardless of their eventual major) described race as a social construct, but such coursework was no guarantee they would adopt that view. Strikingly, the most common approach to defining race among undergraduates was to equate races with culture-specific groups, which sociologists would label "ethnic groups." Students' frequent use of this culturalist model of race, which was virtually nonexistent among the social and biological scientists I interviewed, suggests that their thinking about racial difference is little altered by the scientific education they receive. However, the interviews also hint that what they said about racial difference was not always the same as the way they actually reasoned about or worked with it. "It's all about different cultures" might be an attractive way to define the race concept in the abstract, but it did not provide a consistent tool for explaining real-life differentials in health or occupational outcomes. Instead, academic study of human genetics and evolutionary history heavily colored their understandings of such outcomes. Overall, then, these interview data do not lend themselves to simple conclusions about the impact of scientists' race concepts on their students.

These findings suggest that understanding American racial conceptualization means investigating why essentialist notions of race are so widespread. Moreover, they provide an answer, at least for the realm of formal education: beliefs about fixed, biological differences remain power-

ful because scientists have yet to form a consensus that decisively refutes that outlook. The same might explain why the other science-based
(or -informed) institutions I survey in Chapter 6 share racial essentialism in common (albeit to varying degrees). This account however leaves
open the question of why racial essentialism has retained such purchase
in the academy. It also exaggerates the separation of science from society, as if beliefs about race were dictated to laypeople by scientists rather
than suffusing the broader culture both inhabit. In the following pages,
I explore aspects of contemporary American society that are likely to
influence the ways that all of us conceptualize the nature of race.

HOW NOT TO ACCOUNT FOR RACIAL ESSENTIALISM

To develop an explanation for why biological understandings of racial
difference are compelling for many Americans today, I begin by eliminating three arguments that are among the first to come to mind.

Racial essentialism as truth?

A straightforward explanation of why essentialist concepts are more
popular than constructivist ones might be simply that the former are
true and the latter false.[1] But there are several reasons to be skeptical
of such a conclusion. First and foremost, many experts believe there is a
great deal of empirical evidence that refutes the biological model of race
(Barbujani 2006; Koenig, Lee, and Richardson 2008; Marks 1995). Analysis of human DNA has not revealed any "race gene" whose alleles (i.e.,
variants) correspond to racial-group membership, nor any complex of
genes that together indicate a person's race (*pace* Leroi 2005).[2] Instead, it
has demonstrated extraordinary similarity in human beings' genetic
makeup, regardless of their outward appearance: 99.9 percent of our genome is identical (Barbujani et al. 1997; Lewontin 1972). The genetic
variation that does exist among human beings can mostly be found
within the boundaries of any one racial group (Feldman and Lewontin
2008). Moreover, the analysis of mitochondrial DNA suggests that all

humans alive today descended from African ancestors (Cann, Stoneking, and Wilson 1987). In short, it would be incorrect to deduce that the essentialist perspective has emerged as the clear winner in the scientific debate about race.

Another reason to be skeptical that racial essentialism's popularity is due to its accuracy comes from historical precedent. In the past, essentialist beliefs about race have managed to endure even though their empirical claims or predictions came to be widely refuted. The scientific predictions that blacks would be unable to survive outside slavery or mulattos to reproduce have not been borne out. Theories of major racial differentials in crania and other skeletal attributes have been disproved (Gould 1996). Racial boundaries have been found in neither blood type nor anthropometric statistics (W. Schneider 1996). And although the debate has now moved on to whether genetic analysis reveals racial patterns, some early expectations have already been clearly overturned. There is no "race gene" that dictates a person's race; there are no alleles that are shared by all members of a single race and not by members of any other (Marks 1995). Given the survival of biological race thinking despite these successive empirical upsets, it is difficult to claim that its popularity can be explained by its "fit" with the physical world.

Racial essentialism still demonstrates a surprising independence from empirical data today. Current biology textbooks make claims about race reflecting genetic difference even when no evidence is offered of such difference, nor is any description provided of exactly the kinds of differences involved. Similarly, studies that note racial differentials in areas such as health or intelligence often presume that genetic difference is the principal cause, even when no genetic data is actually examined. Scrutiny of the claims that are made about essential race differences on the one hand, and of the empirical data used to bolster them on the other, suggests that the appeal of essentialism hardly lies in its having made more plausible or solid factual claims than other schools of thought about race.

Racial essentialism as cognitive framework?

Hirschfeld (1996) argues that racial thinking is a powerful instance of a broader human capacity—indeed, necessity—to categorize people into kinds. He reasons that we possess "a domain-specific competence for creating knowledge of and reasoning about human kinds" (12)—a kind of cognitive module that underpins and facilitates our belief in essential human races. This theory might suggest that racial essentialism is powerful in the United States today because our brains are "hardwired" to perceive or create intrinsic racial groups.

While such a faculty may help account for the endurance of essentialist notions of racial difference, it does not explain change very well. Why the shift from phenotypic to genetic models of race over the course of the twentieth century? For that matter, why has the race notion come to satisfy this psychological need for kind-making in the modern era, instead of the civic versus barbaric distinction of antiquity or the Christian versus heathen distinction of medieval Europe (Hannaford 1996)? As Hirschfeld recognizes, "conditions of political, economic, legal, and cultural relations" interact with our kind-making faculty "to transform one system of adult belief into another" over time (16–17). Thus we cannot explain contemporary racial essentialism as the inevitable and timeless product of human psychology. Our human disposition to "make kinds" no doubt facilitates our lasting belief in biological races, but it does not answer the question of why a particular concept of human difference predominates at any given time.

Racial essentialism as legacy?

A final explanation for today's racial essentialism might simply be that it is a holdover from the past, the product of custom or societal inertia. This view seriously underestimates however the extent to which the biological model of race has been challenged and consequently reformulated in the twentieth century (Barkan 1992). The idea of racial essentialism as little more than an old habit that dies hard does not explain how it managed to weather considerable post–World War II antagonism toward "race science" (Reardon 2005). Moreover, the biological view of race has proved to be anything but static, as it has undergone changes in the empirical claims upon which it rests and in the authoritative expertise on which it calls. The historical dynamism of racial essentialism challenges the premise that it exists today simply because it existed yesterday. Such malleability calls instead for careful investigation of the factors, past and present, which play a role in the currency of essentialist thinking in the early twenty-first century.

Racial essentialism as historical phenomenon

As textbooks illustrate, American race thinking changed considerably over the course of the twentieth century (Reardon 2005; Smedley 2007; Winant 2001). As a result, explanations that attribute today's racial essentialism to its timeless accuracy, innate psychological appeal, or invariant preservation of long-standing beliefs all miss the mark because they overlook the crucial dimension of time. Understanding why the biological model of race is so powerful today involves asking how it came to be this way—how the past has yielded this present.

There are two important historical changes to consider when contemplating racial essentialism today. First, why is it so popular now when it came under attack after World War II and faced competition from racial constructivism? Second, why did the biological model shift from its older phenotypic to its current genetic form? These questions are interrelated because the transformation in the essentialist model's framework likely played a vital role in its survival in the second half of the twentieth century.

THE REDEMPTION OF RACIAL ESSENTIALISM

Various observers have described today's racial concepts as reflecting the "return" or "revival" of essentialist beliefs about race in the United States (Duster 2003a; P. Martin et al. 2007; Müller-Wille and Rheinberger 2008). This phrasing captures the sense that explanations for inequality that were based on racial "blood," "type," or "character" were decidedly shunted aside in the post–World War II period by accounts of discrimination, and later by genetic evidence of considerable homogeneity within the human species. In biology textbooks, this turn away from racial essentialism is apparent in the steady decline in the discussion of race from the mid-twentieth century until its last decade. But the imagery of return after an absence obscures the fact that belief in deep-rooted, permanent racial differences never left us. As Troy Duster (2003b) has put it, the biological race concept was simply "buried alive"—not decisively finished off—and subsequently was resuscitated.

More than simply revived, however, the essentialist race concept has been "redeemed" in recent years: made good again with the passage of time. The term has several connotations that are particularly apt, and which are neglected in the more basic reference to the "return" of racial essentialism. First, redemption can mean "to release from blame," "to expiate," and even "to free from the consequences of sin." This set of definitions helps convey the extent to which debates about the nature of race in general have been freighted with moral concerns, and the essentialist notion of race in particular has had to overcome pejorative associations with eugenics in order to become socially acceptable again. As my interviews with both scientists and students suggest, the biological model of race cannot become entirely viable without being ethically redeemed.

Second, redemption can also mean "to exchange for something of value," "to make good," and "to make worthwhile." This interpretation captures the ways in which the return of racial essentialism has meant figuring as a useful and even crucial tool, an instrument for understanding important dimensions of the human experience. Nothing captures the ostensible utility of racial essentialism better than the contemporary claim that health care is most effective when it takes inherent racial differences into account (Burchard et al. 2003; Satel 2002; Wood 2001). This reasoning is a key element in the federal laws and policies that now mandate "research inclusiveness and the measurement of difference" in biomedical research (Epstein 2007, 5; see also S. S. J. Lee, Mountain, and Koenig 2001). As Epstein demonstrates, the "inclusion and difference" paradigm has been institutionalized not just through law and policy but through "the accompanying creation of bureaucratic offices, procedures, and monitoring systems" (6). Although the exact mechanism through which race is relevant for health may not be clear in these practices (does race matter as an indicator of cultural habits? exposure to discrimination? or genetic proclivities?) the inclusion-and-difference framework facilitates the linkage of racial essentialism to medical benevolence. In this way, essentialism is redeemed both as a morally worthy stance and a useful approach.

Finally, "redemption" also brings to mind political life, and particularly the postbellum moment when the federal experiment in civil rights known as Reconstruction drew to a close. Southern white elites saw their salvation as lying in the reinstatement of the harsh racial hierarchy of slavery, and once freed from Northern intervention, they set about building "the house of Jim Crow" (Howard 2008). The South's Redemption, then, involved the reconsolidation of racial hierarchy after a concerted attempt to expand the freedoms guaranteed Americans regardless of color. One parallel with our own post–civil rights era, then, is the risk of reestablishing racial hierarchies that some observers believe is posed by the return of essentialist thinking.

There is another connection to political redemption, however, that may be at work in the return of racial essentialism. The biological model of race has been embraced once more, I suggest, because of the redemption it offers us as a nation: it absolves us of guilt for the racial inequality that continues to plague our society. In the pages to follow, I will draw on my interviewees' understandings of race difference on one hand, and scholars' linkage of racial conceptualization to political orientation on the other, to formulate and evaluate two hypotheses about just how political developments in recent years may have favored racial essentialism.

The post–civil rights political appeal of racial essentialism

Scholars often associate race concepts with political orientation. Essentialism is frequently linked to political conservatism, because it appears to justify the status quo, while constructivism is associated with liberalism due to its tenet that social structures are ultimately flexible (Cartmill

1999; Harrison 1999). From this perspective, the widespread racial essentialism I observed at the turn of the twenty-first century could be interpreted as the product of the political conservatism of the late twentieth century, from the 1980 presidential election of Ronald Reagan through the 2008 end of President George W. Bush's term, and including major Congressional gains by the Republican party in this period. The conservative ideology of rolling back government—especially social spending—in order to reduce its "interference" in Americans' lives is consistent with a recurring stream of essentialist thought whereby race differences are so permanent and irrevocable that policy attempts to eliminate racial inequalities are a pointless waste of money. Contemporary incarnations of this theory can be found in the 1994 bestseller *The Bell Curve: Intelligence and Class Structure in American Life* (Herrnstein and Murray 1994; see also its forerunner, "How Much Can We Boost I.Q. and Scholastic Achievement?" [Jensen 1969]) and in *Race: The Reality of Human Difference* (Sarich and Miele 2004). Another illustration of this reasoning comes from the 2007 controversy sparked by Nobel prize winner James Watson, previously described in the Introduction of this book. His judgment that Africans were inherently unintelligent was intertwined with his assessment that public spending on foreign aid to Africa was futile (Nugent 2007). I also return to the comments of Andrew Sullivan (2005) because they neatly sum up the linkage between essentialism and anti-interventionist conservatism: "The problem [of innate, biological inequality] is intractable," he wrote, "and the more we try and solve this problem, the worse it can get. The better we get at improving the educational or social environment, or enlarging opportunity, the more tenacious and obvious our genetic differences will seem." In summary, one explanation for the renewed prominence of racial essentialism in the United States could well be its affinity with the conservative political ideology that was embraced at the highest levels of government during much of the last thirty years.

I would argue however that another account is more likely, one that is related but subtly distinct, and rooted in the civil rights era and its aftermath. This second argument, which comes out of theories of "new racism," contends that racial essentialism appeals to Americans today because it offers an explanation for enduring, post–civil rights racial inequalities that takes the blame away from our society, its culture, and institutions. Rather than implying that racial discrimination is still alive and well, essentialism attributes socioeconomic inequalities between races to differences in their innate abilities.

Contemporary sociological and psychological theories of racism—for example, "aversive racism" (Gaertner and Dovidio 1986), "symbolic racism" (Sears 1988), "differentialist racism" (Taguieff 1988), "neo-racism" (Balibar 1991), "new racism" (Sniderman et al. 1991), "color-blind racism" (Frankenberg 1993; Schofield 1986), and "racism without racists" (Bonilla-Silva 2003)—commonly claim that although modern racism seeks to avoid appearing like the overt and brutal prejudices of the past, it embodies a continued reluctance to grant full equality to racialized others.[3] These "new racism" theories focus on the complex strategies required to maintain institutional racism and individual prejudice alongside the values of equality and liberty, not to mention the belief in one's own lack of bias. This psychological tension between the principle of equality and complicity in inequality could be considered the individual, personal manifestation of the societal malaise that Gunnar Myrdal (1944) labeled "the American dilemma." One frequently theorized solution is that many Americans prefer to ascribe race differentials in outcomes such as income or education to the shortcomings of the disadvantaged themselves, rather than taking into consideration the possibility of larger systems of social stratification (Kluegel 1986). As Bobo, Kluegel, and Smith (1997, 38) put it in their theory of *"laissez-faire* racism":

> This new ideology concedes basic citizenship rights to African Americans; however, it takes as legitimate extant patterns of black-white socioeconomic inequality and residential segregation, viewing these conditions, as it does, not as the deliberate products of racial discrimination, but as outcomes of a free-market, race-neutral state apparatus and the freely taken actions of African Americans themselves.

Bonilla-Silva (2003) found empirical evidence that white interviewees adopted this strategy by minimizing the existence of racism and thus naturalizing racial inequalities by implying they were the expectable by-product of the impersonal and laudable forces of political and economic liberalism. Together, "new racism" theories and the empirical survey data that support them make it clear that the idea of a "postracial" United States is not a new one; for decades, a large proportion of white Americans has felt that discrimination plays a small role if any in accounting for the differences between whites' and blacks' life chances.

Although it may not be immediately apparent, these theories about contemporary racism presume that certain concepts of racial difference are contained in racist perspectives. "New racism" is thought to include the belief that significant and unchanging differences exist between racial groups, leaving minorities with abilities and behaviors that create racial socioeconomic inequality. More specifically, two types of racial concept fit neatly into "new racist" reasoning, which requires exculpation of the white majority and the attribution of inequality to minorities' shortcomings or to impersonal institutions. On one hand is the genetic explanation for racial difference, which preempts the consideration of discrimination. On the other is the concept of races as cultural entities whose particular values guide the behaviors in which they choose to engage, free of discriminatory constraints. Balibar (1991, 21) describes the latter concept as fueling the rise of "a racism whose dominant theme is not biological heredity but the insurmountability of cultural differences, a racism which, at first sight, does not postulate the superiority of certain groups or peoples in relation to others but 'only' the harmfulness of abolishing frontiers, the incompatibility of life-styles and traditions." In other words, "biological or genetic naturalism is not the only means of naturalizing human behaviour and social affinities . . . *culture can also function like a nature*" (22). The idea that races are marked by distinct and incompatible cultural practices and values thus offers Americans a rationale for racial separatism and inequality that seems free of the trappings of older biological claims of racial hierarchy. And while some researchers suggest that cultural racism has replaced biology-based racism in the United States (e.g., Bobo, Kluegel and Smith 1997; Bonilla-Silva 2003), Balibar's analysis suggests that the two might peacefully coexist as essentialist rationales that both disavow the existence of racial discrimination.

My interviews with college students were quite consistent with these theoretical expectations about contemporary race thinking. Not only were cultural and biological definitions of race the most popular ones among my undergraduate interviewees, but they were hardly mutually exclusive. Instead, the culturalist concept and the biological concept seemed to "go together" for many students. In fact, they may simply have been two facets of the same essentialist understanding of racial difference. Their fundamental commonality is further suggested by the students attributing the same fixedness and permanence to culture that they ascribed to biology when it came to describing racial differences. In addition, even when they chose to define racial difference as "cultural," the kinds of groups they listed as races were the traditional large and culturally heterogeneous continental groupings such as "African" and "Asian" rather than the smaller ethnic groups that are usually associated with specific cultural practices.

The student interviews also support the hypothesis that such racial essentialism is linked to belief that racial discrimination has vanished from American society. As we saw, prejudice toward racial minorities played a minor, virtually nonexistent role in the predominantly white undergraduates' explanations for why race differentials exist in health outcomes or professional sports. Although socioeconomic stratification might be mentioned, it was depicted in the "laissez-faire" style that Bobo, Kluegel, and Smith (1997, 38) described, namely as a "legitimate extant" situation that was not the product of discrimination. Indeed, racial discrimination was only plausible to students in one of three ways: as a phenomenon of the past ("like twenty years ago," in one interviewee's estimation), as a characteristic of other places (especially the U.S. South), or as a racism targeted against whites. In short, my undergraduate interviewees were not unaware of continued socioeconomic inequality between whites and blacks, but they did not connect it to anti-black racism. Instead, ostensibly intrinsic, inherited biological differences between blacks, whites, and others provided the explanatory framework for understanding why racial groups have different life outcomes. This finding is highly consistent with "new racism" theory's premise that essentialism helps reconcile individuals' principles to their attitudes and actions by squaring a racially unequal society with a virtuous, racism-free people.

As stated previously, the two political explanations I have offered for the resurgence of racial essentialism are not unrelated. True, the first emphasizes the role of post-1980 political conservatism, whereas the second stresses the legacy of the civil rights movement of the 1950s, 1960s, and 1970s, particularly the subsequent acknowledgment that the nation had failed to eradicate racial inequality. But the two eras are not unconnected: the Reagan Revolution of the 1980s was very much a response to the civil rights movement, one intended to reassure whites who felt threatened politically, economically, and socially by minorities' gains. The ideological roots of this "revolution" can be traced back to the "Southern Strategy" attributed to Richard Nixon, namely the wooing of white electoral support by playing to fears of desegregation and of equal rights for blacks more generally. It is no surprise then that Reagan launched his presidential campaign in Mississippi with the promise to roll back the federal government's encroachment on "states' rights"—in that context, an invocation of southerners' resistance to civil rights legislation—or that he would go on to veto the Civil Rights Restoration Act of 1988. In other words, the conservative movement of the late twentieth century can be understood as a retrenchment or reversal of the gains made by minorities in the civil rights era—indeed, as the Redemption of our times (Kousser 1999; Western 2006).

Having said that, the two political explanatory accounts for today's racial essentialism focus on different aspects of the post–civil rights period. The first suggests that essentialism has returned because it has an affinity with the conservative movement that came to power in the 1980s; it fits with that ideology's promotion of small government and especially of reduced social spending. The second political hypothesis is that racial essentialism has gained strength in recent decades because it serves an instrumental purpose: it rationalizes away the possibility that racial discrimination might play a role in the socioeconomic inequality that has endured despite civil rights legislation. In this view, racial essentialism has become especially appealing because it exculpates American society of racism.

Although these two political explanations are not mutually exclusive, I believe the second, "laissez-faire" account for the renewal of racial essentialism is more plausible for both theoretical and empirical reasons. In terms of logic, it is harder to see what causal link might be at work in the first, "conservatism" hypothesis. If I am in favor of smaller government, is it likely I will adapt my race concept to one that facilitates or justifies cutting back government? It seems more probable that the causality works the other way, where I start with a belief in deep-rooted racial differences that leads me to oppose civil rights measures, and thus to support the political philosophy (conservatism) that also objects to them. In that case, though, racial essentialism drives political orientation, rather than being explained by it. Reflecting on the potential causal mechanisms at work, the second, "laissez-faire" hypothesis seems more persuasive. In this scenario, my awareness of racial inequality makes me feel uncomfortable or guilty, and to avoid that feeling, I embrace a race concept that rationalizes away my discomfort: it's not my fault—as an individual, or as a white person, or as an American—it is in fact "their" fault, due to innate shortcomings that I am powerless to redress.

Empirically, my interviews lend greater support to the "laissez-faire" hypothesis than the "conservatism" account. Belief in the absence of racial discrimination appeared to be a much more salient feature of students' societal outlook than any right-leaning political orientation. Only a small minority of the undergraduate interviewees described themselves as "right of center," and this percentage was even lower among their professors. The "laissez-faire" account also fits another striking aspect of my data: the centrality of moral concerns to individuals' evaluation and elaboration of various racial concepts. At the heart of this explanation is the idea that concern with guilt or blame can make the essentialist concept of race an appealing one, as it displaces responsibility for inequality from the advantaged to the disadvantaged. The theme of guilt or responsibility is much less prominent in the "conservatism" hypothesis. Yet in my interviews with both students and faculty, ethical questions clearly figured in their considerations of how best to define the nature of race.

This moral dimension lends further support, moreover, to the characterization of racial essentialism as having undergone a "redemption" in recent years and not merely a resurgence. Given its negative image in the decades immediately following World War II, the essentialist biological model of race could only have regained widespread acceptance by shedding its associations with eugenic practices that are now morally condemned, including forced sterilization and at its extreme, genocide. What comes out strongly in the comments of people I interviewed is this ongoing process of redemption, whereby not only is the relationship between racial essentialism and ethically abhorrent activities being re-negotiated (or loosened, really), but essentialism is also becoming the pillar of a morally virtuous depiction of our society. Belief in intrinsic, fundamental, and unchanging differences between races is a valuable element if our consciences are to be assuaged that racism is no longer afoot in the United States—and by extension, that we as individuals are not guilty of this sin.

The lack of competition from racial constructivism

Before concluding the discussion of why racial essentialism has come to be widespread today despite a mid-twentieth century crisis in authority, it is important to consider what competing concepts of race were available. My interviews and analysis of textbooks suggest that proponents of con-structivism and anti-essentialism have not mounted an effective chal-lenge. Scientists have not come to a consensus on the constructed nature of race, and consequently, they have not transmitted that perspective co-herently or comprehensively to the public. Although constructivism is perhaps more strongly associated with anti-racism, it has not "taken" as a lens through which everyday people can make sense of racial stratifica-tion. Although many students I interviewed had heard of the idea that race is socially constructed, it did not seem to serve them when they tried to account for the racial differentials that characterize our society. Instead, they reached for the familiar tool of essentialism.

TRANSFORMATION IN THE BIOLOGICAL
MODEL OF RACE: SOCIAL CONTEXT AND
DEMOGRAPHIC LANDSCAPE

Essentialist thinking about race has not only gained new legitimacy in recent years, but it underwent a striking change in its content in the second half of the twentieth century. As biology textbooks vividly illustrate, race used to be rooted in phenotypic difference, such as eye or hair color, but is now widely ascribed to genetic variation. This was true in my conversations not only with academics, but with their students, who often mentioned surface physical differences yet traced these ultimately to DNA. How can we understand this historic shift in the conceptual basis for biological race?

In part the recasting of race reflects a broader twentieth-century transformation in the life sciences (Kay 1993; E. Keller 2000). As numerous scholars describe, the discipline of biology was "molecularized" during this period (de Chadarevian and Kamminga 1998; Shostak 2005), meaning that its attention turned to a significant extent to microscopic processes at the cellular level, including interactions between deoxyribonucleic acid (DNA) and ribonucleic acid (RNA). Rose (2001, 13) captures the thoroughgoing nature of this shift by describing it as involving the "reorganization of the gaze of the life sciences, their institutions, procedures, instruments, spaces of operation and forms of capitalization." It is no surprise then that race was eventually translated from the language of phenotype to that of genotype, mirroring new thinking in biology as a whole.

The world beyond the laboratory also played an important role in this conceptual shift. Reardon (2004) argues that a genetic definition of race appealed to biologists because it resonated with a wider political ideology that gained currency in the 1950s and 1960s: the principle that institutions (and people) should be "color-blind," impartial in their treatment of individuals regardless of surface traits.

> Human population geneticists . . . [posited] that, independent of genetic analysis, physical traits commonly used to distinguish races (e.g., head form, skin color, etc.) revealed nothing about human biology or the evolution of the human species. In other words, drawing upon distinctions made possible partially through the advent of molecular biology, population geneticists crafted new discursive resources that enabled them to join lawyers, government officials, and even many social scientists in arguing that race, when it is held to be merely a cluster of visible physical traits, is meaningless—both in science and in society. (56)

Reardon concludes that this "rejection of a visible physical concept of race . . . enabled a genetic definition of race to emerge in its place" (56).

My analysis of biology textbooks from the 1950s to the present suggests two additional factors behind the phenotype-to-genotype shift. One was the promise that genetics seemed to hold for addressing certain challenges that faced the traditional phenotypic model of race. The other was the burgeoning demographic diversity of the United States, which a genetic definition of race could accommodate much more easily than a phenotypic one.

Genetic race to the rescue of the phenotypic model

One of the most striking characteristics of biology textbooks published in the 1950s and '60s is how confident the authors were of the transparent or self-evident nature of human racial classifications. A photographic collage from 1958, for example, features a black-and-white jumble of about thirty faces, with a caption that triumphantly concludes, "There are, as you can see, three races with variations within each of them" (Figure 9).

This buoyancy was eventually brought down to earth by increasing concerns about the accuracy of such taxonomies. One reason was that scientific experts could not agree on racial categories: which existed and who they included. As the authors of *Biology and Human Progress* informed students, "there is no definite agreement about the number of races" (Eisman and Tanzer 1972, 431), while the textbook *New Dynamic Biology* pointed out the inconsistencies across different researchers' classification schemes: "Some scientists consider yet another group, the Australoids, as a fourth race" (Baker, Mills, and Tanczos 1959, 448). Another pedagogical problem for the biological race concept was the rigidity of the phenotypic taxonomies that were popular at mid-century. Their visual presentation of races as a series of discrete, mutually exclusive categories, where all "Nordic" people had "light, fine" hair and all "Alpine" people had "thick-set, medium" stature (Smallwood et al. 1952, 265) was easily refuted. Some textbooks tried to address this inaccuracy; *Biology Serving You* explained, "Racial traits are based on the study of many thousands

How do scientists learn the history of the Earth?

How do scientists learn about life on Earth in the very distant past?

How have living things on Earth changed?

How has Man changed?

UNIT X: THE ORIGINS OF LIVING THINGS

Fig. X-1. Races of Man. Man dominates the plants and animals that live on the Earth. There are, as you can see, three races with variations within each of them. Who were the ancestors of these men?

Figure 9. "Races of Man," 1958. The caption for the photo collage at left reads in part, "There are, as you can see, three races with variations within each of them."

SOURCE: Charles Gramet and James Mandel, *Biology Serving You* (Englewood Cliffs, NJ: Prentice Hall, 1958), 538–39. Photo credit: American

of people. A racial trait is therefore a kind of average description. A particular individual in a race may not have all the racial traits" (Gramet and Mandel 1958, 578). And *Elements of Biology* (Smallwood et al. 1952, 262) suggested, "Skin color considered alone is not an adequate basis of classification, because it varies so much with exposure to the sun's rays. Other physical traits upon which groups are classified are color and texture of hair, color and shape of eyes, form of skull, jaw, teeth, prominence of cheekbones, and width of nose." Eventually, though, the apparent shortcomings of phenotypic classification led textbook authors in search of new markers of racial difference.

Their first stop was not genotype but serotype.[4] American biology textbooks began to include blood type as a marker of racial identity in the 1960s, and continued to do so into the 1980s. The appearance of blood-type discourse in this period cannot be ascribed to new advances in scientific knowledge, for "racial serology" had originated before 1920— and been dismissed as a viable science of race shortly thereafter (Marks 1996; W. Schneider 1996). Instead, the introduction of blood groups coincided with textbook authors' declining confidence in surface physical characteristics as indicators of racial membership.

Serotype offered a way out of the deterministic taxonomies of discrete group differences that had characterized—and ultimately discredited— phenotypic definitions of race. Blood-group research tended to define racial groups in terms of the percentage of members with a particular blood type or allele, rather than in terms of some serological characteristic that all members of a race supposedly shared. By no longer requiring that racial groups demonstrate uniformity, the serotype concept of race replaced the phenotypic model of *absolute* difference with one of *relative* difference. This approach of describing races as distinctive in their relative tendencies to embody particular variants endures in today's textbook discussions of genetic racial variation.

The serotype definition of race also had a pedagogical advantage over the older phenotype concept because it drew on the authority of a new branch of science. Even though racial serology was not in fact new in the 1960s, it *was* fresh in textbooks as a source of scientific authority on the nature of race. Blood group research then represented a body of knowledge that had not yet been discredited—as phenotype research had—as being a capable and accurate guide to racial difference. Its credibility as expert science was further reinforced by the fact that it moved the identification of race out of the hands of laypeople into those of specialists. While the previous phenotypical race categories were based on surface physical characteristics such as skin color and hair type that anybody—even schoolchildren—could see, serotype classification relied on measurements that only trained technicians armed with the necessary equipment could take.

This twofold operation of deflecting criticism by shifting a contested racial concept from one empirical basis and scientific field to another basis and field was soon repeated. Claims about racial blood-type differences ran into problems, just as discrete phenotypical categories had before them, and they were eventually superseded by genetic definitions. It turned out that blood-group variation did not map very neatly onto the prevailing racial categories of the day, thus failing to delineate the group boundaries that educators sought to illustrate. The subsequent invocation of broader genetic race markers got around the serotypic mapping problem—by not furnishing any actual guidelines to the specific DNA markers of race. As I emphasized earlier, textbooks' equation of racial difference with genetic variation has actually meant providing students with less, rather than more, information about the nature of race, so there is little that can be criticized. Textbooks no longer offer students lists of races, so there are no boundary lines to scrutinize. In today's textbooks, there are genetic races—but we do not know which they are, who they include, or how one differs from another.

This shielding of gene-based claims about race is possible because they are grounded in an elite science that is practiced only by those with the requisite training and equipment. Few can authoritatively participate in today's discussion about the bases of racial categories. Moreover, the very invisibility of today's genetic racial markers may paradoxically reinforce their credibility. Whereas the power of the older phenotypic accounts lay in their ability to make obvious the reality of race to any viewer, the legitimacy of the contemporary genetic definition of race lies in its inaccessibility to all but a limited number of scientific authorities.

Discerning race now requires expertise. Who then can join the debate about the nature of race?

Geneticization also protected the essentialist model of race by yoking it to an authoritative scientific field. When textbook writers embraced the notion of genetic races in the 1980s, it was hardly new; American scientific interest and belief in racial genetic differences went back for decades. The well-known Eugenics Record Office, for example, had investigated the classical genetics of "race crossing" since its establishment in 1910 (Kevles 1995/1985). But in the 1950s, the field of human genetics began to attract new prestige, funding and practitioners in the United States, having managed to disassociate itself from the discredited eugenics movement by emphasizing its potential medical applications (Kevles 1995/1985). Especially after Crick and Watson's 1953 unraveling of the structure of DNA, advances in genetic research have revolutionized the study of biology and brought immense prestige to the field. In that light, textbook authors may well have sought to bolster claims about race by invoking a branch of human biology that was growing increasingly prominent both among scientists and in the public eye.

The importance of this double operation of shifting both the empirical and the authoritative bases of racial claims should not be underestimated, for it has historically been central to the perpetuation of race science. In long-term perspective, the geneticization of race can be seen as the latest iteration in an ongoing process in which racial difference is corroborated by (and gives impetus to) the most respected scientific techniques. When refuted in one field, the race concept migrates to higher ground, where new evidence for racial difference is inevitably sought and found. As Young (1995, 94) observed in his history of American and British scientific racialism, "Scientific theories measuring the differences between the races and their capacities could come and go, but what they always did was to develop earlier ideas according to a new, merciless economy in which the multiple meanings of race were grafted incrementally on to each other."

As Young's comment suggests, successive perspectives on race contain elements of the frameworks that precede them. Serology, for example, was a conceptual bridge that shared many common elements with both the preceding and subsequent methods of classifying race. Like its predecessor, the phenotype, blood was a long-standing symbol of the essence of individual qualities and thus difference from others (Wailoo 1997). It was also a component of human physiology that was familiar and tangible. Its successor, the genotype, came in turn to share blood's mystical symbolism as the repository or essence of individuality; Nelkin and Lindee (1995) argue that DNA has become something akin to the Christian "soul." Blood type also shared with genotype a certain invisibility or imperceptibility for the average person. Both are biological characteristics that are "buried" below the surface of the human body, anchoring boundaries of racial difference that only specialized experts can excavate. Finally, racial taxonomies based on serotype and genotype are further linked by the intertwined relationships of their underlying scientific fields; blood disorders were among the first subjects of study for early geneticists (Kevles 1995/1985). In considering how the essentialist model of race has changed shape over time, then, it is important to recognize that meaningful conceptual continuities have paved the way for transitions.

Genetic race: An essentialist model for a multiracial America

A final reason that the biological model of race is no longer based on phenotype but on genotype may have to do with the growing racial and ethnic diversity of the United States. Demographic change has made the old phenotypic version of race less defensible but the new genetic framework more plausible. In a sense, this argument reprises my claim that the rigidity of phenotypical taxonomies led to their demise in American biology textbooks. But here I seek to explain why their sharply bounded, mutually exclusive categories came to seem problematic when they did, in the 1960s and 1970s. Three factors likely played a role in these texts' ultimate rejection of phenotype-based race definitions: textbook authors' ongoing concern with the complexity of racial classification, their belated acknowledgment that racial heterogeneity existed within the United States and not just abroad, and the changes in immigration and intermarriage trends that made the nation even more phenotypically complex than it was before.

When mid-century textbook authors lamented the challenges of racial categorization, two kinds of people were most often presented as stymieing scientists' classificatory efforts. On one hand were those, such as Australian aborigines or Asian Indians, who did not fit neatly into the traditional Linnaean "white," "black," "yellow" or "red" categories; on the other were "mixed" groups. As Smith (1954) reported in a section of *Exploring Biology* entitled "Mixed Peoples":

> There are many peoples living today whom anthropologists cannot classify in any one of the main stocks of men. They seem to fit somewhere between two or more of these stocks . . . The Polynesians seem to be a blend of Caucasoids with Malayan Mongoloids and with Negritos and Negroes. The Melanesians seem to be an old blend of several stocks. Some of the peoples of India are considered blends of Mediterraneans with Negritos or some primitive group of Mongoloids. (494)

The classificatory challenges posed by such peoples might have been manageable as long as American textbooks continued to envision racial diversity as a global phenomenon rather than one that obtained within our national borders. The sculptor Malvina Hoffman's 1930s' series "The Races of Mankind"—some of whose busts and figures were reproduced in the American biology textbooks I studied—exemplifies this earlier, global positioning of racial difference. As she recounted in *Heads and Tales* (1936), Hoffman traveled around the world in search of models of each race in what we might call their "natural habitats." Her sculptures aimed to capture not only their representative phenotypical characteristics but the accoutrements she believed were part and parcel of their racial nature: the Chinese man with his rickshaw, the African with his drum, the Native American with his headdress. For the readers of mid-twentieth century biology textbooks, racial difference was something that was located overseas in markedly different cultural settings.

Gradually, however, American textbook authors came to depict racial heterogeneity as a national rather than solely an international phenomenon. Compare the racial taxonomies presented in Figures 5 and 6: for example, the first, from 1952, identifies whites as "Nordic," "Mediterranean," "Alpine," and "Hindu"—in other words, linking each (sub)race to a geographic region outside the United States. In contrast, the second taxonomy, from 1976, features representatives of the "Caucasoid" and "Negroid" races whose dress identifies them as both American, rather than inhabitants of two distinct and distant continents. In short, "the races of man" came home in the civil rights era.

Biology textbooks' new depiction of racial diversity as a home-grown (and not just overseas) phenomenon appeared just as Americans were becoming aware of the impact of two important demographic events of the 1960s. Both brought the dilemma of classifying mixed-race or "non-Linnaean" groups to American shores, making clear this was as much of a challenge at home as it had seemed abroad.

The first demographic development to note is the Immigration and Nationality Act of 1965, which lifted national-origin quotas that had encouraged northwestern European immigration and discouraged inflows from Asia and elsewhere (Massey 1995). Coupled with ongoing immigration streams from Latin America (especially Mexico), the 1965 Act ushered in an era of large-scale immigration that is making the United States ever more heterogeneous in racial and ethnic terms—and consequently more difficult to classify using our long-standing Linnaean taxonomy. In 1950, 90 percent of the population was classified as white on the census; in 2000, that figure had dropped to 75 percent, and it would be below 70 percent if it did not include Hispanics (U.S. Census Bureau 1953, 2001a). Moreover, the nonwhite segment of the population has itself become increasingly diverse, with much of that heterogeneity coming from people who do not fit neatly in traditional American racial categories. Latinos, who now make up the largest minority group in the nation (U.S. Census Bureau 2001b), are difficult to classify in our standard racial terms, especially since there is no "Hispanic" racial option on the census. For decades many people of Hispanic descent have refused to be corralled into the black / white / Asian / American Indian census boxes and have instead described themselves as "Some other race" in large numbers (Rodríguez 2000). They are not the only group that tests the U.S. classification framework, however: South Asians such as Indians and Pakistanis, whose numbers have increased dramatically in the wake of the 1965 immigration act, as well as people of Middle Eastern or North

African descent, also raise questions about our usual race categories (Morning 2001; Samhan 1999). Such groups "fill in" or represent the geographic areas between the spatially separate groups we have labeled races—such as Western European-origin "whites," sub-Saharan African "blacks," and Eastern Asians—and whose boundaries and differences therefore seemed obvious (Marks 1995). By admitting members of spatially intermediary groups, such as North Africans or South Asians, our current immigration regime calls the distinctiveness of racial boundaries—and thus essential race itself—into question.

The other event with demographic repercussions—or interpretations—to be noted is the 1967 Supreme Court decision *Loving v. State of Virginia*, which struck down all state bans on interracial marriage (F. Davis 1991). The importance of the *Loving* case lies not in its actual impact on the number of interracial marriages or the size of the multiracial population, but rather in its raising popular awareness of multiraciality. Given the long history of interracial unions in the United States (Forbes 1993; Nash 1995; Sollors 2000) in spite of legal bans, there was already a large multiracial population prior to 1967. As far back as 1918, the Census Bureau estimated that three-quarters of the Negro population was in fact of mixed-race heritage, and large numbers of other Americans combined white and American Indian ancestry. Using 1990 census data, I have estimated that taking such historical patterns of intermixture into account, roughly 40 percent of the U.S. population could be considered to be mixed-race (Morning 2000). Thus it is unlikely that post-1967 interracial marriages, which remain in the single digits as a share of all married couples (U.S. Census Bureau 1994, 2003), have significantly increased that already-large base of multiracial people.

What has changed more radically than the size of the multiple-race population is the societal recognition of multiraciality (DaCosta 2007). Ever since interracial marriage was legalized throughout the nation, we have increasingly acknowledged mixed-race identity in its own right rather than insisting on the long-standing convention of assigning mixed people to one race or the other. Nowhere has this new recognition been more apparent than in the 1997 revision of the Office of Management and Budget's racial classification standards to permit individuals to identify themselves on federal forms with more than one race, including most importantly the decennial census.

Again, this "new," mixed-race demographic group, like the post-1965 immigrants, challenges our conventional racial categories. Although the federal government has addressed this complication by allowing people to identify with multiple races on the census and other official forms, the growing recognition of multiraciality, like the increasing presence of immigrants who are not clearly black or white (or "yellow" or "red"), still entails a diversification of the phenotypes that Americans attempt to classify in their everyday comings and goings. The question "What are you?" that mixed-race people frequently encounter speaks to the way in which our demographic diversification—whether through immigration or interracial mixing—calls into question the old textbook assumption that racial categories are obvious, straightforward, or immediately recognizable from one's physiognomy.

Why didn't immigration and intermarriage trends completely discredit biological notions of race? I have argued that political life—especially post–civil rights era ideology—better explains the return or redemption of racial essentialism, while population shifts better account for the particular (genetic) form it has taken. As many noted scholars have observed, race is fundamentally a political idea, a tool for distributing and justifying rights and privileges (Hannaford 1996; Omi and Winant 1994). Its endurance is thus more closely tied to the structure of the societies it inhabits (Bonilla-Silva 1996) than it is to the empirical logic or scientific pronouncements of the day.

The genetic recasting of biological race, however, has made its return possible. Geneticization associated race with a new and prestigious branch of science—human genetics—which is effectively closed to scrutiny by outsiders without the requisite professional training and materiel. Furthermore, it removed the rigid requirement of discrete, clear-cut difference that the phenotypic model of race had embodied. Grounding race in DNA helped preserve racial essentialism by decoupling it from surface phenotypes that were becoming ever more varied—and thus more difficult to place—and linking it instead to biological characteristics that few can examine and question. On one hand, if my neighbor is

Mexican American and my doctor is Pakistani, I may find the traditional phenotype-based "Caucasoid"/"Negroid"/"Mongoloid" scheme questionable: how can I neatly put the people around me into these boxes? If on the other hand I learn that racial membership is determined at the genetic level, and not by some algorithm for weighing people's surface traits, I may be more confident that scientists have come up with a reliable and accurate method for detecting race through the analysis of DNA. According to a genetic model, race need not be visually, phenotypically apparent in order to exist; even if I personally cannot tell what race my neighbor is just by looking at her, that does not mean that she does not have a race, or that it is not encoded in some way in her body. It removes the requirement that racial membership be visible or obvious to the common person—that it "look like" anything in particular at all. For this reason, genetic race—at least as it is taught today—is the perfect kind of race for a multiracial America.

Explaining essentialism in a "postracial" era

In the Introduction to this book, I remarked on the irony of biological race flourishing in our ostensibly postracial and multiracial era. Considering how racial essentialism came to be redeemed leads me to conclude however that belief in physical race fits comfortably with the rosy self-portrait of our nation as beyond racism. Racial essentialism is not only perfectly consistent with the claim that societal discrimination no longer exists, it is a helpful tool for explaining why race differentials still obtain in income, education, and just about any other measure of social status. In fact, it would be much harder to maintain that the U.S. is postracial if we did not have inherent biological difference to fall back on as an explanation for inequality. Similarly, despite claims that the existence of multiracial people challenges or refutes traditional race thinking, the nation's growing awareness of multiracialism may have reinforced essentialist belief in biological race. Not just because as Spencer (1999, 2006) points out, the very notion of multiracial identity presupposes the biological mixing of "pure" or single races, but because the complexity of multiracial ancestry made surface-oriented phenotypic definitions of race less persuasive and consequently "buried" or invisible genetic markers of race more plausible. The existence of biological race in a supposedly postracial and multiracial society thus reveals the form and attributes that racial concepts must take on today—the ways in which they must be reconstructed—to make sense in our society as we understand it.

APPENDIX A Textbook Sample Selection and List

The high-school textbooks studied here were selected to represent the most widely used texts in their fields. In the absence of publicly available publisher information on the circulation or revenues of particular textbooks, however, I had to use alternate strategies to determine which books were most popular in the United States.

For the sample of contemporary textbooks in the biological and social sciences, I turned to the curricular lists of "textbook adoption" states to determine which texts are most frequently mandated or recommended. These twenty-three states have centralized their schools' choice or purchase of textbooks to varying degrees, usually by circulating lists of books from which schools are required or encouraged to choose.[1] To determine which texts were most widely used in 2002, I consulted the high-school adoption lists of the six largest adoption states[2]—California, Texas, Florida, North Carolina, Illinois, and Georgia—and noted the frequency with which each biology and social science textbook was listed by a state. For the biology textbooks, I also noted which books had been included in the American Association for the Advancement of Science 2000 assessment of ten "widely-used and newly developed" high-school biology textbooks (Project 2061 2000). Although the original project goal was to acquire not only equal numbers of biology and social-science texts, but equal representation for each social science included, only one anthropology textbook is included because only one such book appeared on the state adoption lists examined, reflecting the rarity with which anthropology is offered at the high-school level in the United States. Although the resulting sample is admittedly a small one, it is used to represent a fairly small underlying population; for example, only about fifty general biology high-school textbooks are in circulation in the United States at present.[3]

To investigate historical developments in textbooks' racial content, I collected a sample of sixty-nine biology textbooks published between 1952 and 1994. Social science texts were not included because courses in anthropology, psychology, and sociology are not only rare in American high schools today, but are likely to have been even more so in the past. Of the sixty-nine historical texts, fifty-two were obtained from a depository library—Columbia University's Teachers College (TC) textbook collection—and seventeen were obtained from the biology department of a private school in Manhattan, the United Nations International School (UNIS), in order to supplement Columbia's holdings from the 1980s and early 1990s.[4] For more information about the historical textbook sample, readers are invited to consult Morning (2008b).

Each textbook studied here was a hardcover that ran several hundred pages long, and it was not unusual for the newest biology textbooks to include over a thousand pages. To narrow down the range of text and illustrations to analyze, I started by simply searching each book's index pages for the terms "race," "ethnicity," human "stocks" or "varieties," and for race group names both current and outmoded, such as "African Americans," "Asians," "blacks," "Caucasoids," "Mongoloids," "Negroids," "Orientals" and "whites." The index pages thus pointed me to sections of the textbooks where race was discussed, and thus to the kinds of topics that came up in conjunction with race. I then drew up a list of all such race-related topics, and after adding to it other topics I thought might prove relevant (for example, Linnaean nomenclature), I systematically searched each textbook's coverage of these topics for mentions of race. In biology books, for example, this meant scrutinizing chapters on heredity, genetics, taxonomy, evolution, populations, and speciation. In particular, I sought out passages that either (1) focused explicitly on race (such as definitions of the term), (2) referred to race without it being the focal topic (e.g., in using racial categories to teach the heredity of skin color), or (3) could be interpreted as making implicit but not explicit references to race (as in linking Europeans to culturally sophisticated hominid ancestors and non-white peoples to "primitive" hominids).[5] Elsewhere I have dubbed these three types of passage "direct," "indirect," and "implicit" discussions of race (Morning 2008b). Pertinent passages (and descriptions of their accompanying visual imagery) were then typed into files that could be coded using the qualitative analysis software program *Atlas.ti*.

1. SOCIAL SCIENCE TEXTBOOKS (BY DISCIPLINE)

Anthropology

Ember, Carol R., Melvin Ember, and Peter N. Peregrine. 2002. *Anthropology*. Upper Saddle River, NJ: Prentice Hall.

Psychology

Kasschau, Richard A. 2001. *Understanding Psychology*. New York: Glencoe/McGraw-Hill.

McMahon, Judith W., and Tony Romano. 2000. *Psychology and You*. Lincolnwood, IL: National Textbook.

Rathus, Spencer. 1998. *Psychology: Principles in Practice*. Austin, TX: Holt, Rinehart and Winston.

Sociology

Calhoun, Craig, Donald Light, and Suzanne Keller. 2001. *Understanding Sociology*. New York: Glencoe/McGraw-Hill.

Macionis, John J. 2001. *Sociology*. Upper Saddle River, NJ: Prentice Hall.

Thomas, W. LaVerne. 1995. *Sociology: The Study of Human Relationships*. Austin, TX: Holt, Rinehart and Winston.

World Culture and Geography

Boehm, Richard G. 2000. *Glencoe World Geography: A Physical and Cultural Approach*. New York: Glencoe/McGraw-Hill.

English, Paul Ward. 1997. *Geography: People and Places in a Changing World*. St. Paul, MN: West.

Farah, Mounir A., Thomas O. Flickema, James Neil Hantula, Ellen C. K. Johnson, Andrea Berens Karls, Abraham Resnick, and Katherine Thermer. 1994. *Global Insights: People and Cultures*. New York: Glencoe/McGraw-Hill.

Helgren, David M., and Robert J. Sager. 2000. *World Geography Today*. Austin, TX: Holt, Rinehart and Winston.

Iftikhar, Ahmad, Herbert Brodsky, Marylee Susan Crofts, and Elisabeth Gaynor Ellis. 2001. *World Cultures: A Global Mosaic*. Upper Saddle River, NJ: Prentice Hall.

2. BIOLOGY TEXTBOOKS (REVERSE CHRONOLOGY)

Contemporary Sample

Biggs, Alton, Kathleen Gregg, Whitney Crispin Hagins, Chris Kapicka, Linda Lundgren, Peter Rillero, and National Geographic Society. 2002. *Biology: The Dynamics of Life*. New York: Glencoe/McGraw-Hill.

Biological Sciences Curriculum Study. 2002. *BSCS Biology: An Ecological Approach (Green Version)*. 9th ed. Dubuque, IA: Kendall/Hunt.

Holt, Rinehart and Winston. *Modern Biology*. 2002. Austin, TX: Holt, Rinehart and Winston.

Miller, Kenneth R., and Joseph S. Levine. 2002. *Prentice Hall Biology*. Upper Saddle River, NJ: Prentice Hall.

Raven, Peter H., and George B. Johnson. 2002. *Biology*. Boston: McGraw-Hill.

Johnson, George B., and Peter H. Raven. 2001. *Biology: Principles and Explorations*. Austin, TX: Holt, Rinehart and Winston.

Strauss, Eric, and Marylin Lisowski. 2000. *Biology: The Web of Life*. Glenview, IL: Scott Foresman–Addison Wesley.

Bernstein, Leonard. 1999. *Globe Biology*. Upper Saddle River, NJ: Globe Fearon.

Johnson, George B. 1998. *Holt Biology: Visualizing Life*. Austin, TX: Holt, Rinehart and Winston.

Leonard, William H., and John E. Penick. 1998. *Biology: A Community Context*. Cincinnati: South-Western Educational.

Biological Sciences Curriculum Study. 1997. *BSCS Biology: A Human Approach*. Dubuque, IA: Kendall/Hunt.

Historic Sample

Curtis, Helena, and N. Sue Barnes. 1994. *Invitation to Biology*. New York: Worth.

Miller, Kenneth R., and Joseph S. Levine. 1993. *Biology*. Englewood Cliffs, NJ: Prentice Hall.

Schraer, William D., and Herbert J. Stoltze. 1993. *Biology: The Study of Life (Annotated Teacher's Edition)*. Needham, MA: Prentice Hall.

Starr, Cecie, and Ralph Taggart. 1992. *Biology: The Unity and Diversity of Life*. Belmont, CA: Wadsworth.

Starr, Cecie. 1991. *Biology: Concepts and Applications*. Belmont, CA: Wadsworth.

Biological Sciences Curriculum Study. 1990. *Biological Science: A Molecular Approach (Blue Version)*. 6th ed. Lexington, MA: D. C. Heath.

Bledsoe, Lucy Jane. 1990. *Fearon's Biology.* Belmont, CA: Fearon Education.

Hopson, Janet L., and Norman K. Wessells. 1990. *Essentials of Biology.* New York: McGraw-Hill.

Arms, Karen, and Pamela S. Camp. 1988. *Biology: A Journey into Life.* Philadelphia: Saunders College.

Biological Sciences Curriculum Study. 1987. *Biological Science: An Ecological Approach (Green Version).* 6th ed. Dubuque, IA: Kendall/Hunt.

Schraer, William D., and Herbert J. Stoltze. 1987. *Biology: The Study of Life (Teacher's Guide).* Newton, MA: Allyn and Bacon.

Alexander, Peter, Mary Jean Bahret, Judith Chaves, Gary Courts, and Naomi Skolky D'Alessio. 1986. *Silver Burdett Biology (Teacher's Edition).* Morristown, NJ: Silver Burdett.

Johnson, Leland G., and Rebecca L. Johnson. 1986. *Essentials of Biology.* Dubuque, IA: William C. Brown.

Otto, James H., and Albert Towle. 1985. *Modern Biology.* New York: Holt, Rinehart and Winston.

Heimler, Charles H., Lucy Daniel, and J. David Lockard. 1984. *Focus on Life Science.* Columbus, OH: Charles E. Merrill.

Kormondy, Edward J., and Bernice E. Essenfeld. 1984. *Addison-Wesley Biology.* Menlo Park, CA: Addison-Wesley.

Smallwood, William L., and Peter Alexander. 1984. *Biology.* Morristown, NJ: Silver Burdett.

Balzer, LeVon, Phyllis L. Goodson, Irwin L. Slesnick, Lois Laver, Ann Collins, and Gretchen M. Alexander. 1983. *Scott, Foresman Life Science.* Glenview, IL: Scott Foresman.

Kimball, John W. 1983. *Biology.* Menlo Park, CA: Benjamin/Cummings.

Magnoli, Michael A., Penelope H. Bauer, and Joyce J. Pinkston. 1983. *Experiences in Life Science (Teacher's Edition).* River Forest, IL: Laidlaw Brothers.

Arms, Karen, and Pamela S. Camp. 1982. *Biology.* Philadelphia: Saunders College.

Baker, Jeffrey J. W., and Garland E. Allen. 1982. *The Study of Biology.* Reading, MA: Addison-Wesley.

Biological Sciences Curriculum Study. 1982. *Biological Science: An Ecological Approach (Green Version, Teacher's Edition).* 5th ed. Boston: Houghton Mifflin.

Kilburn, Robert E., and Peter S. Howell. 1981. *Exploring Life Science.* Boston: Allyn and Bacon.

Biological Sciences Curriculum Study. 1980. *Biological Science: A Molecular Approach (Blue Version).* 4th ed. Lexington, MA: D. C. Heath & Co.

Carter, Joseph, Howard P. Goodman, Danny D. Hunter, and Leroy J. Schelske. 1979. *Life Science: A Problem Solving Approach.* Lexington, MA: Ginn.

Stone, A. Harris, and Lloyd R. Sherman. 1978. *Spaceship Earth Life Science.* Boston: Houghton Mifflin.

Baker, Jeffrey J. W., and Garland E. Allen. 1977. *The Study of Biology.* Reading, MA: Addison-Wesley.

Weinberg, Stanley L., and Herbert J. Stoltze. 1977. *Action Biology.* Boston: Allyn and Bacon.

Oram, Raymond F., Paul J. Hummer Jr., and Robert C. Smoot. 1976. *Biology: Living Systems.* Columbus, OH: Charles E. Merrill.

Kimball, John W. 1974. *Biology.* Reading, MA: Addison-Wesley.

Rahn, Joan E. 1974. *Biology: The Science of Life.* New York: Macmillan.

Weinberg, Stanley L., and Herbert J. Stoltze. 1974. *Action Biology.* Boston: Allyn and Bacon.

Biological Sciences Curriculum Study. 1973. *Biological Science: An Ecological Approach (Green Version).* 3rd ed. Chicago: Rand McNally.

Biological Sciences Curriculum Study. 1973. *Biological Science: An Inquiry into Life (Yellow Version).* 3rd ed. New York: Harcourt Brace Jovanovich.

Biological Sciences Curriculum Study. 1973. *Biological Science: Molecules to Man (Blue Version).* 3rd ed. Boston: Houghton Mifflin.

Otto, James H., and Albert Towle. 1973. *Modern Biology.* New York: Holt, Rinehart and Winston.

Eisman, Louis, and Charles Tanzer. 1972. *Biology and Human Progress.* Englewood Cliffs, NJ: Prentice Hall.

Morholt, Evelyn, Paul F. Brandwein, and Lawrence S. Ward. 1972. *Biology: Patterns in the Environment.* New York: Harcourt Brace Jovanovich.

Brown, Walter R., and Norman D. Anderson. 1971. *Life Science: A Search for Understanding.* Philadelphia: J. B. Lippincott.

Trump, Richard F., and Roger Volker. 1971. *Foundations of Life Science.* New York: Holt, Rinehart and Winston.

Brandwein, Paul F., Alfred D. Beck, Violet Strahler, Matthew J. Brennan, and Daniel S. Turner. 1970. *The Earth: Its Living Things.* New York: Harcourt Brace Jovanovich.

Jacobson, Willard J., Gladys S. Kleinman, Paul S. Hiack, Albert B. Carr, and John S. Sugerbaker. 1969. *Inquiry into Biological Science.* New York: American Book.

Weisz, Paul B. 1969. *Elements of Biology.* New York: McGraw-Hill.

Biological Sciences Curriculum Study. 1968. *Biological Science: Molecules to Man (Blue Version).* Revised. Boston: Houghton Mifflin.

Brandwein, Paul F., R. Will Burnett, and Robert Stollberg. 1968. *Life: Its Forms and Changes.* New York: Harcourt, Brace & World.

Smallwood, William L., and Edna R. Green. 1968. *Biology.* Morristown, NJ: Silver Burdett.

Nelson, Gideon E., Gerald G. Robinson, and Richard A. Boolotian. 1967. *Fundamental Concepts of Biology*. New York: John Wiley.

Fitzpatrick, Frederick L., Thomas D. Bain, and Harold E. Teter. 1966. *Living Things*. New York: Holt, Rinehart and Winston.

Fitzpatrick, Frederick L., and John W. Hole. 1966. *Modern Life Science*. New York: Holt, Rinehart and Winston.

Smith, Ella T., and Thomas G. Lawrence. 1966. *Exploring Biology: The Science of Living Things*. New York: Harcourt, Brace & World.

Gregory, William H., and Edward H. Goldman. 1965. *Biological Science for High School*. Boston: Ginn.

Nason, Alvin. 1965. *Textbook of Modern Biology*. New York: John Wiley.

Brandwein, Paul F., Alfred D. Beck, Violet Strahler, Leland G. Hollingworth, and Matthew J. Brennan. 1964. *The World of Living Things*. New York: Harcourt, Brace & World.

MacCracken, Helen D., Donald G. Decker, John G. Read, Alton Yarian, and William H. Creswell Jr. 1964. *Basic Life Science*. Syracuse, NY: L. W. Singer.

American Institute of Biological Sciences Biological Sciences Curriculum Study. 1963. *Biological Science: Molecules to Man (Blue Version)*. Boston: Houghton Mifflin.

Moon, Truman J., James H. Otto, and Albert Towle. 1963. *Modern Biology*. New York: Holt, Rinehart and Winston.

Smith, Ella T., and Lorenzo Lisonbee. 1962. *Your Biology*. New York: Harcourt, Brace & World.

American Institute of Biological Sciences Biological Sciences Curriculum Study. 1961. *High School Biology (Blue Version)*. Revised. Boulder, CO: American Institute of Biological Sciences.

American Institute of Biological Sciences Biological Sciences Curriculum Study. 1961. *High School Biology (Green Version)*. Revised. Boulder, CO: American Institute of Biological Sciences.

American Institute of Biological Sciences Biological Sciences Curriculum Study. 1961. *High School Biology (Yellow Version)*. Revised. Boulder, CO: American Institute of Biological Sciences.

Weisz, Paul B. 1961. *Elements of Biology*. New York: McGraw-Hill.

Kroeber, Elsbeth, Walter H. Wolff, and Richard L. Weaver. 1960. *Biology*. Boston: D. C. Heath.

Baker, Arthur O., Lewis H. Mills, and Julius Tanczos Jr. 1959. *New Dynamic Biology*. New York: Rand McNally.

Gramet, Charles, and James Mandel. 1958. *Biology Serving You*. Englewood Cliffs, NJ: Prentice Hall.

Curtis, Francis D., and John Urban. 1955. *Biology in Daily Life*. Boston: Ginn.

Smith, Ella Thea. 1954. *Exploring Biology*. New York: Harcourt, Brace.

Whaley, W. Gordon, Osmond P. Breland, Charles Heimsch, Austin Phelps, and Glenn Rabideau. 1954. *Principles of Biology*. New York: Harper & Brothers.

Smallwood, William M., Ida L. Reveley, Guy A. Bailey, and Ruth A. Dodge. 1952. *Elements of Biology*. Boston: Allyn and Bacon.

APPENDIX B Interview Research Design
and Methodology

To locate faculty and undergraduates to interview, I made a series of decisions about which universities to target, and within that group, which kinds of professors and students to approach. In the next few pages, I briefly describe the procedures by which I selected particular campuses and sampled specific individuals.

SELECTION OF UNIVERSITY SITES

I decided to conduct research at more than one institution of higher learning in order to widen the range of scientists and undergraduates with whom I might speak, and to explore whether different campus settings seemed to foster different ways of thinking about race. At the same time, I limited my sample by focusing only on PhD-granting universities, rather than including community colleges that grant two-year degrees or colleges that offer only four-year bachelor's programs. This requirement was motivated by my expectation that PhD-granting departments would be larger than others and thus facilitate my interviewing multiple faculty members within the same discipline on the same campus. I also limited the list of institutions to consider by focusing, for budgetary reasons, on campuses in the northeastern United States.

Another central feature of the project design was my decision to compare concepts of race between the social and natural sciences by focusing on anthropologists on one hand and biologists on the other. These two disciplines are among the scientific fields that have historically been most involved in debate concerning the nature of racial difference, and consequently I expected their practitioners might be particularly likely to convey notions of race to their students, directly or indirectly. To investigate the ideas of race that anthropological or biological training tended to transmit, in my interviews with undergraduates I also concentrated on anthropology and biology majors, but I included equal numbers of randomly selected students from other majors for purposes of comparison. The decision to target anthropology and biology instruction had an impact on the kinds of universities I considered because it prodded me to concentrate on campuses with large enough faculties in these disciplines to cover several relevant subfields, which I could compare to each other. Specifically, I searched for schools whose anthropology departments had both physical and cultural or linguistic anthropologists on the faculty, and whose biological scientists included specialists in both evolutionary biology and genetics. The result of this winnowing process was a list of nine campuses from which to choose (American Anthropological Association 2000; Peterson's 2001a; The College Board 2000).

From these I eventually selected four universities that would permit me to compare racial conceptualization at institutions that differed in two important respects. First, I wanted to contrast "elite" versus "non-elite" universities, since previous research suggested their differences might be meaningful when it came to ideas of race. To gauge university eliteness, I used college tuition prices, admissions selectivity, and entrance difficulty as indicators (see Peterson's 2001b). Second, I sought to compare universities in terms of their racial diversity.[1] Although previous researchers had done little work in this area, I wondered whether the greater or lesser presence of nonwhite students might be related to the ways that faculty and undergraduates conceive of racial difference. With these two factors in mind, I chose three campuses to serve as main interview sites: "City" University to represent non-elite, nondiverse institutions; "State" University to represent non-elite, diverse campuses; and "Ivy" University to represent elite and diverse universities. A fourth "Pilot" University, selected for convenience, has characteristics similar to Ivy University but is less racially diverse. Table 6 summarizes the characteristics of the four schools in my sample.

Table 6.   University Undergraduate Data, AY 2001–02

University	Undergraduates Enrolled	% White*	Acceptance Rate	University Status	Tuition (In-State)
State	30,000	60	60%	Public	$5,000
City	15,000	85	60%	Public	$5,000
Ivy	5,000	65	10%	Private	$25,000
Pilot	5,000	70	10%	Private	$25,000

SOURCE: National Center for Education Statistics, Integrated Postsecondary Education Data System (College Opportunities On-Line).

*Percentage of undergraduate student body excluding "Foreign" and "Other" race responses.

NOTE: For confidentiality, figures rounded to the nearest multiple of 5,000 (or 5 in the case of percentage white and acceptance rate).

SAMPLING OF FACULTY INTERVIEWEES

At each university site, publicly available lists of anthropology and biology department faculty served as sampling frames from which to select professors to interview.[2] In each department, I identified faculty who either taught introductory general courses in the 2000–02 period, or who specialized and/or taught in either of two fields of interest. In anthropology departments, these special fields were physical and sociocultural or linguistic anthropology; in biology departments, they were evolutionary biology or genetics. Thus I shaped the sample by teaching and research interest in order to focus on the faculty whose teaching I expected to be either most accessible to undergraduate students (through introductory courses) or most likely to touch in some way on the topic of race.

In each department (except at the Pilot campus), my goal was to interview six randomly sampled professors: two teachers of introductory coursework, and two specialists each in the subfields of interest. To do so, I used stratified random sampling. In addition, I solicited biologists and anthropologists not otherwise sampled whose online research descriptions explicitly referred to race or racial categories. Finally, I made a special effort to include women in the sample, in order to compare male and female perspectives. Despite such efforts, however, the gender composition of the departments I targeted meant that only slightly over one-third of the faculty interviewees were women.

SAMPLING OF STUDENT INTERVIEWEES

At the same time as I interviewed professors at City, State, Ivy, and Pilot Universities, I also conducted interviews with fifty-two undergraduate students—juniors or seniors—on the same campuses. The sample included primarily those students majoring in either anthropology or biology, but a smaller number of students in other majors were randomly selected from the undergraduate body for purposes of comparison. Anthropology and biology students were generally randomly selected from their departments' lists of majors, and students in other majors were sampled randomly from campus directories.

An important difference in my recruitment of students relative to faculty was that I did not use "follow-up" procedures with students, that is, e-mails or phone calls to solicit interviews from individuals who had not yet responded to the initial invitation letter I had mailed them. As a result, response rates for undergraduates were considerably lower than those for faculty: 44 percent for students versus a 77 percent response rate for professors. (This is an unweighted departmental mean, averaging across the minimum response rate of 46 percent at State University anthropology to the maximum of 100 percent at State University biology and City University anthropology.) However, I used the incentive of a $20 payment for each student interview to encourage participation.

SAMPLE REPRESENTATIVENESS

My intent in constructing the sample of college professors was to talk to people who were not necessarily experts on the topic of race, or even particularly interested in it, but who were representative of the academics who teach undergraduate courses that are likely to touch in some way on the nature of race. In short, I wanted to interview "rank and file" instructors who might be most likely to grapple with defining race as part of their teaching duties or to convey ideas about race to undergraduate audiences.

By tailoring my sample to this objective, however—for example, by purposely shaping it in terms of professors' discipline, teaching portfolios, and research specialization—it is not easy to generalize findings from this research to an immediately recognizable population such as "U.S. college professors." Not only is the sample small, but it is limited to one region (the Northeast), two disciplines (anthropology and biology), and PhD-granting institutions only. In 2002, when this research was conducted, only 6 percent of U.S. postsecondary institutions granted doctoral degrees; in contrast, 44 percent were two-year colleges (National Center for Education Statistics 2003, Table 244). However, limiting the sample to faculty in PhD-granting departments has the advantage of focusing on the segment of the professoriate most easily equated with the "producers" of racial knowledge—those who "control professional training" as Littlefield et al. (1982) put it. In other words, this sample opens a window into the concepts of race held by the social and biological scientists whose ideas are most likely to be disseminated in their disciplines' research literature and to influence future generations of scholars in their fields.

Similarly, the undergraduate students I spoke with cannot be considered simply representative of the American lay public at large. They included just a thin slice of the general population's age range—a cohort of youth aged roughly nineteen to twenty-two—and were largely from the northeastern United States. Equally important, their college enrollment (especially in PhD-granting universities) set them apart; in 2002, only 27 percent of Americans twenty-five and older had completed four years of college (National Center for Education Statistics 2004). However, I turn to this college population in order to examine the encounter between research scientists and the segment of the public that is most directly exposed to their views. In other words, I trade the generalizability of my sample for the vantage point it offers on the transmission of scientific concepts to nonscientists. This relatively privileged, young sample is also significant for another reason: it is precisely from the ranks of the college-educated that we can expect future professionals, policy makers, and academics to be drawn, making it likely that their eventual understandings of race will be disproportionately influential in the years to come.

INTERVIEW STRATEGY

I conducted and audiotaped private interviews in campus offices, laboratories, and conference rooms between November 2001 and April 2002, with each interview usually lasting a little over an hour. My interview questionnaire was structured around a series of open-ended questions (rather than, say, multiple-choice items) in order to gather data in an exploratory mode that avoided imposing a preconceived range of answers or arguments. Open-ended questions combined with frequent probes (i.e., impromptu follow-up questions to elicit detail or clarification) made it possible to investigate the nuances of respondents' views, including the arguments, claims, and values that underpinned their beliefs. The interview instruments can be found in Appendices C (faculty questionnaire) and D (student questionnaire).

APPENDIX C Faculty Questionnaire

A. ACADEMIC BACKGROUND AND RESEARCH

I'd like to start off asking about your academic background and research.

F1   I saw on the Web that you earned your Ph.D. at _____. Is that correct?

F2   Which field(s) was your graduate degree in?

F3   Did you major in the same field in college?

F4   Where did you go to college?

F5   How would you describe the kind of research you currently specialize in?

F6   What topics do you usually teach here, say in the last three years?

F7   Do you teach undergraduate students? Graduate students?

As I mentioned, I'm interested in exploring with you today the ways in which the topic of race may come up in research and teaching in your discipline.

A1   Let's start with the undergraduate courses your department offers: do you think the topic of race (or race-related issues) comes up much in those classes?

A2   When race is discussed in your department's undergraduate classes, what kinds of issues is it usually connected to?

F8   How about research in your field—do you think race is used much?

F9   Can you think of examples of how race is used in research in your field?

B.   CONCEPTUALIZATION OF RACE

At this point I'd like to ask you a little more about how you define the term "race."

A3   For example, if a student in one of your classes asked you to give a definition of the term "race," what would you say?

A4   What kind of evidence do you think best illustrates or supports this understanding of race?

A5   In your view, what are the primary differences that distinguish racial groups?

A6   And how would you say racial differences come about—what causes them?

A7   Do you think there are biological differences between different races? Why or why not?

C.   RACE IN CONTEXT

I've been asking you for your views on the concept of race, but now I'd like to ask you about how other people on campus talk about race. To start off, I'd like to move outside the classroom and ask you a little about how the topic of race may come up in everyday conversations on campus.

A8   In general, would you say the topic of race comes up often at this university?

A9   In connection with what kinds of topics is race usually brought up?

Now I'm going to ask you how you think various groups of academics might define the concept of race. I'll do this by showing you a printed statement and first asking for your opinion, but then asking you to guess how other groups of academics would react.

A10 The statement I am going to ask you about is taken from a survey that was conducted among college professors. After you've read it, I'd like to know whether you agree or disagree with it. (*Hand over card, which reads: "There are biological races within the species Homo sapiens."*) Now, how would you describe your reaction to this statement—agree or disagree?

A11 *Why* do you [agree]/[disagree]?

A12 Let's stick with this statement for a minute. How do you think that most of your colleagues in your discipline would react to it—in general, do you think they would agree or disagree? Why?

F10 And what about academics in the social sciences/the biological sciences (*choose grouping that is not the respondent's*)—in general, do you think they would agree or disagree with this statement? Why?

A13 What about Americans in general, the public—do you think most Americans would agree or disagree with the statement I showed you?

F11 Do you think that the kind of research that is now being conducted on the human genome will have an effect on what or how people think about race?

D. BACKGROUND

Thank you so much for your patience so far. For this last part of the interview, I'd like to ask you a few questions about your background.

A14 How old are you?

A15 What part of the country are you from originally?

A16 Is that where you spent most of your childhood?

A17 What were your parents' occupations when you were growing up?
Father: _____ Mother: _____

A18 Do you know how much education your parents completed?
Father: _____ Mother: _____

A19 What was the racial makeup of your community like?

A20 Were ethnic or religious identities important to people in your community?

A21 Did your elementary and secondary schools tend to have the same racial and ethnic makeup as your home community?

A22 How do you usually describe yourself in terms of race?

A23 Would you say you have any religious affiliation? If so, what is it?

A24 How would you describe your political leanings—for example, in terms of political party affiliation or a liberal-to-conservative spectrum?

. . . . .

A24 Those are all the questions I have for you. Is there anything else that
     you'd like to add—maybe a comment on a related topic I didn't think to
     ask you about?
A25 And are there any questions that you'd like to ask me?

APPENDIX D Student Questionnaire

A1 I know I checked that you are 18 or older, but please remind me how old you are?

A2 So you are a senior or a junior here at the university?

A3 What part of the country are you from originally?

A4 Is that where you spent most of your childhood?

A5 What are your parents' occupations?
Father: _____ Mother: _____

A6 Do you know how much education your parents have completed?
Father: _____ Mother: _____

A7 A lot of the questions I'll ask you today will have to do with how race might come up in the classroom here. But before we get to that, I'm curious to know a little about the racial makeup of the community where you grew up—how would you characterize it?

A8   Are ethnic or religious identities important to people in your home community?

A9   Did your elementary and secondary schools tend to have the same racial and ethnic makeup as your home community?

A10   How do you usually describe yourself in terms of race?

A11   Would you say you have any religious affiliation? If so, what is it?

A12   How would you describe your political leanings—for example, in terms of political party affiliation or a liberal-to-conservative spectrum?

B. EDUCATION

S1   You are majoring in (*name major*)—do you have a second major as well?

S2   How would you characterize your academic experience here at (*name university*): positive, negative, or somewhere in between?

S3   Why do you characterize it that way?

S4   Here I have a list of all the undergraduate majors here at the university. Would you please check off all the areas in which you can recall having completed at least one class so far?

As I mentioned, I'm interested in exploring with you today the ways in which the topic of race may come up in the classroom setting.

S5   Would you say that the topic of race has come up much in the classes you have taken here?

S6   Is race more likely to be a topic of discussion in certain subject areas than others? To answer, you might want to look back at the list of departments in which you've taken classes.

S7   What kinds of issues is race usually connected to in each of these subject areas?

A13   Now let's turn to your department (*name department field*) in particular. In the undergraduate courses offered by your department, does the topic of race (or race-related issues) come up much?

A14   When race is discussed in (*name department*) classes, what kinds of issues is it usually connected to?

In addition to your academic work, I'm also interested in discussions about race that students might have <u>outside</u> the classroom.

A15   In general, would you say the topic of race comes up often at this university?

A16   In connection with what kinds of topics is race usually brought up?

C. CONCEPTUALIZATIONS OF RACE

So far I've asked you several questions related to race and how people talk about it, but I haven't asked you how you define the meaning of the word "race." This might seem like a strange question, since race is such an everyday idea in the United States that we generally don't think very often about how it is defined. But research has shown that different people have different ideas about things like what determines a person's race, or which groups should be considered races.

A17   First of all, if you had to give a definition of the word "race," or explain what it was, what would you say?

A18   What kind of information or facts would you use to support that definition?

A19   What are the main kinds of differences that exist between racial groups; that is, what kinds of things make racial groups different from each other?

A20   Do you think there are biological differences between different races? Why or why not?

A21   How would you say racial differences come about—what causes them?

At this point, I'd like to ask you how you think some other groups of people would define the concept of race. I'll do this by showing you a printed statement, and then asking you first for your opinion about it, and then I'll ask you how you think some other people would react to it.

A22   First I'm going to give you a card with a short statement printed on it; this sentence is taken from a survey that was conducted in the 1980s. After you've read the statement, I'd like to know whether you agree or disagree with it. (*Hand over card, which reads: "There are biological races within the species Homo sapiens."*) Now, how would you describe your reaction to this statement: do you agree or disagree?

A23   Why do you [agree]/[disagree]?

A24   Let's stick with this statement for a minute. How do you think that most of your peers—other students here at (*name university*)—would react to it? In general, do you think other students would agree or disagree? Why?

A25   What about Americans in general, the public—do you think most Americans would agree or disagree with the statement I showed you? Why?

Now I'm going to describe to you two scenarios—taken from real life—where racial groups differ in terms of some outcome or phenomenon. In each case, I'll describe the facts of the situation to you, and then ask you to give me a couple of possible explanations for the differences in the experiences of different racial groups. That is, I'd like you to give a couple of plausible reasons that might explain the situations I'll describe to you.

S8   The first scenario I'll describe refers to a biomedical outcome, namely, the weight of babies at birth. Researchers have discovered that at birth, babies of different racial groups tend to have different weights. For example, white babies have among the highest median weight, black babies among the lowest, and Asian babies' weights tend to be in the middle. In your opinion, what are some possible explanations for this finding?

S9   Which do you think is the most likely explanation? Why?

S10   The second scenario I'll describe has to do with sports, and the overrepresentation, or underrepresentation, of certain racial groups in certain sports, compared to their share of the total population of the country. To give you an example from football: in the NFL, blacks make up 67 percent of the players and white athletes are in the minority. But in the total population of the United States as a whole, whites make up the majority and blacks count for only 12 percent of the population. In your opinion, what could be some plausible explanations for why the racial composition of the National Football League is so different from the racial makeup of the country as a whole?

S11   Which explanation do you think is the most likely one? Why?

·   ·   ·   ·   ·

A26   Those are all the questions I have for you. Is there anything else that you'd like to add—maybe a comment on a related topic I didn't think to ask you about?

A27   And are there any questions that you'd like to ask me?

Notes

CHAPTER ONE

1. See "Cystic Fibrosis DNA Testing," Genzyme Genetics 8.99 (n.d.).

2. I use the term *science* to refer to knowledge, to our "systematic attempt[s] to produce knowledge about the natural world" (Harding 1998, 10), and to the people and institutions that contribute to this process—the "scientific enterprise" in short.

3. See the undated "Statement on the Use of DNA Testing to Determine Racial Background" issued jointly by the British Society for Human Genetics and the British Association for Adoption and Fostering. I thank Fiona Peters for bringing it to my attention.

4. I have borrowed these labels for stages in the knowledge dissemination process from literature in the sociology of knowledge that develops such systemic frameworks (e.g., Goldman 1999; Gurvitch 1971; Holzner and Marx 1979).

CHAPTER TWO

1. This abbreviated synopsis is no substitute for the many excellent works that explore in great depth the historical evolution of racial thinking. Readers interested in such accounts might consult the following, among others: *Race: The History of an Idea in the West* (Hannaford 1996); *Racism: A Short History* (Fredrickson 2002); *Race: A Theological Account* (Carter 2008); *The Racial State* (Goldberg 2002); *Human Biodiversity: Genes, Race, and History* (Marks 1995); *Race in North America: Origin and Evolution of a Worldview* (Smedley 2007); *Race: The History of an Idea in America* (Gossett 1997/1963); *Shades of Citizenship: Race and the Census in Modern Politics* (Nobles 2000); *The Retreat of Scientific Racism: Changing Concepts of Race in Britain and the United States between the World Wars* (Barkan 1992); and *Race to the Finish: Identity and Governance in an Age of Genomics* (Reardon 2005).

2. Forerunner of the modern U.S. Census Bureau.

3. The portrayal of race as a misguided fiction endures today. Consider the following titles: *Race: How Blacks and Whites Think and Feel about the American Obsession* (Terkel 1992), *Race and Other Misadventures* (Reynolds and Lieberman 1996), *One Drop of Blood: The American Misadventure of Race* (Malcomson 2000), and "America's Worst Idea" (Patterson 2000).

4. The original 1950 "Statement on Race" was followed by UNESCO's 1951 "Statement on the Nature of Race and Race Differences," its 1964 "Proposals on the Biological Aspects of Race," and the 1967 "Statement on Race and Racial Prejudice" (Montagu 1972).

5. In his own words, Hirschfeld (1996) argues that "human kinds predicated on intrinsicality are a category of the mind which human beings are prepared to hold. The notion of race is the outcome, the consequence, of this preparedness as it makes contact with contexts in which complex relations of power and authority are played out on the group level" (188–89). Moreover, he stresses: "I do not suggest that race is an inevitable consequence of our conceptual endowment. I argue that racial thinking is derived from the operation of a human-kind-creating module, rather than being the output of a racial-kind-creating one" (196). Critiques of Hirschfeld's hypothesis from both within and outside psychology can be found, for example in the 1997 issue of *Ethos* devoted to his work (volume 25, issue 1).

6. This paragraph is taken largely from Ann Morning, "Reconstructing Race in Science and Society: Biology Textbooks, 1952–2002," *American Journal of Sociology* 114 (s1): s106–s137. © 2008 by The University of Chicago. All rights reserved.

7. Excerpts of this section were originally published in Ann Morning, "The Nature of Race: Teaching and Learning about Human Difference" (PhD thesis, Department of Sociology, Princeton University, 2004).

8. However, these persistent gender differences did not drive the social sciences' tilt away from racial essentialism; women made up a smaller percentage (18 percent) of the cultural anthropologists interviewed than they did of biologists (where they represented 23 percent).

9. Although social desirability effects might be seen as obscuring individuals' true beliefs about racial difference, their presence is nonetheless informative. The fact that concern about appearing racist is so pervasive is not only important testimony to changing social mores (Schuman et al. 1997, 8), but the fact that it inhibits biological formulations of racial difference in particular suggests that the link that academics tend to make between essentialist race concepts and racist attitudes is shared by the public.

10. The remainder did not specify their race or ethnicity.

11. A note on terminology: In keeping with sociological practice, I distinguish the terms *prejudice* and *discrimination* by using the former to denote individual-level attitudes and the latter to refer to actions, both of individuals and institutions (Bobo 2001; Bonilla-Silva 1996). *Racism* includes prejudice and discrimination. However, when citing other researchers' arguments I reproduce the language they have used.

12. Interestingly, these results are the mirror opposite of Jayaratne et al.'s (2006) finding that genetic lay theories were associated with more anti-black and less anti-gay prejudice.

CHAPTER THREE

1. In 2000, 93 percent of American adults aged twenty-five and over had attended high school, and 84 percent were high-school graduates (National Center for Education Statistics 2002, 18).

2. Excerpts of this section were originally published in Ann Morning, "The Nature of Race: Teaching and Learning about Human Difference" (PhD thesis, Department of Sociology, Princeton University, 2004).

3. Anthropologist Eugenia Shanklin (2000) studied fifteen college textbooks of cultural anthropology and judged that only five presented "good discussions of both race and racism" (99), by which she meant a constructivist account. The rest either did not mention race, or simply denied its biological validity without giving clear or meaningful explanation. Overall, Shanklin concluded that the introductory texts' approach to race "makes our profession look ignorant, backward, deluded, or uncaring" (101).

4. The majority of the books sampled were designed for high-school curricula, but the sample also includes a few textbooks that were intended for a college audience yet were used to teach advanced high-school courses.

5. Note moreover that three of the four biology textbooks that included definitions of race were coauthored by the same person (George B. Johnson).

6. The sociology textbooks also render race timeless and unchanging by tracing racial classification back to "ancient times" (Thomas 1995, 232) and locating racism in antiquity (Macionis 2001, 359).

7. Troy Duster also uses this metaphor in "Buried Alive: The Concept of Race in Science" (2003).

CHAPTER FOUR

1. Unless specifically indicated otherwise, I apply the term *professor* to all faculty members and teaching staff regardless of their tenure status.

2. Calculations of student racial composition are based on the responses of U.S.-citizen undergraduates who reported a race. The data come from the U.S. Department of Education's online database, Integrated Postsecondary Education Data System (College Opportunities On-Line), at http://nces.ed.gov/collegenavigator/.

3. He attributed the use of the phrase in this context to Vincent Sarich, anthropologist at the University of California at Berkeley and coauthor of *Race: The Reality of Human Differences* (2004).

4. Barbujani (2006) notes that other species have patterns of biological variation that correspond much more closely to our notion of discrete races.

5. The findings of marked subfield differences between anthropologists is not surprising given the strain that the discipline's traditional four-field structure—encompassing cultural anthropology, linguistic anthropology, archaeology, and physical (or biological) anthropology—has come under in recent decades. As Morell (1993, 1798) put it, "biological anthropologists have become deeply involved with the latest tools of molecular biology and theories of evolutionary ecology, while many cultural anthropologists have become caught up in the wave of deconstructionist thinking that has been sweeping the humanities." In other words, the major anthropological subfields have grown more closely aligned with the objectives and practices of other disciplines than with each other.

6. The idea that fear can dissuade people from pursuing truth is central to what Reanne Frank (forthcoming) calls "forbidden knowledge" discourse. According to this narrative about race and human biology, researchers who investigate genetic racial differences are a brave minority who are willing to defy social or political convention—in other words, political correctness—to discover realities that others are unwilling to stomach.

7. See Reardon (2004) for a historical discussion of how changing notions of race have been grounded in an enduring acknowledgment of scientists as the authoritative arbiters of the race concept.

CHAPTER FIVE

Some material in this chapter first appeared in Ann Morning, "Toward a Sociology of Racial Conceptualization for the 21st Century," *Social Forces* 87 (March 2009): 1167–92.

1. Details on the sampling of universities and interviewees can be found in Appendix B.

2. The major exception to the census taxonomy was students' frequent references to Jews as a race apart, distinct from whites. For example, a State University student described her home community as having "a lot of Jewish-descent people," where in contrast "Caucasians and blacks were definitely a minority." A few students, Jewish and non-Jewish, recounted debates with peers about whether Jews constituted a race.

3. Note however that not all fifty-two students interviewed were asked to comment on the Lieberman question; due to time pressure, this question was omitted in three interviews.

4. I did not, however, put these two "real-life" questions to all fifty-two students in the sample. When interviews had run particularly long, I omitted one or both. I asked the first question of thirty-seven (71 percent) and the second question of forty-six (or 89 percent) of the students.

5. In the United States in 1997, babies identified as white had a median weight of 7 lbs. 7 oz., while Asian babies had a median weight of 7 lbs. 2 oz. and black newborns' median weight was 6 lbs. 15 oz. (National Center for Health Statistics 2001).

6. Similarly, Wilson (1996) found that respondents' perceptions of the racial composition of the poor had an effect on how they accounted for poverty.

7. The data cited come from Lapchick and Matthews (2001) and U.S. Census Bureau (2001b).

8. This supposition that the physical results of an individual's activities can be imprinted on their offspring is known as Lamarckianism; for a summary, see Marks (1995).

9. Herrnstein and Murray (1994), *The Bell Curve: Intelligence and Class Structure in American Life*.

CHAPTER SIX

1. No. 88-339 (Sup. Jud. Ct. Suffolk County, Mass. July 25, 1989).

2. Duro v. Reina, 821 F.2d 1358, 1363 (9th Cir. 1987), quoted in Ford (1994, 1264).

CHAPTER SEVEN

1. Part of this section was previously published in Ann Morning, "Reconstructing Race in Science and Society: Biology Textbooks, 1952–2002." *American Journal of Sociology* 114 (2008,s1): s106–37. © 2008 by The University of Chicago. All rights reserved.

2. Genetic genealogy firms effectively claim to be able to identify racial origins in DNA, but their private algorithms are not subject to outside scrutiny, nor have they converged on any single agreed-upon mapping of genes to race.

3. For a comparative overview of modern racism theories, see Sears, Sidanius, and Bobo (2000).

4. Although serotype (blood type) is technically a phenotype as well—that is, an expression of genetic information—I use "phenotype" here in its lay sense of surface or somatic traits.

APPENDIX A

1. The precise number of textbook-adoption states varies slightly over time. Although southern and western states make up the overwhelming majority of adoption states, their textbook selections are not a bad reflection of textbook purchasing around the country. For one thing, the adoption states' large purchasing contracts direct textbook publishers' production so extensively that their choices effectively determine which textbooks are available to the rest of the nation (Keith 1991; Squire and Morgan 1990; Stille 2002). For another, the compression of the American textbook publishing industry to a handful of large conglomerates in recent decades means that the same reduced pool of textbooks is being marketed to both adoption and non-adoption states (Ravitch 1996; Walsh 2000). In 2000, McGraw-Hill (U.S.), Pearson (U.K.), Harcourt/Vivendi (France), Houghton Mifflin/Reed Elsevier (U.K.-Netherlands), and Scholastic (U.S.) earned approximately 90 percent of the sales in the $4.5 billion U.S. textbook market (Education Market Research 2001).

2. Largest in terms of high-school age population aged 15–19 in 2000, according to the U.S. Census Bureau (2001).

3. Author's calculation based on Bowker's *El-Hi Textbooks and Serials in Print 2002.*

4. As a graduate of the high school, I was permitted access to its teaching collection.

5. Hominids are generally considered to include humans and their closest ancestors, comprising the genera *Australopithecus* and *Homo. Homo sapiens* is the only hominid species alive today.

APPENDIX B

1. I labeled "diverse" the campuses with a share of white undergraduates below the national college mean of 75 percent (National Center for Education Statistics 2001).

2. In order to reduce variation introduced by training in diverse cultural backgrounds, however, faculty with doctoral degrees obtained outside the United States were eliminated from consideration.

References

Note: Bibliographic information for the textbooks analyzed in this study is provided in Appendix A.

Abu El-Haj, Nadia. 2007. "The Genetic Reinscription of Race." *Annual Review of Anthropology* 36:283–300.

Ahdied, L., and R. A. Hahn. 1996. "Use of the Terms 'Race', 'Ethnicity', and 'National Origins': A Review of Articles in the *American Journal of Public Health*, 1980–1989." *Ethnicity and Health* 1 (1): 95–98.

Alesina, Alberto, and Edward L. Glaeser. 2004. *Fighting Poverty in the U.S. and Europe: A World of Difference*. Oxford: Oxford University Press.

Allport, Gordon. 1954. *The Nature of Prejudice*. Cambridge, MA: Addison-Wesley.

American Anthropological Association. 1999. "Statement on 'Race.'" *American Anthropologist* 100 (3): 712–13.

———. 2000. *Guide 2000–2001: A Guide to Programs, a Directory of Members*. Arlington, VA: American Anthropological Association.

American Association of Physical Anthropologists. 1996. "Statement on Biological Aspects of Race." *American Journal of Physical Anthropology* 101:569–70.

American Committee for Democracy and Intellectual Freedom. 1939. *Can You Name Them?* New York: American Committee for Democracy and Intellectual Freedom.

American Sociological Association. 2003. *The Importance of Collecting Data and Doing Social Scientific Research on Race.* Washington, DC: American Sociological Association.

Anderson, M. R., and Susan Moscou. 1998. "Race and Ethnicity in Research on Infant Mortality." *Family Medicine* 30 (3): 224–27.

Anderson, Warwick. 2008. "Teaching 'Race' at Medical School: Social Scientists on the Margin." *Social Studies of Science* 38 (October): 785–800.

Angier, Natalie. 2000. "Do Races Differ? Not Really, Genes Show." *New York Times.* August 22, 2000.

Apostle, Richard A., Charles Y. Glock, Thomas Piazza, and Marijean Suelzle. 1983. *The Anatomy of Racial Attitudes.* Berkeley: University of California Press.

Balibar, Etienne. 1991. "Is There a 'Neo-Racism'?" Pp. 17–28 in *Race, Nation, Class: Ambiguous Identities,* edited by Etienne Balibar and Immanuel Wallerstein. London: Verso.

Bamshad, Michael J. 2005. "Genetic Influences on Health: Does Race Matter?" *Journal of the American Medical Association* 294 (8): 937–46.

Bamshad, Michael J., and Steve E. Olson. 2003. "Does Race Exist?" *Scientific American* (December): 80–85.

Barbassa, Juliana. 2009. Mixed-Race Patients with Cancer Struggle to Find Marrow Donors. *Boston Globe,* May 28, 2009. Accessed September 3, 2010. http://www.boston.com/news/health/articles/2009/05/28/mixed_race_pa tients_struggle_to_find_marrow_donors/.

Barbujani, Guido. 2006. *L'invenzione delle razze.* Milan: Bompiani.

Barbujani, Guido, A. Magagni, E. Minch, and L. L. Cavalli-Sforza. 1997. "An Apportionment of Human DNA Diversity." *Proceedings of the National Academy of Sciences* 94:4516–19.

Barkan, Elazar. 1992. *The Retreat of Scientific Racism: Changing Concepts of Race in Britain and the United States between the World Wars.* Cambridge: Cambridge University Press.

Barr, Donald A. 2005. "The Practitioner's Dilemma: Can We Use a Patient's Race to Predict Genetics, Ancestry, and the Expected Outcomes of Treatment?" *Annals of Internal Medicine* 143:809–15.

Bastian, Brock, and Nick Haslam. 2006. "Psychological Essentialism and Stereotype Endorsement." *Journal of Experimental Social Psychology* 42: 228–35.

————. 2007. "Psychological Essentialism and Attention Allocation: Preferences for Stereotype-Consistent versus Stereotype-Inconsistent Information." *Journal of Social Psychology* 147 (October): 531–41.

————. 2008. "Immigration from the Perspective of Hosts and Immigrants: Roles of Psychological Essentialism and Social Identity." *Asian Journal of Social Psychology* 11 (2): 127–40.

Beatty, P. G., K. M. Boucher, M. Mori, and E. L. Milford. 2000. "Probability of Finding HLA-Mismatched Related or Unrelated Marrow or Cord Blood Donors." *Human Immunology* 61:834–40.

Ben-David, Joseph. 1962. "Scientific Productivity and Academic Organization in Nineteenth-Century Medicine." Pp. 305–28 in *The Sociology of Science*, edited by Bernard Barber and Walter Hirsch. New York: Free Press of Glencoe.

Benedict, Ruth, and Gene Weltfish. 1943. *The Races of Mankind*. New York: Public Affairs Committee.

Bhopal, R. 1997. "Is Research into Ethnicity and Health Racist, Unsound, or Important Science?" *British Medical Journal* 314:1751–56.

Blanchard, Pascal, and Nicolas Bancel. 1998. *De l'indigène à l'immigré*. Paris: Gallimard.

Blangiardo, Gian Carlo. 2009. "Gli aspetti quantitativi della presenza straniera in Italia: aggiornamenti e prospettive." Pp. 33–53 in *Quattordicesimo Rapporto sulle migrazioni 2008*, edited by Fondazione ISMU. Milan: FrancoAngeli.

Bobo, Lawrence D. 2001. "Racial Attitudes and Relations at the Close of the Twentieth Century." Pp. 264–301 in *America Becoming: Racial Trends and Their Consequences*, edited by Neil J. Smelser, William Julius Wilson, and Faith Mitchell. Washington, DC: National Academy Press.

Bobo, Lawrence D., James R. Kluegel, and Ryan A. Smith. 1997. "Laissez-Faire Racism: The Crystallization of a Kinder, Gentler, Antiblack Ideology." Pp. 15–42 in *Racial Attitudes in the 1990s: Continuity and Change*, edited by Steven A. Tuch and Jack K. Martin. Westport, CT: Praeger.

Bobo, Lawrence D., and Ryan A. Smith. 1998. "From Jim Crow Racism to Laissez-Faire Racism: The Transformation of Racial Attitudes." Pp. 182–220 in *Beyond Pluralism: The Conception of Groups and Group Identities in America*, edited by Wendy F. Katkin, Ned Landsman, and Andrea Tyree. Urbana and Chicago: University of Illinois Press.

Bolnick, Deborah A., Duana Fullwiley, Troy Duster, Richard S. Cooper, Joan H. Fujimura, Jonathan Kahn, Jay Kaufman, Jonathan Marks, Ann Morning, Alondra Nelson, Pilar Ossorio, Jenny Reardon, Susan M. Reverby, and Kimberly TallBear. 2007. "The Science and Business of Genetic Ancestry." *Science* (October 19): 399–400.

Bonham, Vence L., Sherrill L. Sellers, Thomas H. Gallagher, Danielle Frank, Adebola O. Odunlami, Eboni G. Price, and Lisa A. Cooper. 2009. "Physicians' Attitudes toward Race, Genetics, and Clinical Medicine." *Genetics in Medicine* 11 (April): 279–86.

Bonilla-Silva, Eduardo. 1996. "Rethinking Racism: Toward a Structural Interpretation." *American Sociological Review* 62 (3): 465–80.

———. 2002. "The Linguistics of Color Blind Racism: How to Talk Nasty about Blacks without Sounding 'Racist.'" *Critical Sociology* 28 (1–2): 41–64.

———. 2003. *Racism without Racists: Color-Blind Racism and the Persistence of Racial Inequality in the United States.* Lanham, MD: Rowman and Littlefield.

Braun, Lundy. 2002. "Race, Ethnicity, and Health: Can Genetics Explain Disparities?" *Perspectives in Biology and Medicine* 45 (Spring): 159–74.

———. 2006. "Reifying Human Difference: The Debate on Genetics, Race, and Health." *International Journal of Health Services* 36 (3): 557–73.

Braun, Lundy, Anne Fausto-Sterling, Duana Fullwiley, Evelynn M. Hammonds, Alondra Nelson, William Quivers, Susan M. Reverby, and Alexandra Shields. 2007. "Racial Categories in Medical Practice: How Useful Are They?" *PLoS Medicine* 4 (September): 1423–28.

Brückner, Hannah, Ann Morning, and Alondra Nelson. 2005. "The Expression of Biological Concepts of Race." Paper presented at the Annual Meeting of the American Sociological Association, Philadelphia, August 14, 2005.

Brues, Alice M. 1992. "Forensic Diagnosis of Race—General Race vs Specific Populations." *Social Science & Medicine* 34 (January): 125–28.

Bucchi, Massimiano. 1998. *Science and the Media: Alternative Routes in Scientific Communication.* London and New York: Routledge.

Burchard, Esteban Gonzalez, Elad Ziv, Natasha Coyle, Scarlett Lin Gomez, Hua Tang, Andrew J. Karter, Joanna L. Mountain, Eliseo J. Perez-Stable, Dean Sheppard, and Neil Risch. 2003. "The Importance of Race and Ethnic Background in Biomedical Research and Clinical Practice." *New England Journal of Medicine* 348 (12): 1170–75.

Campbell, Bruce A. 1981. "Race-of-Interviewer Effects among Southern Adolescents." *Public Opinion Quarterly* 45 (Summer): 231–44.

Cann, Rebecca L., M. Stoneking, and A. C. Wilson. 1987. "Mitochondrial DNA and Human Evolution." *Nature* (325): 31–36.

Cao, K., J. Hollenbach, X. Shi, W. Shi, M. Chopek, and M. A. Fernández-Viña 2001. "Analysis of the Frequencies of HLA-A, B, and C Alleles and Haplotypes in the Five Major Ethnic Groups of the United States Reveals High Levels of Diversity in These Loci and Contrasting Distribution Patterns in these Populations." *Human Immunology* 62:1009–30.

Carter, J. Kameron. 2008. *Race: A Theological Account.* New York: Oxford University Press.

Cartmill, Matt. 1999. "The Status of the Race Concept in Physical Anthropology." *American Anthropologist* 100 (3): 651–60.

Cavalli-Sforza, Luigi Luca. 2000. *Genes, Peoples, and Languages*. New York: North Point Press.

Cavalli-Sforza, Luigi Luca, Paolo Menozzi, and Alberto Piazza. 1994. *The History and Geography of Human Genes*. Princeton, NJ: Princeton University Press.

Chamberlain, Houston Stewart. 1911. *The Foundations of the Nineteenth Century*. London and New York: John Lane.

Chowkwanyun, Merlin. 2007. "Race against History: Why Genes Don't Determine Race." *The New Republic Online*, June 11, 2007. Accessed September 3, 2010. http://www.tnr.com/article/race-against-history.

Clark, William. 2006. *Academic Charisma and the Origins of the Research University*. Chicago: University of Chicago Press.

The College Board. 2000. *The College Board Index of Majors and Graduate Degrees*. New York: The College Board.

Condit, Celeste M. 2004. "The Meaning and Effects of Discourse about Genetics: Methodological Variations in Studies of Discourse and Social Change." *Discourse & Society* 15 (4): 391–407.

Condit, Celeste M., Roxanne L. Parrott, B. R. Bates, Jennifer Bevan, and P. J. Achter. 2004a. "Exploration of the Impact of Messages about Genes and Race on Lay Attitudes." *Clinical Genetics* 66 (5): 402–08.

Condit, Celeste M., Roxanne L. Parrott, and Tina M. Harris. 2002. "Lay Understandings of the Relationship between Race and Genetics: Development of a Collectivized Knowledge through Shared Discourse." *Public Understanding of Science* 11 (October): 373–87.

Condit, Celeste M., Roxanne L. Parrott, Tina M. Harris, John Lynch, and Tasha Dubriwny. 2004b. "The Role of 'Genetics' in Popular Understandings of Race in the United States." *Public Understanding of Science* 13 (3): 249–72.

Condit, Celeste M., Alan Templeton, Benjamin Bates, Jennifer Bevan, and Tina M. Harris. 2003. "Attitudinal Barriers to Delivery of Race-Targeted Pharmacogenomics among Informed Lay Persons." *Genetics in Medicine* 5:385–92.

Conner, Clifford D. 2005. *A People's History of Science: Miners, Midwives, and "Low Mechanicks"*. New York: Nation Books.

Cooper, Richard S. 2003. "Race, Genes, and Health—New Wine in Old Bottles?" *International Journal of Epidemiology* 32:23–25.

Cooper, Richard S., Jay S. Kaufman, and Ryk Ward. 2003. "Race and Genomics." *New England Journal of Medicine* 348 (March 20): 1166–70.

Cosmides, Leda, John Tooby, and Robert Kurzban. 2003. "Perceptions of Race." *TRENDS in Cognitive Sciences* 7 (April): 173–79.

Cotter, Patrick R., Jeffrey Cohen, and Philip B. Coulter. 1982. "Race-of-Interviewer Effects in Telephone Interviews." *Public Opinion Quarterly* 46 (Summer): 278–84.

Council on Interracial Books for Children. 1977. *Stereotypes, Distortions and Omissions in U.S. History Textbooks: A Content Analysis Instrument for Detecting Racism and Sexism, Supplemental Information on Asian American, Black, Chicano, Native American, Puerto Rican, and Women's History.* New York: Racism and Sexism Resource Center for Educators.

DaCosta, Kimberly McClain. 2007. *Making Multiracials: State, Family, and Market in the Redrawing of the Color Line.* Stanford, CA: Stanford University Press.

Daniel, G. Reginald. 2002. *More Than Black? Multiracial Identity and the New Racial Order.* Philadelphia: Temple University Press.

Dávila, Arlene. 2001. *Latinos, Inc: The Marketing and Making of a People.* Berkeley: University of California Press.

Davis, Darren W. 1997. "Nonrandom Measurement Error and Race of Interviewer Effects among African Americans." Special Issue on Race, *Public Opinion Quarterly* 61 (Spring): 183–207.

Davis, Floyd James. 1991. *Who Is Black? One Nation's Definition.* University Park: Pennsylvania State University Press.

de Chadarevian, Soraya, and Harmke Kamminga, eds. 1998. *Molecularizing Biology and Medicine: New Practices and Alliances, 1910s–1970s.* Amsterdam: Harwood Academic.

DeGenova, Nicholas. 2006. "Introduction: Latino and Asian Racial Formations at the Frontier of U.S. Nationalism." Pp. 1–20 in *Racial Transformations: Latinos and Asians Remaking the United States,* edited by Nicholas DeGenova. Durham, NC: Duke University Press.

Demoulin, Stéphanie, Jacques-Philippe Leyens, and Vincent Yzerbyt. 2006. "Lay Theories of Essentialism." *Group Processes & Intergroup Relations* 9 (1): 25–42.

Dubriwny, Tasha N., Benjamin R. Bates, and Jennifer L. Bevan. 2004. "Lay Understandings of Race: Cultural and Genetic Definitions." *Community Genetics* 7 (4): 185–95.

Duster, Troy. 1984. "A Social Frame for Biological Knowledge." Pp. 1–40 in *Cultural Perspectives on Biological Knowledge,* edited by Troy Duster and Karen Garrett. Norwood, NJ: Ablex.

———. 2003a. *Backdoor to Eugenics.* New York: Routledge.

———. 2003b. "Buried Alive: The Concept of Race in Science." Pp. 258–77 in *Genetic Nature/Culture: Anthropology and Science beyond the Two-Culture Divide,* edited by Alan Goodman, Deborah Heath, and Susan Lindee. Berkeley: University of California Press.

———. 2005. "Race and Reification in Science." *Science* 307 (February 18): 1050–51.

———. 2006. "American Sociological Association 2005 Presidential Address: Comparative Perspectives and Competing Explanations: Taking on the Newly Configured Reductionist Challenge to Sociology." *American Sociological Review* 71 (February): 1–15.

Education Market Research. 2001. "Educational Lineup for 2000 Poised for Change in 2001." *The Complete K–12 Newsletter* Sample Issue.

Ellison, George T. H. 2005. "'Population Profiling' and Public Health Risk: When and How Should We Use Race/Ethnicity?" *Critical Public Health* 15 (March): 65–74.

Ellison, George T. H. , Jay S. Kaufman, Rosemary F. Head, Paul A. Martin, and Jonathan D. Kahn. 2008a. "Flaws in the U.S. Food and Drug Administration's Rationale for Supporting the Development and Approval of BiDil as a Treatment for Heart Failure Only in Black Patients." *Journal of Law, Medicine & Ethics* (Fall): 2–10.

Ellison, George T. H., Andrew Smart, Richard Tutton, Simon M. Outram, Richard Ashcroft, and Paul Martin. 2007. "Racial Categories in Medicine: A Failure of Evidence-Based Practice?" *PLoS Medicine* 4 (September): 1434–36.

Ellison, George T. H., Richard Tutton, Simon M. Outram, Paul Martin, Richard Ashcroft, and Andrew Smart. 2008b. "An Interdisciplinary Perspective on the Impact of Genomics on the Meaning of 'Race', and the Future Role of Racial Categories in Biomedical Research." *N.T.M. Journal of the History of Science, Technology and Medicine* 16: 378–86.

Emerson, Michael O., Christian Smith, and David Sikkink. 1999. "Equal in Christ, But Not in the World: White Conservative Protestants and Explanations of Black-White Inequality." *Social Problems* 46 (3): 398–417.

Epstein, Steven. 2007. *Inclusion: The Politics of Difference in Medical Research.* Chicago: University of Chicago Press.

———. 2008. "The Rise of 'Recruitmentology': Clinical Research, Racial Knowledge, and the Politics of Inclusion and Difference." *Social Studies of Science* 38 (October): 801–32.

Eurostat. 2010. "Migration Statistics." May 27, 2010. Accessed August 25, 2010. http://epp.eurostat.ec.europa.eu/statistics_explained/index.php/Migration_statistics#Further_Eurostat_information.

Fausto-Sterling, Anne. 2004. "Refashioning Race: DNA and the Politics of Health Care." *Differences* 15 (3): 1–37.

———. 2008. "The Bare Bones of Race." *Social Studies of Science* 38 (October): 657–94.

Feldman, Marcus W., and Richard C. Lewontin. 2008. "Race, Ancestry, and Medicine." Pp. 89–101 in *Revisiting Race in a Genomic Age*, edited by Barbara A. Koenig, Sandra Soo-Jin Lee, and Sarah S. Richardson. New Brunswick, NJ: Rutgers University Press.

Ferber, Abby L. 1999. *White Man Falling: Race, Gender, and White Supremacy.* Lanham, MD: Rowman and Littlefield.

Fleck, Ludwik. 1979/1935. *Genesis and Development of a Scientific Fact.* Chicago, IL and London: University of Chicago Press. First published 1935 by Benno Schwabe (Basel, Switzerland).

Forbes, Jack D. 1993. *Africans and Native Americans: The Language of Race and the Evolution of Red-Black Peoples.* Urbana and Chicago: University of Illinois Press.

Ford, Christopher A. 1994. "Administering Identity: The Determination of 'Race' in Race-Conscious Law." *California Law Review* 82:1231–85.

Foshay, Arthur W. 1990. "Textbooks and the Curriculum during the Progressive Era: 1930–1950." Pp. 23–41 in *Textbooks and Schooling in the United States*, edited by David L. Elliott and Arthur Woodward. Chicago: University of Chicago Press.

Foster, Morris W., and Richard R. Sharp. 2002. "Race, Ethnicity, and Genomics: Social Classifications as Proxies of Biological Heterogeneity." *Genome Research* 12:844–50.

Foucault, Michel. 1973. *The Order of Things: An Archaeology of the Human Sciences.* New York: Vintage Books.

Frank, Reanne. Forthcoming. "Forbidden or Forsaken? The (Mis)Use of a Forbidden Knowledge Argument in Research on Race, DNA and Disease." In *Genetics and the Unsettled Past: The Collision between DNA, Race, and History*, edited by Keith Wailoo, Alondra Nelson, and Catherine Lee. New Brunswick, NJ: Rutgers University Press.

Frankenberg, Ruth. 1993. *White Women, Race Matters: The Social Construction of Whiteness.* Minneapolis: University of Minnesota Press.

Fredrickson, George M. 2002. *Racism: A Short History.* Princeton, NJ: Princeton University Press.

Fullwiley, Duana. 2007a. "The Molecularization of Race: Institutionalizing Human Difference in Pharmacogenetics Practice." *Science as Culture* 16 (1): 1–30.

———. 2007b. "Race and Genetics: Attempts to Define the Relationship." *Biosocieties* 2 (2): 221–37.

———. 2008. "The Biologistical Construction of Race: 'Admixture' Technology and the New Genetic Medicine." *Social Studies of Science* 38 (October): 695–735.

Gaertner, Samuel L., and John F. Dovidio. 1986. "The Aversive Form of Racism." Pp. 61–90 in *Prejudice, Discrimination, and Racism*, edited by John F. Dovidio and Samuel L. Gaertner. Orlando, FL: Academic Press.

Garcia, R.S. 2004. "The Misuse of Race in Medical Diagnosis." *Pediatrics* 113:1394–95.

GenSpec LLC. 2006. "GenSpec Formulates the World's First Genetically Specific Vitamins and Weight Loss Supplements." *PR Newswire*, February 7, 2006. Accessed November 13, 2009. http://sev.prnewswire.com/supplementary-medicine/20060207/NYTU04207022006-1.html.

Gergen, Kenneth J. 1998. "Constructionist Dialogues and the Vicissitudes of the Political." Pp. 33–48 in *The Politics of Constructionism*, edited by Irving Velody and Robin Williams. London: SAGE.

Gieryn, Thomas F. 1999. *Cultural Boundaries of Science: Credibility on the Line.* Chicago: University of Chicago Press.

Gifford-Gonzalez, Diane. 1995. "The Real Flintstones? What Are Artists' Depictions of Human Ancestors Telling Us?" *Anthro Notes: National Museum of Natural History Bulletin for Teachers* 17 (Fall): 1–5.

Ginzburg, Carlo. 1992. *The Cheese and the Worms: The Cosmos of a Sixteenth-Century Miller.* Baltimore: Johns Hopkins University Press

Gissis, Snait B. 2008. "When Is 'Race' a Race? 1946–2003." *Studies in History and Philosophy of Biological and Biomedical Sciences* 39 (December): 437–50.

Glazer, Nathan, and Reed Ueda. 1983. *Ethnic Groups in History Textbooks.* Washington, DC: Ethics and Public Policy Center.

Glick Schiller, Nina. 2005. "Blood and Belonging: Long-Distance Nationalism and the World Beyond." Pp. 289–312 in *Complexities: Beyond Nature and Nurture*, edited by Susan McKinnon and Sydel Silverman. Chicago: University of Chicago Press.

Goldberg, David Theo. 2002. *The Racial State.* Malden, MA and Oxford: Blackwell.

Goldman, Alvin I. 1999. *Knowledge in a Social World.* Oxford: Clarendon Press.

Goodman, Alan H. 1997. "Bred in the Bone?" *The Sciences* (March–April): 20–25.

Gossett, Thomas F. 1997. *Race: The History of an Idea in America.* New York: Oxford University Press. First published 1963 by Southern Methodist Press.

Gould, Stephen Jay. 1996. *The Mismeasure of Man.* New York: Norton.

Grant, Madison. 1916. *The Passing of the Great Race; or, The Racial Basis of European History.* New York: C. Scribner's Sons.

Graves, Joseph L. 2001. *The Emperor's New Clothes: Biological Theories of Race at the Millennium.* New Brunswick, NJ: Rutgers University Press.

Graves, Joseph L., and Michael R. Rose. 2006. "Against Racial Medicine." *Patterns of Prejudice* 40 (September): 481–93.

Greely, Henry T., Daniel P. Riordan, Nanibaa' A. Garrison, and Joanna L. Mountain. 2006. "Family Ties: The Use of DNA Offender Databases to Catch Offenders' Kin." *Journal of Law, Medicine, & Ethics* 34 (Summer): 248–62.

Gross, Neil. 2002. "Becoming a Pragmatist Philosopher: Status, Self-Concept, and Intellectual Choice." *American Sociological Review* 67 (February): 52–76.

Gross, Paul R., and Norman Levitt. 1998. *Higher Superstition: The Academic Left and Its Quarrels with Science.* Baltimore: Johns Hopkins Press.

Gurvitch, Georges. 1971. *The Social Frameworks of Knowledge.* Oxford: Blackwell.

Hacking, Ian. 1999. *The Social Construction of What?* Cambridge, MA: Harvard University Press.

———. 2005. "Why Race Still Matters." *Daedalus* 134 (Winter): 102.

Haney López, Ian F. 1996. *White by Law: The Legal Construction of Race.* New York: New York University Press.

Hannaford, Ivan. 1996. *Race: The History of an Idea in the West.* Washington, DC: Woodrow Wilson Center Press.

Happe, Kelly E. 2006. "The Rhetoric of Race in Breast Cancer Research." *Patterns of Prejudice* 40 (September): 461–80.

Harding, Sandra. 1998. *Is Science Multicultural? Postcolonialisms, Feminisms, and Epistemologies.* Bloomington: Indiana University Press.

Harrison, Faye V. 1999. "Introduction: Expanding the Discourse on 'Race.'" *American Anthropologist* 100 (3): 609–31.

Haslam, Nick, Louis Rothschild, and Donald Ernst. 2000. "Essentialist Beliefs about Social Categories." *British Journal of Social Psychology* 39 (1): 113–127.

———. 2002. "Are Essentialist Beliefs Associated with Prejudice?" *British Journal of Social Psychology* 41 (March): 87–100.

Herrnstein, Richard J., and Charles Murray. 1994. *The Bell Curve: Intelligence and Class Structure in American Life.* New York: Free Press.

Hey, Jody. 2001. *Genes, Categories, and Species: The Evolutionary and Cognitive Causes of the Species Problem.* New York: Oxford University Press.

Hirschfeld, Lawrence A. 1996. *Race in the Making: Cognition, Culture and the Child's Construction of Human Kinds.* Cambridge, MA: MIT Press.

———. 1997. "The Conceptual Politics of Race: Lessons from Our Children." *Ethos* 25 (1): 63–92.

———. 1998. "Natural Assumptions: Race, Essence, and Taxonomies of Human Kinds." *Social Research* 65 (Summer): 331–49.

Hochschild, Jennifer L. 1995. *Facing Up to the American Dream: Race, Class, and the Soul of the Nation.* Princeton, NJ: Princeton University Press.

Hodgson, Dennis. 1991. "The Ideological Origins of the Population Association of America." *Population and Development Review* 17 (March): 1–34.

Hoffman, Malvina. 1936. *Heads and Tales.* New York: Charles Scribner's Sons.

Holden, Constance. 2003. "Race and Medicine." *Science* 302:594–96.

Holzner, Burkhart, and John H. Marx. 1979. *Knowledge Application: The Knowledge System in Society.* Boston: Allyn and Bacon.

Howard, John. 2008. *Concentration Camps on the Home Front: Japanese Americans in the House of Jim Crow.* Chicago: University of Chicago Press.

Hunt, Matthew O. 2007. "African American, Hispanic, and White Beliefs about Black/White Inequality, 1977–2004." *American Sociological Review* 72 (June): 390–415.

Hutchinson, Janis Faye. 1997. "The Resurgence of Genetic Hypotheses to Explain Social Behavior among Ethnic Minorities." Pp. 5–25 in *Cultural Portrayals of African Americans: Creating an Ethnic/Racial Identity*, edited by Janis Faye Hutchinson. Westport, CT: Bergin & Garvey.

Isaac, Benjamin. 2004. *The Invention of Racism in Classical Antiquity.* Princeton, NJ: Princeton University Press, 2004.

Jackson, John L., Jr. 2008. "The Racial Impasse." *The Chronicle Review*, May 30, 2008.

Jacobi, Daniel. 1986. *Diffusion et Vulgarisation: Itinéraires du Texte Scientifique.* Paris: Les Belles Lettres.

Jasanoff, Sheila, ed. 2004. *States of Knowledge: The Co-Production of Science and Social Order.* London and New York: Routledge.

Jayaratne, Toby E. 2002. "White and Black Americans' Genetic Explanations for Perceived Gender, Class and Race Differences: The Psychology of Genetic Beliefs." Paper presented at 2002 Human Genome Lecture Series, National Human Genome Research Institute, NIH, Bethesda, MD, June 2002.

Jayaratne, Toby E., Oscar Ybarra, Jane P. Sheldon, Tony N. Brown, Merle Feldbaum, Carla A. Pfeffer, and Elizabeth M. Petty. 2006. "White Americans' Genetic Lay Theories of Race Differences and Sexual Orientation: Their Relationship with Prejudice toward Blacks, and Gay Men and Lesbians." *Group Processes and Intergroup Relations* 9 (1): 77–94.

Jefferson, Thomas. 1784. *Notes on the State of Virginia.* Paris.

Jensen, Arthur. 1969. "How Much Can We Boost I.Q. and Scholastic Achievement?" *Harvard Educational Review* 39: 1–123.

Jewell, Elizabeth J., and Frank Abate, eds. 2001. *The New Oxford American Dictionary.* New York: Oxford University Press,

Kahn, Jonathan. 2006. "Patenting Race." *Nature Biotechnology* 24 (November): 1349–51.

———. 2007. "Race in a Bottle." *Scientific American* (August): 40–45.

———. 2008. "Exploiting Race in Drug Development: BiDil's Interim Model of Pharmacogenomics." *Social Studies of Science* 38 (October): 737–58.

Kay, Lily E. 1993. *The Molecular Vision of Life: Caltech, the Rockefeller Foundation, and the Rise of the New Biology.* New York: Oxford University Press.

Keita, S.O.Y., and Rick A. Kittles. 1997. "The Persistence of Racial Thinking and the Myth of Racial Divergence." *American Anthropologist* 99, no. 3: 534–44.

Keith, Sherry. 1985. "Choosing Textbooks: A Study of Instructional Materials Selection Processes for Public Education." *Book Research Quarterly* 1 (Summer): 24–37.

———. 1991. "The Determinants of Textbook Content." Pp. 43–60 in *Textbooks in American Society: Politics, Policy, and Pedagogy*, edited by Philip G. Altbach, Gail P. Kelly, Hugh G. Petrie, and Lois Weis. Albany: State University of New York Press.

Keller, Evelyn Fox. 2000. *The Century of the Gene*. Cambridge, MA: Harvard University Press.

Keller, Johannes. 2005. "In Genes We Trust: The Biological Component of Psychological Essentialism and Its Relationship to Mechanisms of Motivated Social Cognition." *Journal of Personality and Social Psychology* 88 (April): 686–702.

Kennedy, Randall. 2003. *Interracial Intimacies: Sex, Marriage, Identity, and Adoption*. New York: Pantheon.

Kerr, Kathleen. 2006. "New Vitamin Line for Blacks and Hispanics Puts Focus on Ethnicity's Role in Health." *New York Newsday*, April 14, 2006. Accessed September 3, 2010. http://www.targetmarketnews.com/storyido4180602.htm.

Kevles, Daniel J. 1995/1985. *In the Name of Eugenics: Genetics and the Uses of Human Heredity*. Cambridge, MA: Harvard University Press. First published 1985 by Alfred A. Knopf.

King, K. E., P. M. Ness, H. G. Braine, and K. S. Armstrong. 1996. "Racial Differences in the Availability of Human Leukocyte Antigen-Matched Platelets." *Journal of Clinical Apheresis* 11:71–77.

King-O'Riain, Rebecca Chiyoko. 2006. *Pure Beauty: Judging Race in Japanese American Beauty Pageants*. Minneapolis: University of Minnesota.

Klein, Gillian. 1985. *Reading into Racism: Bias in Children's Literature and Learning Materials*. London: Routledge & Kegan Paul.

Kluegel, James R. 1986. *Beliefs about Inequality: Americans' Views of What Is and What Ought to Be*. New York: Aldine de Gruyter.

———. 1990. "Trends in Whites' Explanations of the Black-White Gap in Socioeconomic Status, 1977–1989." *American Sociological Review* 55 (4): 512–25.

Koenig, Barbara A., Sandra Soo-Jin Lee, and Sarah S. Richardson. 2008. *Revisiting Race in a Genomic Age*. New Brunswick, NJ: Rutgers University Press.

Kollman, C., C. W. S. Howe, and C. Anasetti. 2001. "Donor Characteristics as Risk Factors in Recipients after Transplantation of Bone Marrow from Unrelated Donors: The Effect of Donor Age." *Blood* 98:2043–51.

Kousser, J. Morgan. 1999. *Colorblind Injustice: Minority Vote Dilution and the Undoing of the Second Reconstruction*. Chapel Hill: University of North Carolina Press.

Krieger, Nancy, and Mary Bassett. 1993. "The Health of Black Folk: Disease, Class, and Ideology in Science." Pp. 161–69 In *The "Racial" Economy of*

Science: Toward a Democratic Future, edited by Sandra Harding. Bloomington and Indianapolis: Indiana University Press.

Kuhn, Thomas S. 1996/1962. *The Structure of Scientific Revolutions*. Chicago, IL: University of Chicago Press. First published 1962 by University of Chicago Press.

Kukla, André. 2000. *Social Constructivism and the Philosophy of Science*. London: Routledge.

Ladd, Everett Carll, and Seymour Martin Lipset. 1975. *The Divided Academy: Professors and Politics*. New York: McGraw-Hill.

Lamont, Michèle. 2000. *The Dignity of Working Men: Morality and the Boundaries of Race, Class, and Immigration*. Cambridge and New York: Harvard University Press and Russell Sage Foundation.

Lamont, Michèle, and Virág Molnár. 2002. "The Study of Boundaries in the Social Sciences." *Annual Review of Sociology* 28:167–95.

Lapchick, Richard E., and Kevin J. Matthews. 2001. *Racial and Gender Report Card, 1998–2001*. Boston: Center for the Study of Sport in Society, Northeastern University.

Latour, Bruno. 1987. *Science in Action: How to Follow Scientists and Engineers through Society*. Cambridge, MA: Harvard University Press.

Lee, Catherine. 2009. "'Race' and 'Ethnicity' in Biomedical Research: How Do Scientists Construct and Explain Differences in Health?" *Social Science & Medicine* 68:1183–90.

Lee, Jennifer, and Frank D. Bean. 2004. "America's Changing Color Lines: Immigration, Race/Ethnicity, and Multiracial Identification." *Annual Review of Sociology* 30:221–42.

Lee, Sandra S. J., Joanna Mountain, and Barbara Koenig. 2001. "The Meanings of 'Race' in the New Genomics: Implications for Health Disparities Research." *Yale Journal of Health Policy, Law and Ethics* 1 (May 3): 33–75.

Lee, Sandra S. J., Joanna Mountain, Barbara Koenig, Russ Altman, Melissa Brown, Albert Camarillo, Luca Cavalli-Sforza, Mildred Cho, Jennifer Eberhardt, Marcus Feldman, Richard Ford, Henry Greely, Roy King, Hazel Markus, Debra Satz, Matthew Snipp, Claude Steele, and Peter Underhill. 2008. "The Ethics of Characterizing Difference: Guiding Principles on Using Racial Categories in Human Genetics." *Genome Biology* 9 (7): 404.1–404.4.

Lee, Sharon M. 1993. "Racial Classifications in the U.S. Census: 1890–1990." *Ethnic and Racial Studies* 16 (1): 75–94.

Lepage-Monette, Amber. 2008. "Black Patients Face Worse Outcomes with Race Mismatch for Donor Hearts." *Medical Post* 44:17.

Leroi, Armand Marie. 2005. "A Family Tree in Every Gene." *New York Times*. March 14, 2005.

Lewis, Earl, and Heidi Ardizzone. 2001. *Love on Trial: An American Scandal in Black and White*. New York: Norton.

Lewontin, Richard C. 1972. "The Apportionment of Human Diversity." *Evolutionary Biology* 6:381–98.

Lieberman, Leonard. 1968. "The Debate over Race: A Study in the Sociology of Knowledge." *Phylon* 29 (2): 127–41.

———. 1997. "Gender and the Deconstruction of the Race Concept." *American Anthropologist* 99 (3): 545–58.

Lieberman, Leonard, Raymond E. Hampton, Alice Littlefield, and Glen Hallead. 1992. "Race in Biology and Anthropology: A Study of College Texts and Professors." *Journal of Research in Science Teaching* 29 (3): 301–21.

Lieberman, Leonard, and Fatimah Linda C. Jackson. 1995. "Race and Three Models of Human Origin." *American Anthropologist* 97 (2): 231–42.

Lippman, Abby. 1993. "Prenatal Genetic Testing and Geneticization: Mother Matters for All." *Reproductive Genetic Testing: Impact upon Women, Fetal Diagnosis and Therapy* 8: S64–S79.

Littlefield, Alice, Leonard Lieberman, and Larry T. Reynolds. 1982. "Redefining Race: The Potential Demise of a Concept in Physical Anthropology." *Current Anthropology* 23 (6): 641–55.

Longino, Helen E. 1990. *Science as Social Knowledge: Values and Objectivity in Scientific Inquiry*. Princeton, NJ: Princeton University Press.

Lowe, Alex L., Andrew Urquhart, Lindsey A. Foreman, and Ian W. Evett. 2001. "Inferring Ethnic Origin by Means of an STR Profile." *Forensic Science International* 119:17–22.

Mahle, W. T., K. R. Kanter, and R. N. Vincent. 2005. "Disparities for Black Patients after Pediatric Heart Transplantation." *Journal of Pediatrics* 147:739–43.

Malcomson, Scott L. 2000. *One Drop of Blood: The American Misadventure of Race*. New York: Farrar, Straus Giroux.

Marks, Jonathan. 1995. *Human Biodiversity: Genes, Race, and History*. New York: Aldine de Gruyter.

———. 1996. "The Legacy of Serological Studies in American Physical Anthropology." *History and Philosophy of the Life Sciences* 18:345–62.

Martin, John Levi, and King-To Yeung. 2003. "The Use of the Conceptual Category of Race in American Sociology, 1937–99." *Sociological Forum* 18 (December): 521–42.

Martin, Paul, Richard Ashcroft, George T. H. Ellison, Andrew Smart, and Richard Tutton. 2007. *Reviving "Racial Medicine"? The Use of Race/Ethnicity in Genetics and Biomedical Research, and the Implications for Science and Healthcare*. London: Faculty of Health and Social Care Sciences at St. George's, University of London.

Massey, Douglas S. 1995. "The New Immigration and Ethnicity in the United States." *Population and Development Review* 21 (3): 631–52.

Mayr, Ernst. 2002. "The Biology of Race and the Concept of Equality." *Daedalus* 131 (Winter): 89–94.

McCann-Mortimer, Patricia, Martha Augoustinos, and Amanda Lecouteur. 2004. "'Race' and the Human Genome Project: Constructions of Scientific Legitimacy." *Discourse & Society* 15 (4): 409–32.

McKee, James. 1993. *Sociology and the Race Problem.* Urbana: University of Illinois Press.

McMahon, Judith W., and Tony Romano. 2000. *Psychology and You.* Lincoln-wood, IL: National Textbook.

Medin, Douglas L., and A. Ortony. 1989. "Psychological Essentialism." Pp. 179–95 in *Similarity and Analogical Reasoning*, edited by S. Vosniadou and A. Ortony. New York: Cambridge University Press.

Merton, Robert K. 1968. *Social Theory and Social Structure.* New York: Free Press.

Molina, Natalia. 2006. *Fit to Be Citizens? Public Health and Race in Los Angeles, 1879–1939.* Berkeley: University of California Press.

Montagu, Ashley. 1942. *Man's Most Dangerous Myth: The Fallacy of Race.* New York: Columbia University Press.

———. 1945. *Man's Most Dangerous Myth: The Fallacy of Race.* New York: Columbia University Press.

———. 1972. *Statement on Race: An Annotated Elaboration and Exposition of the Four Statements on Race Issued by the United Nations Educational, Scientific, and Cultural Organization.* New York: Oxford University Press.

Montoya, Michael J. 2007. "Bioethnic Conscription: Genes, Race and Mexicana/o Ethnicity in Diabetes Research." *Cultural Anthropology* 22 (1):94–128.

Morell, Virginia. 1993. "Anthropology: Nature-Culture Battleground." *Science* 261 (September 24): 1798–802.

Morning, Ann. 2000. "Who Is Multiracial? Definitions and Decisions." *Sociological Imagination* 37 (4): 209–29.

———. 2001. "The Racial Self-Identification of South Asians in the United States." *Journal of Ethnic and Migration Studies* 27 (January): 61–79.

———. 2005. "On Distinction." *Is Race "Real"?* Accessed September 3, 2010. http://raceandgenomics.ssrc.org/Morning/.

———. 2007. "'Everyone Knows It's a Social Construct': Contemporary Science and the Nature of Race." *Sociological Focus* 40 (November): 436–54.

———. 2008a. "Ethnic Classification in Global Perspective: A Cross-National Survey of the 2000 Census Round." *Population Research and Policy Review* 27 (2):239–72.

———. 2008b. "Reconstructing Race in Science and Society: Biology Textbooks, 1952–2002." *American Journal of Sociology* 114 (s1): s106–37.

———. 2009. "Toward a Sociology of Racial Conceptualization for the 21st Century." *Social Forces* 87 (March): 1167–92.

Morning, Ann, and Daniel Sabbagh. 2005. "From Sword to Plowshare: Using Race for Discrimination and Antidiscrimination in the United States." *International Social Science Journal* 57 (183): 57–73.

Morris, Aldon D. 2007. "Sociology of Race and W.E.B. Dubois: The Path Not Taken." Pp. 503–34 in *Sociology in America: A History*, edited by Craig Calhoun, Chicago: University of Chicago Press.

Morrow, Lance. 2001. "Controversies: The Provocative Professor." *TIME.* Accessed January 8, 2008. http://www.time.com/time/magazine/article/0,9171,157721,00.html.

Mukhopadhyay, Carol C., and Yolanda T. Moses. 1997. "Reestablishing 'Race' in Anthropological Discourse." *American Anthropologist* 99 (3): 517–33.

Müller-Wille, Staffan, and Hans-Jörg Rheinberger. 2008. "Race and Genomics: Old Wine in New Bottles? Documents from a Transdisciplinary Discussion." *N.T.M. Journal of the History of Science, Technology and Medicine* 16:363–86.

Murphy, Gregory L., and Douglas L. Medin. 1985. "The Role of Theories in Conceptual Coherence." *Psychological Review* 92 (July): 289–316.

Myrdal, Gunnar. 1944. *An American Dilemma: The Negro Problem and Modern Democracy.* New York: Harper and Brothers.

Nash, Gary B. 1995. "The Hidden History of Mestizo America." *Journal of American History* 82 (December): 941–62.

Nash, Gary B., Charlotte Crabtree, and Ross E. Dunn, eds. 1997. *History Trials: Culture Wars and the Teaching of the Past.* New York: A. A. Knopf.

National Center for Education Statistics. 2001. *Digest of Education Statistics, 2000.* Washington, DC.

———. 2002. *Digest of Education Statistics, 2001.* Washington, DC.

———. 2003. *Digest of Education Statistics, 2002.* Washington, DC.

———. 2004. *Digest of Education Statistics, 2003.* Washington, DC.

———. 2009. *Digest of Education Statistics, 2008.* Washington, DC.

National Center for Health Statistics. 2001. "Vital Statistics of the United States, 1997. Natality: Volume 1." January 11, 2007. Accessed April 2, 2007. http://www.cdc.gov/nchs/datawh/statab/unpubd/natality/natab97.htm.

Nelkin, Dorothy, and M. Susan Lindee. 1995. *The DNA Mystique: The Gene as Cultural Icon.* New York: Freeman.

Nelson, Alondra. 2008. "Bio Science: Genetic Genealogy Testing and the Pursuit of African Ancestry." *Social Studies of Science* 38 (October): 759–83.

Nerlich, Brigitte, Robert Dingwall, and Paul Martin. 2004. "Genetic and Genomic Discourses at the Dawn of the 21st Century." *Discourse & Society* 15 (4): 363–68.

Ng, P. C., Q. Zhao, S. Levy, R. L. Strausberg, and J. C. Venter. 2008. "Individual Genomes Instead of Race for Personalized Medicine." *Clinical Pharmacology & Therapeutics* 84 (September): 306–9.

Nicholas, George P. 2001. "On Representations of Race and Racism." *Current Anthropology* 42 (February): 140–2.

Nitromed. 2007. "Patient Home Page." Accessed September 15, 2009. http://www.bidil.com/pnt/.

No, Sun, Ying-yi Hong, Hsin-Ya Liao, Kyoungmi Lee, Dustin Wood, and Melody Manchi Chao. 2008. "Lay Theory of Race Affects and Moderates Asian Americans' Responses Toward American Culture." *Journal of Personality and Social Psychology* 95 (4): 991–1004.

Nobles, Melissa. 2000. *Shades of Citizenship: Race and the Census in Modern Politics.* Stanford, CA: Stanford University Press.

Nugent, Helen. 2007. "Black People 'Less Intelligent' Scientist Claims." *The Times,* October 17, 2007. Accessed November 26, 2007. http://www.timesonline.co.uk/tol/news/uk/article2677098.ece?token=null&offset=0.

Obach, Brian K. 1999. "Demonstrating the Social Construction of Race." *Teaching Sociology* 27 (July): 252–57.

Obasogie, Osagie K. 2009. *Playing the Gene Card? A Report on Race and Human Biotechnology.* Oakland, CA: Center for Genetics and Society.

Odocha, Okay. 2000. "Race and Racialism in Scientific Research and Publication in the *Journal of the National Medical Association.*" *Journal of the National Medical Association* 92 (February): 96–97.

Office of Management and Budget. 1997. "Revisions to the Standards for the Classification of Federal Data on Race and Ethnicity." In *Federal Register.* Washington, DC.

Olson, Steve. 2001. "The Genetic Archaeology of Race." *Atlantic Monthly* 287 (April): 69–80.

Omi, Michael, and Howard Winant. 1994. *Racial Formation in the United States: From the 1960s to the 1990s.* New York: Routledge.

Osborne, Newton G., and Marvin D. Feit. 1992. "The Use of Race in Medical Research." *Journal of the American Medical Association* 267 (January 8): 275–79.

Ossorio, Pilar N. 2006. "About Face: Forensic Genetic Testing for Race and Visible Traits." *Journal of Law, Medicine, & Ethics* 34 (Summer): 277–92.

Ossorio, Pilar N., and Troy Duster. 2005. "Race and Genetics: Controversies in Biomedical, Behavioral, and Forensic Sciences." *American Psychologist* 60 (1): 115–28.

Outram, Simon M., and George T. H. Ellison. 2006a. "Anthropological Insights into the Use of Race/Ethnicity to Explore Genetic Contributions of Disparities in Health." *Journal of Biosocial Science* 38:83–102.

———. 2006b. "Improving the Use of Race and Ethnicity in Genetic Research: A Survey of Instructions to Authors in Genetics Journals." *Science Editor* 29 (May–June): 78–81.

———. 2006c. "The Truth Will Out: Scientific Pragmatism and the Geneticization of Race and Ethnicity." Pp. 157–79 in *The Nature of Difference: Science, Society and Human Biology,* edited by George T. H. Ellison and Alan H. Goodman. Boca Raton, FL: Taylor and Francis.

Palmié, Stephan. 2007. "Genomics, Divination, 'Racecraft.' " *American Ethnologist* 34 (2):205–22.

Pálsson, Gísli. 2007. "How Deep Is the Skin? The Geneticization of Race and Medicine." *Biosocieties* 2 (2):257–72.

Pascoe, Peggy. 1996. "Miscegenation Law, Court Cases, and Ideologies of 'Race' in Twentieth-Century America." *Journal of American History* 83 (June): 44–69.

Patterson, Orlando. 2000. "America's Worst Idea." *New York Times.* October 22, 2000.

Peterson's. 2001a. *Peterson's Graduate & Professional Programs: An Overview 2001.* Princeton, NJ: Peterson's.

———. 2001b. *Peterson's Guide to Four-Year Colleges 2002.* Lawrenceville, NJ: Peterson's.

Pettigrew, Thomas F. 2009. "Post-Racism? Putting President Obama's Victory in Perspective." *Du Bois Review* 6 (2): 279–92.

Phimister, Elizabeth G. 2003. "Medicine and the Racial Divide." *New England Journal of Medicine* 348 (March 20): 1081–82.

Plous, S., and Tyrone Williams. 1995. "Racial Stereotypes from the Days of American Slavery: A Continuing Legacy." *Journal of Applied Social Psychology* 25 (9): 795–817.

Popenoe, Paul, and Roswell Hill Johnson. 1918. *Applied Eugenics.* New York: Macmillan.

Preiswerk, Roy. 1980a. "Ethnocentric Images in History Books and Their Effect on Racism." Pp. 131–39 in *The Slant of the Pen: Racism in Children's Books,* edited by Roy Preiswerk. Geneva: World Council of Churches.

———, ed. 1980b. *The Slant of the Pen: Racism in Children's Books.* Geneva: World Council of Churches.

Prentice, Deborah A., and Dale T. Miller. 2007. "Psychological Essentialism of Human Categories." *Current Directions in Psychological Science* 16 (4): 202–6.

Project 2061. 2000. "Big Biology Books Fail to Convey Big Ideas, Reports AAAS's Project 2061." June 27. Accessed April 11, 2001. http://www.project2061.org/newsinfo/press/rl000627.htm.

Putnam, Robert D. 2007. "*E Pluribus Unum*: Diversity and Community in the Twenty-First Century." *Scandinavian Political Studies* 30 (2): 137–74.

Quine, W. V. O. 1977. "Natural Kinds." Pp. 155–75 in *Naming, Necessity, and Natural Kinds*, edited by S. P. Schwartz. Ithaca, NY: Cornell University Press.

Race, Ethnicity and Genetics Working Group (National Human Genome Research Institute). 2005. "The Use of Racial, Ethnic, and Ancestral Categories in Human Genetics Research." *American Journal of Human Genetics* 77 (4): 519–32.

Ravitch, Diane. 1996. "50 States, 50 Standards: The Continuing Need for National Voluntary Standards in Education." *Brookings Review* 14 (3): 6–9.

Reardon, Jenny. 2004. "Decoding Race and Human Difference in a Genomic Age." *Differences: A Journal of Feminist Cultural Studies* 15 (3): 38–65.

———. 2005. *Race to the Finish: Identity and Governance in an Age of Genomics*. Princeton, NJ: Princeton University Press.

Reuben, Julie A. 1996. *The Making of the Modern University: Intellectual Transformation and the Marginalization of Morality*. Chicago: University of Chicago Press.

Reynolds, Larry T., and Leonard Lieberman, eds. 1996. *Race and Other Misadventures: Essays in Honor of Ashley Montagu in His Ninetieth Year*. Dix Hills, NY: General Hall.

Risch, Neil, Esteban Burchard, Elad Ziv, and Hua Tang. 2002. "Categorization of Humans in Biomedical Research: Genes, Race and Disease." *Genome Biology*, 7. Accessed July 1, 2002. http://genomebiology.com/2002/3/7/comment/2007.1.

Rizzuto, G., L. Li, N. Steiner, R. Slack, T. Tang, U. Heine, Y. S. J. Ng, R. Hartzman, and C. K. Hurley 2003. "Diversity within the DRB1*08 Allele Family in Four Populations from a United States Hematopoietic Stem Cell Donor Database and Characterization of Five Novel DRB1*08 Alleles." *Human Immunology* 64:607–13.

Roberts, J. P., R. A. Wolfe, J. L. Bragg-Gresham, S. H. Rush, J. J. Wynn, D. A. Distant, V. B. Ashby. P. J. Held, and F. K. Port. 2004. "Effect of Changing the Priority for HLA Matching on the Rates and Outcomes of Kidney Transplantation in Minority Groups." *New England Journal of Medicine* 350:545–51.

Roberts, Sam. 2008. "A Nation of None and All of the Above." *New York Times*. August 17, 2008.

Rodríguez, Clara E. 2000. *Changing Race: Latinos, the Census, and the History of Ethnicity in the United States*. New York: New York University Press.

———. 2004. *Heroes, Lovers, and Others: The Story of Latinos in Hollywood.* Washington, DC: Smithsonian Books.

Root, Michael. 2007. "Race in the Social Sciences." Pp. 735–53 in *Philosophy of Anthropology and Sociology,* edited by Stephen P. Turner and Mark W. Risjord. Oxford: Elsevier.

Rose, Nikolas. 2001. "The Politics of Life Itself." *Theory, Culture and Society* 18 (December): 1–30.

Rowe, David C., and Joseph (Ed) Rodgers. 2005. "Under the Skin: On the Impartial Treatment of Genetic and Environmental Hypotheses of Racial Differences." *American Psychologist* 60 (January): 60–70.

Royster, Deirdre. 2003. *Race and the Invisible Hand: How White Networks Exclude Black Men from Blue-Collar Jobs.* Berkeley: University of California Press.

Rushton, J. Philippe, and Arthur R. Jensen. 2008. "James Watson's Most Inconvenient Truth: Race Realism and the Moralistic Fallacy." *Medical Hypotheses* 71:629–40.

Samhan, Helen Hatab. 1999. "Not Quite White: Race Classification and the Arab-American Experience." Pp. 209–26 in *Arabs in America: Building a New Future,* edited by Michael W. Suleiman. Philadelphia: Temple University Press.

Sanders, Edith R. 1969. "The Hamitic Hypothesis; Its Origins and Functions in Time Perspective." *Journal of African History* X (4): 521–32.

Sankar, Pamela, and Mildred K. Cho. 2002. "Toward a New Vocabulary of Human Genetic Variation." *Science* 298 (November 15): 1337–38.

Sarich, Vincent, and Frank Miele. 2004. *Race: The Reality of Human Differences.* Boulder, CO: Westview Press.

Satel, Sally. 2002. "I Am a Racially Profiling Doctor." *The New York Times Magazine.* May 5, 2002, 56–58.

Sauer, Norman J. 1992. "Forensic Anthropology and the Concept of Race: If Races Don't Exist, Why Are Forensic Anthropologists So Good at Identifying Them?" *Social Science and Medicine* 34 (2): 107–11.

Schneider, David J. 2004. *The Psychology of Stereotyping.* New York: Guilford Press.

Schneider, William H. 1996. "The History of Research on Blood Group Genetics: Initial Discovery and Diffusion." *History and Philosophy of the Life Sciences* 18: 277–303.

Schofield, Janet Ward. 1986. "Causes and Consequences of the Colorblind Perspective." Pp. 231–53 in *Prejudice, Discrimination, and Racism,* edited by John F. Dovidio and Samuel L. Gaertner. Orlando, FL: Academic Press.

Schuman, Howard, Charlotte Steeh, Lawrence Bobo, and Maria Krysan. 1997. *Racial Attitudes in America: Trends and Interpretations.* Cambridge, MA: Harvard University Press.

Schwartz, Robert S. 2001. "Racial Profiling in Medical Research." *New England Journal of Medicine* 344 (May 3): 1392–93.

Sears, David O. 1988. "Symbolic Racism." Pp. 53–84 in *Eliminating Racism: Profiles in Controversy*, edited by Phyllis A. Katz and Dalmas A. Taylor. New York: Plenum Press.

Sears, David O., Jim Sidanius, and Lawrence Bobo, eds. 2000. *Racialized Politics: The Debate about Racism in America*. Chicago, IL: University of Chicago Press.

See, Katherine O'Sullivan, and William Julius Wilson. 1989. "Race and Ethnicity." Pp. 223–42 in *Handbook of Sociology*, edited by Neil J. Smelser. Beverly Hills, CA: SAGE.

Segev, Dorry L., Sommer E. Gentry, Daniel S. Warren, Brigitte Reeb, and Robert A. Montgomery. 2005. "Kidney Paired Donation and Optimizing the Use of Live Donor Organs." *Journal of the American Medical Association* 293:1883–90.

Selden, Steven. 1999. *Inheriting Shame: The Story of Eugenics and Racism in America*. New York: Teachers College Press.

Shakespeare, Tom. 1998. "Social Constructionism as a Political Strategy." Pp. 168–181 in *The Politics of Constructionism*, edited by Irving Velody and Robin Williams. London: SAGE.

Shanklin, Eugenia. 1999. "The Profession of the Color Blind: Sociocultural Anthropology and Racism in the 21st Century." *American Anthropologist* 100 (3): 669–79.

———. 2000. "Representations of Race and Racism in American Anthropology." *Current Anthropology* 41 (1): 99–103.

Shields, Alexandra, Michael Fortun, Evelyn M. Hammonds, Patricia A. King, Caryn Lerman, Rayna Rapp, and Patrick F. Sullivan. 2005. "The Use of Race Variables in Genetic Studies of Complex Traits and the Goal of Reducing Health Disparities: A Transdisciplinary Perspective." *American Psychologist* 60 (1):77–103.

Shinn, Terry, and Richard Whitley, eds. 1985. *Expository Science: Forms and Functions of Popularisation*. Dordrecht, Holland: Reidel.

Shostak, Sara. 2005. "The Emergence of Toxicogenomics: A Case Study of Molecularization." *Social Studies of Science* 35 (3): 367–403.

Shryock, Richard Harrison. 1962. "American Indifference to Basic Science during the Nineteenth Century." Pp. 98–110 in *The Sociology of Science*, edited by Bernard Barber and Walter Hirsch. New York: Free Press of Glencoe.

Sigelman, Lee, and Susan Welch. 1991. *Black Americans' Views of Racial Inequality: The Dream Deferred*. Cambridge: Cambridge University Press,

Skerry, Peter. 2000. *Counting on the Census? Race, Group Identity, and the Evasion of Politics*. Washington, DC: Brookings Institution Press.

Skoog, Gerald D. 1992. "The Coverage of Evolution in Secondary School
Biology Textbooks, 1900–1989." Pp. 71–87 in *The Textbook Controversy: Issues,
Aspects and Perspectives*, edited by John G. Herlihy. Norwood, NJ: Ablex.

Smedley, Audrey. 2007. *Race in North America: Origin and Evolution of a Worldview.*
Boulder, CO: Westview Press.

Sniderman, Paul M., and Thomas Piazza. 1993. *The Scar of Race*. Cambridge,
MA: The Belknap Press of Harvard University Press.

Sniderman, Paul M., Thomas Piazza, Philip E. Tetlock, and Ann Kendrick. 1991.
"The New Racism." *American Journal of Political Science* 35:423–47.

Snowden, Frank M., Jr. 1983. *Before Color Prejudice: The Ancient View of Blacks.*
Cambridge, MA: Harvard University Press.

Sollors, Werner, ed. 2000. *Interracialism: Black-White Intermarriage in American
History, Literature, and Law*. Oxford: Oxford University Press.

Spencer, Rainier. 1999. *Spurious Issues: Race and Multiracial Identity Politics in the
United States*. Boulder, CO: Westview Press.

———. 2006. *Challenging Multiracial Identity*. Boulder, CO: Lynne Rienner.

Squire, James R., and Richard T. Morgan. 1990. "The Elementary and High
School Textbook Market Today." Pp. 107–126 in *Textbooks and Schooling in the
United States*, edited by David L. Elliott and Arthur Woodward. Chicago:
University of Chicago Press.

Stark, Jerry A., Larry T. Reynolds, and Leonard Lieberman. 1979. "The Social
Basis of Conceptual Diversity: A Case Study of the Concept of 'Race' in
Physical Anthropology." *Research in Sociology of Knowledge, Sciences and Art*
2:87–99.

Stewart, Angela. 2008. "Heart Drug's Racial Focus Proves a Liability Rather
than an Asset." *Star-Ledger*, May 31, 2008. Accessed September 3, 2010.
http://www.geneticsandsociety.org/article.php?id=4108.

Stille, Alexander. 2002. "Textbook Publishers Learn: Avoid Messing with
Texas." *New York Times*. June 29, 2002.

Stolberg, Sheryl Gay. 2001. "Skin Deep: Shouldn't a Pill Be Colorblind?" *New York
Times*, May 13, 2001. Accessed September 3, 2010. http://www.nytimes.com/
2001/05/13/weekinreview/the-world-skin-deep-shouldn-t-a-pill-be-colorblind
.html.

Sullivan, Andrew. 2005. "Daily Express: Provocations." *TNR Online*, January 19,
2005. Accessed April 2, 2007. http://www.tnr.com/doc.mhtml?i=express&s=
sullivan011905.

Sundstrom, Ronald. 2008. *The Browning of America and the Evasion of Social
Justice*. Albany: State University of New York Press.

Swidler, Ann, and Jorge Arditi. 1994. "The New Sociology of Knowledge."
Annual Review of Sociology 20: 305–29.

Taguieff, Pierre-André. 1988. *La Force du Préjugé: Essai sur le Racisme et Ses Doubles*. Paris: Éditions La Découverte.

Tate, Sarah K., and David B. Goldstein. 2004. "Will Tomorrow's Medicines Work for Everyone?" *Nature Genetics Supplement* 36 (November): S34.

Temple, Robert, and Norman L. Stockbridge. 2007. "BiDil for Heart Failure in Black Patients: The U.S. Food and Drug Administration Perspective." *Annals of Internal Medicine* 146 (January 2): 57–62.

Terkel, Studs. 1992. *Race: How Blacks and Whites Think and Feel about the American Obsession*. New York: New Press.

Thomas, W. I., and D. S. Thomas. 1928. *The Child in America: Behavior Problems and Programs*. New York: Alfred A. Knopf.

Todd, Knox H., Christi Deaton, Anne P. D'Adamo, and Leon Goe. 2000. "Ethnicity and Analgesic Practice." *Annals of Emergency Medicine* 35 (January): 11–16.

Travis, John. 2009. "Scientists Decry Isotope, DNA Testing of 'Nationality.' " *Science* 326 (October 2): 30–31.

Tyson-Bernstein, Harriet. 1988. *A Conspiracy of Good Intentions: America's Textbook Fiasco*. Washington, DC: The Council for Basic Education.

United Network for Organ Sharing. 2009. "Questions and Answers." *Transplant Living*. Accessed September 3, 2010. http://www.transplantliving.org/beforethetransplant/qa.aspx#donMinority.

U.S. Census Bureau. 1953. *U.S. Census of Population: 1950*. Washington, DC: U.S. Government Printing Office.

———. 1994. "Table 1. Race of Wife by Race of Husband: 1960, 1970, 1980, 1991, and 1992." Interracial Tables. July 5, 1994. Accessed September 3, 2010. http://www.census.gov/population/socdemo/race/interractab1.txt.

———. 2001a. *DP-1 Profile of General Demographic Characteristics*. Washington, DC.

———. 2001b. *Population by Race and Hispanic or Latino Origin for the United States: 1990 and 2000*. Washington, DC.

———. 2003. "Table 1. Hispanic Origin and Race of Wife and Husband in Married-Couple Households for the United States: 2000." Census 2000 PHC-T-19. Hispanic Origin and Race of Coupled Households: 2000. Accessed September 3, 2010. http://www.census.gov/population/cen2000/phc-t19/tab01.pdf.

U.S. Census Office. 1872. *The Statistics of the Population of the United States*. Washington, DC: Government Printing Office.

Velody, Irving, and Robin Williams, eds. 1998. *The Politics of Constructionism*. London: SAGE.

Vera, Hernán, and Andrew Gordon. 2002. *Screen Saviors: Hollywood Fictions of Whiteness*. Lanham, MD: Rowman & Littlefield.

Verkuyten, M. 2003. "Discourses about Ethnic Group (De-)Essentialism: Oppressive and Progressive Aspects." *British Journal of Social Psychology* 42 (3): 371–91.

Visweswaran, Kamala. 1998. "Race and the Culture of Anthropology." *American Anthropologist* 100 (1): 70–83.

Voyles, Karen. 2010. "Ex-Dixie Official to Serve 7 Years." *Ocala.com*, February 6, 2010. Accessed September 3, 2010. http://www.ocala.com/article/20100206/articles/2061010.

Wade, Nicholas. 2004. "Articles Highlight Different Views on Genetic Basis of Race." *New York Times*. October 27, 2004.

Wadman, Meredith. 2004. "Geneticists Struggle towards Consensus on Place for 'Race.'" *Nature* 431 (October 28): 1026.

Wailoo, Keith. 1997. *Drawing Blood: Technology and Disease Identity in Twentieth-Century America*. Baltimore: Johns Hopkins University Press.

Wailoo, Keith, and Stephen Pemberton. 2006. *The Troubled Dream of Genetic Medicine: Ethnicity and Innovation in Tay-Sachs, Cystic Fibrosis, and Sickle Cell Disease*. Baltimore: Johns Hopkins University Press.

Walsh, Mark. 2000. "Harcourt General Inc. Agrees to Terms of Sale." *Education Week* 20 (November 8): 13.

Waters, Mary C. 1990. *Ethnic Options: Choosing Identities in America*. Berkeley: University of California Press.

Weber, Max. 1978/1956. *Economy and Society: An Outline of Interpretive Sociology*. Berkeley: University of California Press. First published 1956 by J. C. B. Mohr (Paul Siebeck), Tübingen, Germany.

Webster, Yehudi O. 1994–1995. "Rethinking Racial Classification in Sociology." *California Sociologist* 17–18 (Winter–Summer): 165–76.

Western, Bruce. 2006. *Punishment and Inequality in America*. New York: Russell Sage.

Williams, Melinda J., and Jennifer L. Eberhardt. 2008. "Biological Conceptions of Race and the Motivation to Cross Racial Boundaries." *Journal of Personality and Social Psychology* 94 (June): 1033–47.

Wilson, George. 1996. "Toward a Revised Framework for Examining Beliefs about the Causes of Poverty." *Sociological Quarterly* 37 (3): 413–28.

Winant, Howard. 2000. "Race and Race Theory." *Annual Review of Sociology* 26 (August): 169–85.

———. 2001. *The World Is a Ghetto: Race and Democracy since World War II*. New York: Basic Books.

———. 2007. "The Dark Side of the Force: One Hundred Years of the Sociology of Race" Pp. 535–71 in *Sociology in America: A History*, edited by Craig Calhoun. Chicago: University of Chicago Press.

Winickoff, David E., and Osagie K. Obasogie. 2008. "Race-Specific Drugs: Regulatory Trends and Public Policy." *Trends in Pharmacological Sciences* 29 (6): 277–79.

Winslow, Olivia. 2001. "Does It All Add Up? New Census Race Categories Raise Questions about How They're Used." *Newsday.* February 11, 2001.

Wittenbrink, Bernd, James L. Hilton, and Pamela L. Gist. 1998. "In Search of Similarity: Stereotypes as Naive Theories in Social Categorization." *Social Cognition* 16 (1).

Witzig, Ritchie. 1996. "The Medicalization of Race: Scientific Legitimization of a Flawed Social Construct." *Annals of Internal Medicine* 125: 675–79.

Wofford, J., J. Kemp, D. Regan, and M. Creer 2007. "Ethnically Mismatched Cord Blood Transplants in African Americans: The Saint Louis Cord Blood Bank Experience." *Cytotherapy* 9:660–66.

Wolfe, Patrick. 2001. "Land, Labor, and Difference: Elementary Structures of Race." *American Historical Review* 106 (June): 866–905.

Wood, Alastair J. J. 2001. "Racial Differences in the Response to Drugs— Pointers to Genetic Differences." *New England Journal of Medicine* 344 (May 3): 1393–96.

Yearley, Steven. 2005. *Making Sense of Science: Understanding the Social Study of Science.* London: Sage.

Young, Robert J. C. 1995. *Colonial Desire: Hybridity in Theory, Culture and Race.* London and New York: Routledge.

Yzerbyt, V., A. Rogier, and S. T. Fiske. 1998. "Group Entitativity and Social Attribution: On Translating Situational Constraints into Stereotypes." *Personality and Social Psychology Bulletin* 24 (10): 1089–1103.

Zimmerman, Jonathan. 2002. *Whose America? Culture Wars in the Public Schools.* Cambridge, MA: Harvard University Press.

Zuberi, Tukufu. 2001. *Thicker Than Blood: How Racial Statistics Lie.* Minneapolis: University of Minnesota Press.

Index

academia, essentialism and, 38. *See also* scientists
academic training, 178–86
affirmative-action measures, 203
African American Heart Failure Trial (A-HeFT), 213
Agassiz, Louis, 28
age, racial conceptualization and, 46, 58, 126
A-HeFT (African American Heart Failure Trial), 213
Allport, Gordon, 59
American Anthropological Association, 41, 101
American Association of Physical Anthropologists, 41, 100–101
American Committee for Democracy and Intellectual Freedom, 67
American Indians, 204
ancestry testing, 205–8

anthropologists / anthropology professors, 33–34, 36, 43–45, 179–80
Anthropology (Ember et al.), 74–76
anthropology, subfields in, 274n5
anthropology majors, 179, 181–85
anthropology textbooks, 70–71, 273n3
anti-essentialism: as academic ideology, 187–88; in *Anthropology* (Ember et al.), 75, 76; anthropology majors and, 184–85; in biology textbooks, 90–91; color-blindness and, 215; development and definition of, 30–32; essentialism and, 235; in formal education, 137, 221–22; gender and, 127–28; racism and, 134–35; scientific racial conceptualization and, 130–32; as scientists' definition of race, 113–17, 121
Apostle, Richard A., 51–55, 58–60, 63
Association of Black Cardiologists, 62, 134
athletics, 161–70

Text: Palatino
Display: Univers Condensed Light 47 and Bauer Bodoni
Compositor: Westchester Book Group
Indexer: Rachel Lyon

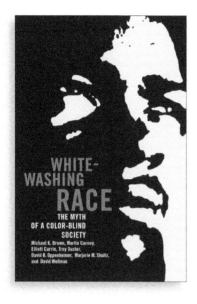

Whitewashing Race

The Myth of a Color-Blind Society

MICHAEL K. BROWN, MARTIN CARNOY, ELLIOTT CURRIE, TROY DUSTER, DAVID B. OPPENHEIMER, MARJORIE M. SHULTZ, and DAVID WELLMAN

"An impressive and diverse group of scholars launch an empirically grounded assault on the vast body of colorblind orthodoxy. The authors harness a medley of disciplinary perspectives into a cogent argument about racial stratification accompanied by a set of practical racial justice policy options. Their aim is both simple and ambitious: to reinvigorate a moribund debate by marshalling their collective intellectual resources to demonstrate that the conservative consensus on race is neither morally sustainable nor logically defensible."

—Lani Guinier, coauthor of *The Miner's Canary*

Gustavus Myers Outstanding Book Award
Benjamin L. Hooks Outstanding Book Award

A George Gund Foundation Book in African American Studies

$21.95 paper   978-0-520-24475-7
$49.95 cloth   978-0-520-23706-3

Being Black, Living in the Red

Race, Wealth, and Social Policy in America

DALTON CONLEY
10th Anniversary Edition

"Compelling.... An important contribution to our overall understanding of social stratification in modern society."

—*American Journal of Sociology*

"Within the race-versus-class framework, this is an outstanding book." —*Social Forces*

"Insightful and thorough.... This book cannot be ignored." —*Contemporary Sociology*

"Conley asserts that wealth is at the heart of the racial inequality that plagues this country, and that focus on comparing income, occupation, and educational status ignores the benefits and access that accrue from having wealth." —*San Francisco Examiner*

$21.95 paper   978-0-520-26130-3

www.ucpress.edu

CPSIA information can be obtained
at www.ICGtesting.com
Printed in the USA
LVHW091302250319
611734LV00001B/248/P

9 780520 270312